Dylan and C

DYLAN AND COHEN

Poets of Rock and Roll

David Boucher

continuum
NEW YORK • LONDON

2004

The Continuum International Publishing Group Inc
15 East 26 Street, New York, NY 10010

The Continuum International Publishing Group Ltd
The Tower Building, 11 York Road, London SE1 7NX

www.continuumbooks.com

Printed in the United States of America

Library of Congress Cataloging-in-Publication Data
Boucher, David.
  Dylan and Cohen : poets of rock and roll / David Boucher.
    p. cm.
    Includes bibliographical references (p.).
    ISBN 0-8264-5980-3 (hardcover : alk. paper) — ISBN 0-8264-5981-1 (pbk. :
alk. paper)
    1. Dylan, Bob, 1941–   2. Cohen, Leonard, 1934–   3. Rock
musicians—United States—Biography.   4. Poets, Canadian—20th
century—Biography.   5. Music and literature.   I. Title.
ML400.B63 2004
782.42164'092'2—dc22   2003017812

CONTENTS

ILLUSTRATIONS

ACKNOWLEDGMENTS

This book has been a long time coming, and it would not have been possible without the help of many people. Michelle Wallace of the Music Experience Project in Seattle was more than generous with her time and actually gave up one of her days off to show me the Robert Shelton Archive. She was also kind enough to copy some of the items for me. The image of the handbill advertising a poetry reading session by Irving Layton and Leonard Cohen in New York is from the Experience Music Project collection. The staff at the Thomas Fisher Rare Book Library, University of Toronto, were extremely helpful when I consulted Leonard Cohen's papers there. Jeff Rosen of Bob Dylan Music Co. was admirably prompt in responding to my request for permission to reprint lyrics, and Lynne Okin was refreshingly efficient in dealing with the paperwork. Christy Ikne of Sony/ATV Music generously granted a license for the reproduction of Leonard Cohen's lyrics. Kelley Lynch and Leonard Cohen graciously gave permission to quote from the works of poetry and prose and use the photographs in the Thomas Fisher Rare Book Library. Kelley Lynch, Cohen's manager, was exceptionally generous with her time, and I am very grateful for all the help that she has given me.

Many of my friends are fans of Bob Dylan and Leonard Cohen, and some have academic interests in them. I have benefited greatly from conversations with Ivan Molloy, Lawrence Wilde, and Gary Browning. I am particularly indebted to my longtime friend Mike Jones, lyricist with Latin Quarter and now of the Institute for Popular Music at Liverpool University. The institute holds the Robert Shelton material that was not sold at Sotheby's to the Experience Music Project. I am indebted to Mike for his hospitality and for his help with my use of the important collection of Dylan-related materials at Liverpool donated by Robert Shelton's sisters. We have had many conversations about this book, and I have learned enormously from his knowledge of the music industry.

The research for this book took me to many places, including Liverpool, New York, Montreal, Toronto, Cleveland, Los Angeles, San Francisco, and Seattle. I'd like to thank Tony and Karen Mughan for their hospitality while I was in Ohio and Karen for driving me to the Rock and Roll Hall of Fame in Cleveland. I am indebted to Dai and Rosie Blatchford, whose abiding interest in Leonard Cohen and in the book kept me to my task. I am grateful to three Lisas: Lisa Davies translated Federico García Lorca's "Imaginatión, inspiración, evasión" for me; Lisa Chivers printed and copied some of the earlier drafts of the book; and in the final stages of this project, Lisa Berni has been invaluable in printing out various versions and in scanning and preparing the images used for the publisher. I much appreciate the time she devoted to helping me. I also got help from Suzi Williams and Fred Marshalsea, for which I am very grateful. I would also like to thank once again Clare, Emma, and Lucy for their abiding forbearance, especially when they found it difficult to comprehend that my job took me to such places as the Experience Music Project in Seattle, the Rock and Roll Hall of Fame in Cleveland, and the Chelsea Hotel in New York. Fraser and Niles took a curious feline interest in the project, usually in the form of being fast asleep in my study as I wrote. It goes without saying that I take full responsibility for the deficiencies that remain in the book.

I would like to thank Sony/ATV Music Publishing LLC for granting a license to quote from the following songs: "The Land of Plenty" © 2001 Sony/ATV Songs LLC and Robin Hill Music. "A Singer Must Die" © 1990 Sony/ATV Songs LLC. "Democracy" © 1993 Sony/ATV Songs LLC. "Suzanne" © 1967 Sony/ATV Songs LLC. "Sisters of Mercy" © 1997 Sony/ATV Songs LLC. "Hallelujah" © 1995 Sony/ATV Songs LLC. "The Future" © 1993 Sony/ATV Songs LLC. "So Long, Marianne" © Sony/ ATV Songs LLC. "First We Take Manhattan" © Sony/ATV Songs LLC. "Everybody Knows" © Sony/ATV Songs LLC. All rights on behalf of Sony/ATV Songs LLC administered by Sony/ATV Music Publishing, 8 Music Square, Nashville, TN 37203. All rights reserved. Used by permission.

I would like to thank Kelley Lynch and Leonard Cohen for granting permission to quote from the Cohen archives, Thomas Fisher Rare Book Library, Toronto University, and from the following poems and books: "The Only Tourist in Havana Turns His Thoughts Homeward," "All There is to Know about Adolph Eichmann," and "Alexander Trocchi, Public Junkie, Prié pour Nous," in *Flowers for Hitler* (London: Jonathan Cape, 1973; first published 1964). *The Favourite Game* (Toronto: McClelland & Stewart, 1994; first published 1963). *Beautiful Losers* (London: Jonathan Cape, 1970;

first published 1966). *The Spice-Box of Earth* (Toronto: McClelland &
Stewart, 1961). Leonard Cohen remembering his first meeting with Troc-
chi in *A Life in Pieces: Reflections on Alexander Trocchi*, edited by Allan
Campbell and Tim Niel (Edinburgh: Rebel Inc., 1997).

I am indebted to the following for permission to reprint Bob Dylan's
lyrics. "Talkin' John Birch Paranoid Blues" © 1970 Special Rider Music.
"It Ain't Me, Babe" © 1964 Warner Bros. Inc. © renewed 1992 by
Special Rider Music. "Masters of War" © 1963 Warner Bros. Inc. ©
renewed 1991 by Special Rider Music. "Slow Train" © 1979 Special Rider
Music. "A Hard Rain's A-Gonna Fall" © 1963 Warner Bros. Inc. ©
renewed 1991 by Special Rider Music. "The Times They Are A-Changin' "
© 1963, Warner Bros. Inc. © renewed 1991 by Special Rider Music.
"Lonesome Death of Hattie Carroll" © Warner Bros. Inc. © renewed
1992 by Special Rider Music. "Who Killed Davey Moore?" © Warner
Bros. Inc. © renewed in 1992 by Special Rider Music. "My Back Pages"
© 1964 Warner Bros. Inc. © renewed 1992 by Special Rider Music. "Lay
Down Your Weary Tune" © 1964, 1965 by Warner Bros. Inc. "Ballad
of a Thin Man" © 1965 Warner Bros. Inc. "She Belongs to Me" © Warner
Bros. Inc. © renewed 1993 by Special Rider Music. "Tombstone Blues"
© 1965 Warner Bros. Inc. © renewed 1993 by Special Rider Music.
"Desolation Row" © 1965 Warner Bros. Inc. © renewed 1993 by Special
Rider Music. "It's Alright, Ma (I'm Only Bleeding)" © 1965 Warner Bros.
Inc. © renewed 1993 by Special Rider Music. "Just Like a Woman" ©
1966 Dwarf Music. "Visions of Johanna" © 1966 Dwarf Music. "I Dreamed
I Saw St. Augustine" © 1968 Dwarf Music. "You're Gonna Make Me
Lonesome When You Go" © 1974 Rams Horn Music. "Trying to Get to
Heaven" © 1997 Special Rider Music. "Lonesome Day Blues" © 2001
Special Rider Music. All rights reserved. International copyright secured.
Reprinted by permission.

David Boucher
Cardiff, Easter 2003

INTRODUCTION

POETS OF A GENERATION

> What remains true is that, if Dylan is, *sui generis*, the greatest
> song-writer of the age, Leonard Cohen is still the *only* name that
> can seriously be mentioned in the same breath.[1]

Poetry is an evaluative descriptive word. It is descriptive in that it signifies an art form that, while being readily identifiable, retains a sufficient degree of ambiguity to have its meaning contested. To claim that something is poetry may often be to claim that it is authentic, that the voice of poetry has a greater claim to be heard than the nonpoetic. Paul Garon has made the emphatic and stipulative pronouncement that all blues is self-evidently poetry and that those who think otherwise must be mentally defective.[2] He argues that poetic art necessarily contains within itself elements of revolutionary ferment manifested as the struggle for freedom. Poetry liberates the mind from ideological structures and repressive constraints, projecting a vision of the possible beyond the actual. Surrealism, in Garon's view, has facilitated this liberation by connecting the imagination to the blind spots of reality through stimulating and irritating nascent and latent faculties of thought by means of fantasy. Garon's argument is stipulative and tautological. In defining poetry in this way, by definition those modes of expression that conform to the definition are more poetic than those that do not. Garon is contemptuously dismissive of those who do not agree with the surrealist position and completely hostile to academics in the formal sense, suggesting that the real business of thinking has to go on outside of the constraints of academia. Not only does Garon wish to compel us to accept that the blues is poetry, but that

1

it is better poetry than that produced by T. S. Eliot, Robert Frost, or Allen Ginsberg.[3]

One way to address the dilemma of resolving what is and what is not poetry is to subscribe to what Cohen says: poetry is a verdict rather than an intention, meaning that it is others who bestow the title of poetry on the poet or poem. If this is to be a criterion, it is undeniable that numerous critics do describe both Bob Dylan and Leonard Cohen as lyric poets. To get a definitive answer to the question What makes Dylan Thomas's "Vision and Prayer," in which the words are shaped into a triangle, poetry? is just as elusive as getting agreement on whether Damien Hirst's dismembered animals suspended in formaldehyde constitute art.

It is nevertheless the case that the concepts of poetry and art carry with them favorable evaluative connotations. They are what philosopher Maurice Cranston called "hooray words." To call something poetic, or artistic, is deliberately to invoke this positive sense of approval. The positive is not, of course, universal, and for some, poetry, and the label *poetry,* may be tainted by unpleasant associations with school and the "high" culture of the establishment. Jonzi D., for example, found the term uncool and performance poetry too anal.[4] In an age when we all too readily manipulate evaluative descriptive terms in order to bask in their appraisive glory, profiteers in the music industry have not been reticent to extend the descriptive referent of poetry in order to capitalize on the evaluative element. A song lyric that might plausibly stand without its music is at risk of being packaged and sold as poetry. This dubious honor has been bestowed upon, among others, Joni Mitchell, Blixa Bargeld, Nick Cave, Marc Almond, and Shane MacGowan. In France, for example, there is a very strong tradition of the poet-singer, with Serge Gainsbourg, Jacques Brel, Charles Aznavour, Brasse, and Hugues Aufray. Brel, for example, strongly influenced Rod McKuen. This French tradition found in the songwriting circles of Montreal and Quebec was quickly identified as the milieu of Cohen's artistry: "Intense, dark-haired Leonard Cohen, acclaimed by some as Canada's leading poet, ends his poetry readings with guitar in hand, singing in the style of the French-Canadian chansonnier."[5]

Poets themselves have not been averse to cross over into song. Homer, for example, was chanted, and so were the Scandinavian epics. Frank Davey argues that poetry and music have historically been closely allied. The heroic poetry of Anglo-Saxons is very likely to have been chanted to the accompaniment of a harpist.[6] Shakespeare liberally punctuated his plays with song. *Twelfth Night* and *A Midsummer Night's Dream*, for example, are sustained by intermittent interludes of song. William Blake's *Poetical Sketches* includes eight poems with *song* in the title, with two of his most famous collections being *Songs of Innocence* and *Songs of Experience*. The San Francisco Beat poets fused jazz and poetry, and in his early career Cohen tried to emulate their style. One of the pioneers in the United States was Kenneth Rexroth, who had experimented in Chicago during the 1930s. He was one of the prime movers of the San Francisco Cellar jazz poetry scene. He was ecstatic about the potential that Dylan had to advance the movement. Fusing music and poetry in the way that Dylan had was not new, Rexroth conceded. In France and Germany it had been traditional since the time of Charlemagne. It was Dylan's influence on the younger generation and their imitation of him that was the important factor.[7] Allen Ginsberg, a great admirer of Blake, sang "The Tiger" to harmonium accompaniment and recited some of his own poems, such as "Father Death," to music. Much of the force of Ginsberg's poetry is in the performance, and without the mantric intonation and musical accompaniment, the words often appear dead on the page. Inspired by Dylan and Happy Traum, a leading figure in the folk revival movement in the United States, Ginsberg wrote songs that folk music anthologist and fellow Beat artist and poet Harry Smith recorded him singing in the Chelsea Hotel around 1971. The album eventually appeared in 1981 as *Allen Ginsberg: First Blues, Rags, Ballads and Harmonium Songs* (Folkways FSS 37560). The Liverpool poets Roger McGough and Adrian Henry both sang their poetry when they were members of Scaffold and the Liverpool scene, respectively.

The book *The Message: Crossing the Tracks between Poetry and Pop*, which celebrated the theme of the 1999 National Poetry Day, spearheaded by the Poetry Society of Great Britain, explored the relation between pop lyrics and poetry, and the contributors, with varying degrees of equivocation, conclude that there is none. Lyrics are distinctive in their way, often gaining their particular force in the performance, the combination of intonation and notation, betraying a dependency on the music that is integral to their appeal. The banality of the lone lyric is atoned in the musical accompaniment, and the romantic death of the author may be positively redemptive. It is the event of the romanticized deaths of Jim Morrison, Jimi Hendrix, Janis Joplin, and Marc Bolan at the height of their fame, for example, rather than the memory of any particular lyric, other than for their sheer banality, that made them enduring icons, whereas with Keats, the beauty of the poetry made his untimely death a tragedy. Stephen Troussé, for instance, suggests that the "splendid banality" of Marc Bolan's lines "I drive a Rolls-Royce / Cos it's good for my voice" is a more profound gift to the history of pop than the contributions of all of the sad-eyed singer-songwriters of the 1970s.[9] He calls it "the aesthetic of the artful artlessness."

Indeed, there may be a great deal of mileage in Simon Reynold's view that popular music gains its power not from the depth and meaning of its lyrics, but from its sheer noise.[10] The critics who analyze it import criteria from the higher culture in which they have been educated and impose rationality, aesthetic value, and depth of meaning on a form of expression devoid of all such things. Instead, it is the extralinguistic elements that refuse to succumb to content analysis that constitute the pop song—a driving bass line, earthy guitar, haunting Hammond organ, wistful wailing slide guitar, and rasping delivery of the lyrics. There has been what Troussé calls a critical shift from text to texture.[11] It would be a mistake to divorce Dylan and Cohen from such a characterization. Instead of making a category distinction in which the so-called poets of rock and roll are different in kind from other performers, they may be seen on a continuum representing the end at which text and texture are mutually supportive and inseparable. As Stephen Scobie points out, in themselves some of Dylan's lyrics may appear awkward or even banal printed on the page, but the music and the phrasing give character and effect: "The music provides a rhythm, a beat, an emotional ambience."[12] The arrangements of songs change, of course, and the mood conveyed, the images projected, and the context invoked take on different nuances, but Dylan is notorious for setting his lyrics to completely different accompaniments, transforming the effect, if not the content, of the words.

Bob Dylan and Leonard Cohen have both been hailed as great poets of their generation. Donald Henahan, commenting on Cohen, asserts that "on the alienation scale, he rates somewhere between [Arthur] Schopenhauer and Bob Dylan, two other prominent poets of pessimism."[13] *Playboy* described Cohen as both the minstrel and the poet laureate of his generation.[14] Harry Rasky, the filmmaker, who produced the film *The Song of Leonard Cohen*, bestowed on him the dubious honor of being "the first great, vaginal poet."[15] Both Dylan and Cohen precipitated heated discussions among academics and practicing poets about whether their lyric poetry was truly poetry at all, let alone good poetry. Neil Corcoran argues that Dylan's lyrics rarely stand alone as poetry. Lyric poetry is meant to be composed and thought of rhythmically. The centrality of music in Dylan's songs means that they cannot be viewed unreservedly as poetry. Corcoran equivocates on Dylan's claim to be a poet and rather evasively suggests that although Dylan is not a conventional poet, he has the same artistry of mind as would a great poet in the clarity of expressions, the forcefulness of the imagery, the gracefulness of the language, and the relevance of the words in different contexts.[16]

George Woodcock, for example, maintained in 1970 that Cohen had become something of an instant Keats, combining the romanticism with the fame that Keats did not enjoy until a half century after his death. Woodcock held that Cohen's poetry had virtues that would keep it alive as "good minor poetry." Combining pop singing with poetry, however, was barely compatible, and the former had had a deleterious affect on Cohen's poetic development. Woodcock cites an interview with Cohen in *Saturday Night* in which he says that he no longer thinks about the words, because in themselves they are completely empty and any emotion can be poured into them. Woodcock argues that Cohen's popular songs have ceased to be poetry because they are merely forms of words that receive life and meaning in the performance of the singer.[17]

Acknowledged poets such as Arthur Rimbaud, Ezra Pound, and Federico García Lorca had sought to restore poetry's place among the lived experiences of the everyday life of a community. The Beat poets emulated them in this aspiration. Kenneth Rexroth declared that intellectuals, that is, college professors, had hijacked poetry, taking it out of the hands of the people. Poetry in the oral traditions of Homer and *Beowulf* were show business, and the Beat poets aspired to reestablish the connection. Lawrence Ferlinghetti complained that the voice of poetry was being drowned by the competition of the mass media, traceable to Johannes Gutenberg's printing press.[18] None succeeded in achieving the aim of reconnecting poetry with the masses, but the irony is that, Rimbaud, Pound, Lorca, and Ferlinghetti, through their influence on Bob Dylan and Leonard Cohen, came to the attention of a much wider reading public than was traditionally associated with poetic appreciation. Although Ferlinghetti acknowledged Dylan's achievement, he was nevertheless resentful of Dylan's success. Once, after attending a Dylan concert in Berkeley, California, with Ginsberg and Ken Kesey, Ferlinghetti was embittered, ranting about a stringy kid with an electric guitar drawing a bigger audience than a major poet such as himself.[19] In an interview with Robert Shelton, Ferlinghetti acknowledged that Dylan has a poet's imagination, but added, "I still think he needs that guitar."[20] In the March 1966 issue of *Ramparts,* Ralph J. Gleason praised Dylan for doing the impossible: for taking poetry out of the classroom and bringing it to the jukebox, from reaching a small circle of friends to having a worldwide audience. The importance of intruding art into popular culture was affirmed by Cohen in acknowledging that what Dylan had done was to put "the word back into the jukebox, which is really where you have to have it, or at least where I like to have it."[21]

What is undoubtedly the case, whether one confirms or denies Dylan's and Cohen's claims to be poets, is that they achieved what their mentors failed to accomplish. They introduced a new audience to the world of poetry, an audience whose horizons were broadened and who contributed to a significant increase in the sales of poetry books. Rexroth acknowledged that "the importance of Dylan is that he is imitated right and left. It is a very important phenomenon that in the new-leisure society of barefoot boys and girls, poetry is dissolving into the community."[22]

The 1999 National Poetry Day, October 7, had as one of its principal themes the relation between poetry and song lyrics. Andrew Motion chose as his favorite lyric of all time the opening lines from Bob Dylan's "Visions of Johanna": "Ain't it just like the night to play tricks when you're trying to be so quiet." (Incidentally, it is also Bono's favorite line from a Dylan song.[23]) The Poetry Society of Great Britain commissioned Roddy Lumsden to explore the relation between pop lyrics and poetry and between their respective "industries." The project drew upon the musings of a disparate crowd of commentators, including Motion, who commented on Bob Dylan's work. The general consensus was that pop lyrics have their own integrity within the much broader texture of music, image, performance, and "attitude." There are exceptions to the rule, and occasionally a success-ful lyricist produces words capable of being read and divorced from their texture. In Motion's view, Bob Dylan is one such exception who does not need to lean on the crutch of his guitar. Despite this, Dylan worked hard at the texture, consciously crafting musical forms to coincide with his obsession with change.

Very early in Dylan's career Robert Shelton, the folk music critic of the *New York Times*, described him as "one of the musical-poetic geniuses of our time."[24] The literary critic Frank Kermode caused a stir in the 1960s when he compared Dylan with Keats and Wordsworth.[25] Paul Williams described Dylan's work as "great art."[26] Leonard Cohen suggested in 1985 that Dylan "is the Picasso of song," and in 1988 in an interview in the *Musician Magazine*, he again likened Dylan to Picasso in his "exuber-ance, range and assimilation of the whole history of music."[27]

The claim that Dylan was a great poet of his generation precipitated a heated debate to which critics and academics contributed. Many academics were disdainful of the claim, suggesting that Dylan was a self-conscious second-rate imitator of Jack Kerouac, who appealed to the feebleminded who knew nothing of poetry. Whatever the merits of the counterclaims, it cannot be denied that Dylan made poetry popular, elevated from its secluded shade in a corner of academia, into the horizon of a new and inquisitive audience, hitherto not renowned for its cultural and artistic discernment. Henrietta Yurchenco argued in 1966 that "if Dylan has done nothing else, he is responsible for the present widespread interest in poetry." She went on to say: "He has given poetry a significance and stature which it has never had in American life. Furthermore, he is a bard—a singing poet in an ancient but thoroughly neglected tradition."[28] Adrian Rawlings, commenting on Dylan's 1966 Australian tour, proclaimed that he had rescued poetry from obscurity "in a way that neither Eliot nor Pound nor the American poetry and jazz movement ever could."[29]

At about the same time that Bob Dylan was listening to American folk and blues he started reading Ginsberg, Gary Snyder, Philip Whalen, and Frank O'Hara. Dylan had come to lyric poetry through Woody Guthrie, who Billy Bragg has suggested is the best American lyric poet since Walt Whitman. In 1960, a friend in Minneapolis, Dave Whitaker, who is credited with having brought about Dylan's first great transformation, from the reluctant university fraternity boy on the margins of the in crowd to one of the coolest men in town, is most likely to have introduced him to Kerouac and the Beat poets, particularly Ginsberg and Ferlinghetti. It was at this time that Dylan read Guthrie's *Bound for Glory*, the effect of which was to metamorphose him into a seasoned traveler with an Oklahoma accent, as well as a new past.

In Greenwich Village the poetic influences were extended. Folk musician Dave Van Ronk stimulated Dylan's interest in the work of the French symbolists. He particularly liked Rimbaud. Rimbaud was a rebel who wanted to reach a wider popular audience with his poetry, in which he questioned all types of establishment authority, including church and state. Like Woody Guthrie, he almost lived the life of a vagrant and drank very heavily. In addition, Rimbaud indulged heavily in marijuana and opium. He claimed that, in order to transform the poet into a seer or visionary, the senses must become disordered or disturbed by a prolonged process of disorientation. Blake, whom both Ginsberg and Dylan admired, expressed similar sentiments in more restrained terms: "The road of excess leads to the palace of wisdom" (from *Proverbs of Hell*). Dylan's own well-documented drunkenness and excessive abuse of drugs coincide with the development of his abstract, almost surreal, poetic phase, or what he described himself as "hallucination . . . atery" songs. Van Ronk also got him interested in Villiers and Bertholt Brecht. Suze Rotolo, who appears on the cover of *The Freewheelin' Bob Dylan* in a pose almost identical to that in a photograph of Dylan and Caitlin Thomas on the same New York street, was involved with a group of actors who staged Brecht plays at the Circle in the Square Theatre in Greenwich Village. She helped out by painting the scenery for a production of *Brecht on Brecht,* and Dylan would go down and watch the six performers rehearsing the poems and the songs Brecht wrote with Kurt Weill. Rotolo has commented that Dylan was most affected by Lotte

Lenya's signature song, "Pirate Jenny."[30] On the album *The Times They Are A-Changin'*, which includes the beautiful "Boots of Spanish Leather," a lament on Suze's lost love, her presence is also indirect: her connection to Brecht is felt in the structure and verse pattern of "The Lonesome Death of Hattie Carroll," which is based on Brecht's *The Black Freighter*.[31]

Rotolo was widely read and introduced Dylan to such poets as François Villon, Yevgeny Yevtushenko, and Robert Graves, whom he met in London when the BBC flew Dylan over to appear in *Madhouse on Castle Street*. Graves wasn't really interested in a pushy, scruffy little American trying to thrust his poetry under his nose. Dylan was deeply offended and went back to New York, describing Graves as an "old bastard." Graves, in fact, had been very rude by turning to four musicians and starting a conversation while Dylan was singing "Hollis Brown."[32]

Dylan consciously tried to go beyond the rhyming of words that was typical of most song forms. He once said in an interview that he wrote his songs so that they could be read or recited even without the beat or melody.[33] As early as 1963 he found the song form restrictive, a medium through which he felt that he was no longer fully able to express his thoughts and feelings, or in which he could draw upon the wealth of influences to which he had now become exposed. Initially his response was to turn away from song, particularly the finger-pointing genre that was coming to stereotype him. Throughout 1963, but with more intensity during the last two months, which partially coincides with his first meeting with Ginsberg in December of that year, and in early 1964, he increasingly expressed himself in free form verse and prose, rarely revising it, and some of which he published not only on the back of his own albums, such as the "Eleven Outlined Epitaphs" on the sleeve cover of *The Times They Are A-Changin'*, but also on albums by Joan Baez and Peter, Paul, and Mary. One of his tributes to poet Dave "Tony" Glover was printed in the program for the 1963 Newport Folk Festival. Much of the early work is loosely autobiographical, including his "Life in a Stolen Moment," printed on the Town Hall concert program, and "Last Thoughts on Woody Guthrie," which he recited as an encore to the concert and culminates in print in his 1966 book *Tarantula*. In the dust jacket notes by Michael Gray the book is described as "surrealism on speed, a phantasmagoric trip through America." Scattered throughout are the more readable prose poems in the form of letters, as well as an epitaph, once again to Bob Dylan, starting with "Here lies bob dylan / murdered."

Dylan even experimented with writing plays at the end of 1963, as a letter from him to *Broadside* magazine testifies, and what appears to be a fragment of the utterly unmemorable play he refers to was discovered

BOB DYLAN

The cover of the 1971 edition of *Tarantula*.

in the Margolis and Moss manuscripts that date from this period. He gradually came to realize that if the song form was too restrictive, it was not to be abandoned, but instead transformed. In February 1964, faithful to the Beat Generation, he went on the road for twenty days with three companions, who took turns driving while Dylan sat in the back of the station wagon and typed. Two of the songs from this excursion were "Chimes of Freedom" and "Mr. Tambourine Man." This marks the most significant transition and extension of his expressive songs, and a conscious adoption of Rimbaud as his model, along with an unequivocal rejection of the genre that he had done so much to popularize, the topical song.

Whereas Dylan never performed as a poet except on the solitary occasion of reading "Last Thoughts on Woody Guthrie" in 1963, Leonard Cohen was first and foremost a poet, but the seriousness with which his poetry was studied became eclipsed by his fame as a singer and performer. For example, his book *Death of a Lady's Man,* published in 1978, was little discussed either by academics or Cohen aficionados, yet his European tours attracted rapturous reviews, fixing him firmly as a pop idol rather than a writer or poet. Ironically, it was *Death of a Lady's Man* that signaled Cohen's return to form as a poet after two indifferent collections. Cohen demonstrated his gift for poetry at an early age by winning the Chester McNaughton Prize (1955) for creative writing for his collections of poems *Thoughts of a Landsman* and *Sparrows.* In contrast, Dylan was first and foremost a singer who came to like the idea of being a poet and gradually grew into the role.

In 1949, while browsing in one of Montreal's secondhand book shops, Cohen came across a collection of poems by Federico García Lorca. For Cohen, it was a more profound experience than the bar mitzvah ceremony he had undergone two years earlier. Lorca's impact was so immense, in terms of style, the disturbing imagery, juxtaposing the sacred and profane, and subject matter. Cohen was later to joke on the 1988 tour when introducing "Take This Waltz," which is based on Lorca's "Little Viennese Waltz," that the Spaniard ruined his life. Two lines had drawn Cohen into Lorca's universe, a landscape that he knew and understood. Those lines were "I want to pass through the arches of Elvira / To see her thighs and begin weeping."

From 1949 Cohen immersed himself in reading and writing poetry. At McGill University in Montreal, Cohen's literary studies led him to Rimbaud, Yeats, Pound, and Eliot, sources that were also to impress indelibly upon Dylan. His first published poem was "A Halloween Poem to Delight My Friends" in *CIV/n,* a quarterly literary magazine. The magazine's title is Ezra Pound's abbreviation for *civilization.*[34] In 1956

Cohen published his first poetry collection, called *Let Us Compare Mytholo-gies*, dedicated to his father and including line drawings by his first serious girlfriend, Freda Guttman. This book reflected the fact that Pound's and Eliot's reigns as the shapers of modern poetry had come to an end. The poems in this collection are faithful to the change in mood effected by the Beat poets and the angry young men of the 1960s. Like them, Cohen is engaged in self-exploration and the relation of the self to immediate experience. There is an emphasis on the politics of the personal, where one's own thoughts and feelings, one's own place in events or in the narrative, are of central significance. Over half of the forty-four poems have *I* or some derivative, such as *he* at the center. This collection betrays what was to become the hallmark of his work, that is, the engagement of the reader at a profoundly personal and intimate level.

After an interlude of five years Cohen published *The Spice-Box of Earth* in 1961, a book liberally spiced with erotic verse. In this work Cohen was acknowledged to be a sensitive poet in the making, capable of conveying sexual passion with a vengeance. One reviewer thought that Cohen should write about love less and think about it more, and that much of the language used to convey the passion of love was decayed in its meanings. Words such as *beauty, golden*, and *glory* were overused and their ambiguity had rendered them obtuse. *Heart,* for example, is a word ruined by bad poets and good songwriters.[35] The reviewer commended Cohen at least for realizing the obsolescence of the word *heart* and for not using it once. Despite the authoritative air that the reviewer exudes, his carelessness is starkly exposed by the fact that the word *heart* is indeed sprinkled through-out *The Spice-Box of Earth*. For example, in "Sing to Fish, Embrace the Beast," we have the line "Animals do not kill for the human heart," and in "Brighter Than our Sun," Cohen talks of the "heart of God." In "Lines from my Grandfather's Journal," the word *heart* appears no fewer than four times.

Cohen published *Flowers for Hitler* in 1964 and *Parasites of Heaven* in 1966, gaining international recognition for them. As if to fly in the face of the critic's advice, he uses the very terms that were said to be obsolete even more liberally, continuing to write about love, the heart, and beauty. In *Flowers for Hitler* the word *beauty,* for example, is used in "Cruel Baby," "Nursery Rhyme," "Kerensky," "The New Leader," "Hydra 1960," "Goebbels Abandons His Novel and Joins the Party," and "Why Commands are Obeyed." "Teachers" in *Parasites of Heaven*, and later on *The Songs of Leonard Cohen* (1968), bounds with references to the heart: "Are you the teacher of my heart / We teach old hearts to break."

The cover of the British edition of *Flowers for Hitler*.

The very title *Flowers for Hitler* would have been abhorrent to the Jewish community from which Cohen hailed. There was a strong political point insinuating itself throughout the poems, a subversive point, that places the Holocaust on a scale that reaches from every domestic relationship in which power and force play a role to the immense savagery of genocide. The theme was suggested to him by Primo Levi, who is quoted at the beginning of *Flowers for Hitler*: "Take care not to let it happen in your own homes." Cohen's understanding of Levi's work was such that in this collection of poems he took the mythology of the concentration camp and screamed that this is indeed what we are doing to each other in our own living rooms.[36] He promoted the idea that *Flowers for Hitler* constituted a radical departure from his previous work. On the back cover he wrote: "This book moves me from the world of golden boy poet into the dung-pile of the front-line writer." Nevertheless, the politics of the personal is still strongly evident in the self-exploratory character of the poetry. In Milton Wilson's view, *Flowers for Hitler* distinguishes itself from *The Spice-Box of Earth* in a more relentless and uncompromising search for "the poetic substance that he exists on, at all the things that he can remember, imagine, absorb, separate, excrete, transmute, forget."[37]

Cohen also wrote two novels, *The Favourite Game* (1963) and *Beautiful Losers* (1966). The novels are far from conventional in that the components of narrative, such as plot, dramatic situation, and character, are subservient to dramatic imagery, thematic visions, and rich language texture. Indeed, as Stephen Scobie suggests, *Beautiful Losers* is about the destruction of characters rather than their creation.[38] The central characters in his novels are priestlike poets struggling for redemption. *The Favourite Game* is semi-autobiographical, a work of autobiography and of fiction. It tells the story of Lawrence Breavman (a combination of *bereaved man* and *brave man*), a Jewish boy from a comfortable Montreal suburb, desperate to escape the stultifying middle-class atmosphere and widen his experience of the world. It is a hormonally driven, emotionally undulating journey through a mind appealing to be liberated.

Jack McClelland, of the publishing house McClelland & Stewart, at first objected to the tedious love affair of Breavman with himself and to the lurid sex scenes. He also wondered to what degree the text was autobiographical. Cohen acknowledged that all of the incidents, with the exception of the death of Robert at the end of the second section, actually happened. He admitted that Breavman and he did many of the same things but reacted differently to them, and therefore they became different men.[39] Cohen was extremely disillusioned by the treatment he got at the hands of McClelland & Stewart. In asking for a reference in support of his application for a second Canada Council grant, Cohen quoted from the readers' reports. One accused him of having a protracted love affair with himself, another of being tedious and disgusting, and yet another of dwelling upon "damp, morbid" sex. He was made to feel that he had not written a book, but rather something dirty at his desk. It was the encouragement he got from the Abelard-Schuman literary agency in New York that inspired him to continue with the project, and which brought into sharp relief the parochialism of Canada.[40]

The game in the title is not what the book itself implies, or what the dust jacket actually says, that is, love and its allied pursuits, but instead the game that the character Lisa liked most, throwing herself and Breavman in soft snow and seeing who makes the best impressions. The snowscape was left with flowerlike impressions with footprint stems. By extension, Cohen's point was that we make an impression upon the world by leaving the imprints of our designs, as well as the traces of our footprints as we walk away.

For one reviewer, *The Favourite Game* was reminiscent of visiting a peep show, where voyeurs witness Breavman seducing the family maid in the cellar, Tamara in a rented room, Norma in the woods, and Wanda in the boathouse. The repetition feeding the poet's imagination is alleviated and redeemed by Cohen's gift for "creating outrageously comic situations and startling and illuminating metaphors. His ability to crystallise the interrelationships of these metaphors allows many of the chapters to be read as individual poems."[41] Another reviewer described the book as "a beautiful story, joyously physical, witty and introspective, written with a wonderful surging intensity."[42] Cohen was not terribly disappointed by its lack of commercial success. Indeed, commercial success was not an expectation for a young Canadian writer in those days, since to be commercially successful was equivalent to selling out. In Montreal in the 1960s there was no notion of superstars, and "the same glittering prizes weren't in the air as there are today, so one had a kind of modest view of what a writing career was."[43]

Cohen described *Beautiful Losers* as a soul-saving, redemptive novel. The *Boston Globe*'s review of *Beautiful Losers* intimated that Cohen was the reincarnation of James Joyce.[44] It is a modern avant-garde novel, many of whose scenes, Dennis Duffy suggests, "have a phantasmagoric, surrealistic quality about them, coupled with a delight in blood and buggery, that reminds one of the novels of William Burroughs." It is, the reviewer says, "a respectable work of its kind," firmly of the '60s but not attaining the heights of Burroughs's *Naked Lunch*, Thomas Pynchon's *V.*, or John Barth's *The Floating Opera*, because of its ultimate "thinness of texture."[45] In the opinion of another reviewer, it was "the most intricate, erudite, and fascinating Canadian novel ever written."[46]

Ironically, it was Cohen's success as a singer and songwriter, for which he was accused of selling out as a poet, that added to his very success as a poet. It was in reviews of his *Parasites of Heaven*, published in 1966, that critical acclaim for his literary and poetic talents began to turn. George Bowering, reviewing the collection in *Canadian Literature*, described it as the least satisfying of Cohen's efforts.[47] Most serious critics after this either ignored the fact that Cohen was a commercially successful singer or descried his status as a rock star. Louis Dudek suggested that Cohen used to be a fine poet until he gave it all up, took up a guitar, and became a popular entertainer.[48] Cohen's *Selected Poems: 1956–1968* (1968) sold over two hundred thousand copies in the first few months after publication, almost unheard of for a book of contemporary poetry, and its success was without a doubt the result of the author's success as a rock star.

Although Dylan had close associations with the Beat poets, particularly Allen Ginsberg, Cohen was never really accepted into this artistic circle. Ginsberg believed that Dylan had almost single-handedly transformed the landscape of American poetry by creating an art out of the roots of the culture.[49] At the age of nineteen Cohen wanted to be accepted by the Canadian followers of the Beat poets because he admired their desultory look, bohemian lifestyles, and affectation of working-class associations. He was extremely well dressed, being the son of a clothing manufacturer, and middle class. He moved out of his home into a rooming house in order to change his style to one more commensurate with his poetic aspirations and burgeoning hormonal obsessions. He became part of the local bohemian literary scene of "underground" writers and poets, which was so underground that it did not demean itself with "subversive inten-tions."[50] The desire to be attractive to women was not unconnected to his ambition to become a poet. Indeed, after the publication of *The Favourite Game*, he reveled in his limited and localized fame. Self-mockingly he said that he could not stand the sound of his own voice, the voice of his generation in Canada. He found it amusing that he was being paid by television stations to iterate any blasphemous nonsense that came into his head.[51]

Cohen's education at McGill University was conventional. There is evidence that he studied Joseph Butler's *Sermons* and H. J. Paton's edition of Immanuel Kant's *Groundwork*. He also studied the English Romantics, Robert Burns, William Blake, Wordsworth, Samuel Coleridge, Charles Lamb, Walter Scott, Thomas De Quincey, Lord Byron, Shelley, Keats, William Hazlitt, Walter Savage Landor, and Thomas Wood. He was able to develop his oratorical and rhetorical skills by becoming a prize-winning debater and president of the school's debating society. He participated in debates such as "This House prefers Woolworth's to Wordsworth" and "This House resolves that TV is a mad moral influence on society."

Cohen's poetic roots, however, were much more deeply embedded, not in the traditions of popular culture, but in the Western religious experience, with all of the guilt, sin, salvation, and redemption that came with it. He explored the horizons of this culture, both subverting and affirming it, exposing its hypocrisy, finding solace in its protectiveness and definition of the self. He was influenced by A. M. Klein's fascination with the Jewish "obsession" with Adolf Hitler. In 1961 Cohen told a correspondent that he was working on "a collection of wild and satiric verse," *Flowers for Hitler,* that he was prepared to publish himself if he could not get a publisher.[52] In 1963 he described the work, now called *Opium for Hitler*, as a collection that "studies the totalitarian spirit for our century."[53] In Cohen's 1964 collection of poetry, *Flowers for Hitler*, he asserted that his own position is beyond that of what he pejoratively called the "traveling pack of poets." He acknowledged his attachment to tradition and his determination not to break free from or reject it before achieving an understanding of what he left behind. He found inspiration in the Bible and in such writers as Miguel de Cervantes, Albert Camus, and Jean-Paul Sartre. He also derived great pleasure from Yeats, Pound, and his teachers at McGill University, Hugh MacLennan and Louis Dudek, but also from the circle of Canadian poets with whom Cohen was associated, particularly his teacher Irving Layton. Layton has been described as a "professional poet and extrovert" and evidently more than compensated in company for Cohen's basic shyness.[54] He was regarded as a likeable, roguish rake by the Montreal cultural set, with a liking for much younger women. In the 1950s he delighted in outraging people and took a perverse pleasure in always trying to do the wrong thing. Cohen met Layton for the first time in 1949, then again as a student at McGill, where Layton organized a poetry workshop class. He was twenty years older than Cohen, but this did not prevent them from establishing an enduring friendship. Layton was a living inspiration to Cohen both as a surrogate father and as an exemplar. Layton's prodigious output particularly impressed Cohen.

The impression one gets from reading about Layton and seeing him on film is of an opinionated, overbearing, pompous, chauvinistic elitist, a man of his times and not above them, as he liked to think, who thought that the Montreal Jewish community was not only different from but far superior to the French or English. He was indeed charismatic, and many of his students, including Cohen, fell under his spell. What differentiates Cohen is the self-effacement, self-mocking ironic, even farcical, adoption of extreme poses that rescue him from the often ridiculously absurd and pathetically naive self-adulation of his poetic talent and sexual magnetism.[55] Whereas Layton cut an almost comic figure of a Romantic, Cohen is what Sandra Diwa described as a Black Romantic.[56] The Romantic delights in his or her personal vision, to some extent in defiance of the conventional. The Romantic explores the irrational, emphasizing emotions, imagination, delusions, and visionary images. In many ways this romanticism dwells on the mysteries and beauties of nature. Black romanticism takes these tendencies to extremes, adulating the sinister and dark moments of reality, as, for example, in Baudelaire's *Fleurs du Mal*, the title of which inspires *Flowers for Hitler*. It is an introspection that precipitates morbid and grotesque images of death and suicide. The poetry of Cohen is characterized by excess. However, Cohen himself claimed to have a more rounded philosophy than that exhibited in black romanticism. The Black Romantic tends to side with Valerie Solanis, who tried to kill artist Andy Warhol in July 1968. In the *SCUM Manifesto*, Solanis contends that men have the negative Midas touch: everything they touch turns to shit. For the Black Romantic like Sartre, nothing turns to gold, whereas for Cohen, some things are transformed into gold, and some degenerate into dirt. Unless the two sides are acknowledged, one's philosophy is incomplete.[57]

After the publication of *The Favourite Game* in 1963 and *Flowers for Hitler* in 1964, Cohen decided to capitalize on his popularity by doing a reading tour with Layton and Canadian poets Earle Birney and Phyllis Gotlieb, all of whom had new books to publicize. The publisher, McClelland and Stewart, an automobile manufacturer, and the Ministry of Tourism sponsored the tour of university campuses, engendering the usual accusations of art prostituting itself to big business. The tour was filmed by the Canadian National Film Board, and the footage forms the basis of Donald Brittain and Dan Owen's 1965 film *Ladies and Gentlemen, Mr. Leonard Cohen*. An unkind reviewer, Louis Dudek, Cohen's teacher at McGill, commented in the *Montreal Star* in October 1964 that the only problem with the tour was that it had little to do with poetry. Layton's book, according to Dudek, was simply popular buffoonery, taken by ignorant Canadians to be poetry, and Cohen's was little better, saved only by a "rudderless fantasy and wit," in that it sailed a little close to Layton's obnoxious egoism. The other two books by Birney and Gotlieb were highly polished and crafted, almost like lessons in creative writing, but lacked the energy of Cohen and Layton, and therefore it was difficult to know which type of poetry was the worse.

Cohen had great admiration for the Beat poets. Cohen was at Columbia University in New York when Ginsberg's *Howl* came out, and his own *Let Us Compare Mythologies* was published in the same year, 1956. In 1985 he described Ginsberg as the greatest contemporary poet in the United States, who, with Jack Kerouac and Gregory Corso, reinvigorated modern poetry. The whole thrust of Beat poetry was anticonventional, railing against the accepted mores of sex, art, and religion. It was a movement that was also anti-intellectual, a trait with which Cohen empathized.

Both Dylan and Cohen could empathize with the Beat poets, because, like themselves, despite the propensity to want to shock, the *raison d'être* of the Beat poets was to be famous and successful. They wanted everyone to be like them, which is not quite the same as wanting to change the world.[58]

Cohen had experienced the beatnik scene of Greenwich Village four years before Dylan. He associated with minor Beat poets and experienced their readings in the coffeehouses around the Village, and was excited by their bohemian lifestyles and irreverent commentaries on the dominant culture. Seeing Kerouac perform with indomitable panache and animated style the year before the publication of his novel *On the Road* (1957) inspired Cohen to couple his poetic tastes with a predilection for prose expression. Evidence for Cohen's fascination with the decadence of Beat and its obsession with fame is his poem on Alexander Trocchi in *Flowers for Hitler*. A Glaswegian Beat poet and novelist, Trocchi was also a notorious junkie and pornographer. During the early '60s Trocchi's main focus was Project Sigma, a worldwide organization of intellectuals, poets, and writers linked to precipitate the revolutionary transformation of the West. Its main theme was the opposition of play to work, urging that others devote themselves to greater creativity in advance of and in anticipation of the greater degree of leisure resulting from increasing automation. Its aim was self-discovery and being equipped to deal with more leisure time. This is basically what Cohen is referring to when he recalled his first meeting with Trocchi. The few days that Trocchi spent in Cohen's apartment on Mountain Street in Montreal seemed like weeks or months because of the Scotsman's certainty of his convictions. "In a certain sense," Cohen reminisced, "he saw himself as the General Secretary of some new subversive worldwide movement which would overthrow the old sensibility and establish a new one, nearer and dearer and closer to the heart than the one we were all forced to live in and indeed are still living."[59]

Trocchi was a born manipulator and fraternized with a wide variety of celebrities. Fellow Scottish writers such as Irvin Welsh and Kevin Williamson liked him because he was as disparaging about the parochialism of Scotland as they were. Welsh had read and enjoyed *Young Adam* but did not care for *Cain's Book*, which is often said to be Trocchi's best, because it was an inferior version of Burroughs's dark mythologizing of drugs. *Trainspotting* was in fact a reaction to the genre of literature associated with Burroughs and Trocchi, the bohemian drug abuser with a dark character.[60] Trocchi reveled in perversion, the repulsive and diseased. He maintained that "men call me mad. It is true that I love bad smells and all sinful unclean things generally. I love bandits and poets and raped women, chinks and diseased negresses. Everything in fact from the navel downwards."[61] Trocchi's high-class pornography as art would have appealed to Cohen, as it later appealed to and influenced Patti Smith. Indeed, all three artists, like Rabelais, abjure the separation of art from the reality of bodily functions and perversions.

The poem "Alexander Trocchi, Public Junkie, *Priez pour Nous*" is a precursor to some of the themes in *Beautiful Losers*. Indeed, Trocchi is himself a beautiful loser, a saint with disciples seeking guidance, but self-destructive and perverse, thinking that gray is the color of healthy skin dedicated to changing the "Law," an allusion to Project Sigma.

Cohen's Jewish upbringing instilled in him a fascination with the Holocaust, and in the months before leaving Columbia University, which he found totally uninspiring, he wrote a short piece of fiction entitled *A Ballet of Lepers*, a melancholic and morbid exploration of his feelings on the Holocaust, which he failed to get published. The theme constantly resurfaces in his songs and poems, often when it is not immediately apparent. There is explicit reference to the Holocaust in, for example, "The Captain's Song," and it is the inspiration behind "Dance Me to the End of Love." On his return to Canada and the completion of his second book of poetry, eventually published in 1961, he unsuccessfully collaborated on play writing with Irving Layton.

Just as the visionary poetry of Blake served as a formative influence and lasting inspiration to Ginsberg, Cohen was similarly inspired, as already suggested, by the imaginative romantic poetry of Federico García Lorca, who had been a friend of Salvator Dalí's since 1925, but whose surrealist phase was summarily dismissed by him. Lorca was a Spanish poet who died at the hands of Nationalist partisans in 1936. He was the first poet who had the power to move Cohen, with whom he felt a deep affinity. Lorca had been in New York at Columbia University from June 1929 to March 1930, and had also visited Havana. Fascinated by Lorca, Cohen also spent some time at Columbia and was in Cuba during the Bay of Pigs fiasco in 1961. Lorca was known in Spain as the Gypsy poet, a term that he once found amusing but later came to detest because of its pejorative connotations. It made him sound, he said, like an uneducated, uncultured savage poet.[62] Cohen alludes to Lorca in one of his early songs, "So Long, Marianne," when he sang "I used to think that I was some kind of Gypsy boy, before I let you take me home." Lorca's New York poems reflect his unease with the landscape of a vast, impersonal city, with its poverty, degradation, segregation, and violence—a suffering that seems to defy explanation. Both in mood and style the New York poems of Lorca have an affinity with Cohen's work. They are somber, graphic, and disturbing, and some are written in the lyrical style of song. Two of them are titled waltzes, and one of these, "Little Viennese Waltz," is the basis for Cohen's tribute to him, a loose translation called "Take This Waltz (after Lorca)."

Although Cohen does not discuss at length the relationship between his novels, poetry, and song, and, to some extent, sees them all as part of the same creative energy, he does want to maintain a difference between the song and poetry proper. In an interview for French television channel French2, *Le Cercle de Minuit,* which aired December 1992, songs, he suggested, have energy, whereas poems, pure poetry, just stand there. The fact that poetry is not popular is no bad thing. The poet can renew language with his or her secret work; that is not a public activity. In Cohen's view, it is important to maintain the distinction, without denying that there is poetry in songs, and that poetry contains the song's spirit. Critics, however, thought that the celebrity status that Cohen had achieved as a singer-songwriter was to the detriment of his poetry. *Flowers for Hitler* and *Beautiful Losers* were regarded as the high-water mark of his writing. Indeed, *Parasites of Heaven* and *The Energy of Slaves* (1972) were deemed to be indicative of his decline. The latter was described by John Robert Colombo, a critic sympathetic to Cohen, as "a charming but limited achievement," and the whole period was described as a lapse into technical and intellectual poverty. The two books were "a desperate gesture telling us that the poet was wiped out."[63] *Death of a Lady's Man* was important in that it came out at a time when his career was beginning to flag, his relationships with his children disintegrated, and the experience of working with music legend Phil Spector on the album *Death of a Lady's Man* had traumatized him. The book signaled Cohen's return to form as a poet: "The old Cohen is back, the jester-saint, with all the resources of the language once more at his disposal."[64]

This introduction has given greater emphasis to Leonard Cohen, mainly because his claim to be a poet predates that of Dylan and because Cohen's literary output was the springboard for his singer-songwriter career. In Chapter One I want to say something about the music industry into which Dylan and Cohen became inducted, and place them in the social and political context that was so receptive to their music and message. Chapters Two and Three characterize the musical and poetic milieu of Greenwich Village, in which Dylan and Cohen at various times located themselves. In these two chapters greater emphasis is given to Dylan's location and the changing persona he affected, because it was he who made it possible for the likes of Cohen to find success in setting lyric poetry to music. I show how Dylan's very raison d'être was transformation and confrontation. He thrives on challenging his audience, on eliciting from them reactions, often hostile. In Chapter Four I trace Cohen's journey to the status of cultural icon, by first showing the extent to which he was an acclaimed writer and poet. I then try to discern in what ways his songs were political, while so obviously not conforming to the finger-pointing genre that the early Dylan exploited so well. In Chapter Five I trace some of the musical influences that inspired Cohen and Dylan in their formative years, taking the opportunity to introduce a distinction between the concepts of origins and originality and relating them to Harry Smith's *Anthology of American Folk Music*, which was first released in 1952.

In Chapter Six I identify two predominant methods of interpreting the work of Dylan and Cohen: first, the search for referents in people, places, and objects and in poetic and musical sources, each of which is significantly flawed when applied to some of the songs and poems. The second approach, which I term the emotional response, rejects equating meaning with outside referents, and often rejects the search for meaning altogether. I go on to develop a vocabulary, with the help of R. G. Collingwood, Michael Oakeshott, and Federico García Lorca, in terms of which to distinguish these approaches, and in order to identify the types of questions appropriate to ask of a poem. In this respect, I attempt not only to distinguish different phases that overlap and run concurrently in Dylan's and Cohen's songwriting careers, but also to be able to determine which questions are appropriate and which are inappropriate in appreciating their works. I demonstrate that these distinctions within the poetic voice are implicit in both Dylan's and Cohen's self-understanding of what they were doing. In Chapters Seven and Eight a selection of themes is explored, first from Dylan's and then from Cohen's oeuvres, in order to determine how the distinctions developed in Chapter Six work out in practice. In Chapter Nine I explore the place of religion in the lives of Dylan and Cohen and suggest that, for Dylan, God is transcendent, whereas for Cohen, He is immanent. Their religious quests have been long and complex, always present, but sometimes surfacing more forcefully at particular times and in particular phases of their work.

Endnotes

1. Stephen Scobie, "The Counterfeit Begs Forgiveness: *Leonard Cohen* and Leonard Cohen," *Canadian Poetry* 33 (Fall/Winter 1993): 16.
2. Paul Garon, *Blues and the Poetic Spirit* (San Francisco: City Lights, 1996), 1.
3. Garon, *Blues and the Poetic Spirit*, 8.
4. Jonzi D., "From the Old School to the Lyrical Fearta," in *The Message: Crossing the Tracks between Poetry and Pop*, ed. Roddy Lumsden and Stephen Troussé (London: The Poetry Society, 1999), 85.
5. *Aspen Magazine* 1(3): 4.
6. Frank Davey, "Leonard Cohen and Bob Dylan: Poetry and the Popular Song," in *Leonard Cohen: The Artist and His Critics*, ed. Michael Gnarowski (Toronto: McGraw-Hill, 1976), 111.
7. Lumsden and Troussé, *The Message*.
8. Rexroth, interviewed by Robert Shelton, *No Direction Home* (New York: Da Capo Press, 1997; first published 1986), 227.

9. Stephen Troussé, "Stupid and Contagious: The Pleasures of the Text," in Lumsden and Troussé, *The Message*, 44.

10. Cited in ibid., 46–48.

11. Ibid., 46.

12. Stephen Scobie, *Alias Bob Dylan* (Alberta: Red Deer Press, 1991), 36.

13. Cited in Harry Rasky, *The Song of Leonard Cohen: Portrait of a Poet, a Friend and a Film* (Oakville, Ontario: Mosaic Press, 2001), 19.

14. *Playboy* (November 1968).

15. Rasky, *Song of Leonard Cohen*, 19.

16. Neil Corcoran, "Introduction, Writing Aloud," in *Do You Mr Jones?: Bob Dylan with the Poets and Professors,* ed. Neil Corcoran (London: Chatto & Windus, 2002), 13.

17. George Woodcock, "The Song of Sirens: Reflections on Leonard Cohen," in Gnarowski, *The Artist and His Critics*, 150, 166.

18. In Ralph J. Gleason, ed., *Jam Session: An Anthology of Jazz* (New York: J. P. Putnam's Sons, 1958), 285–286.

19. See Shelton, *No Direction Home*, 333.

20. Interview in *SNA San Francisco* (March 1965) (Robert Shelton Archives, Liverpool University Institute for Popular Music).

21. Cited in Michael Ondaatje, *Leonard Cohen* (Toronto: McClelland & Stewart, 1970), 4.

22. Rexroth, interview by Shelton, *No Direction Home*, 227.

23. Bono, "He's Got You from Cradle to Grave," *Q Dylan* (October 2000): 2.

24. Robert Shelton, "The Man behind the Songs," in *Bob Dylan Songbook* (London: Warner Bros., n.d.), 14.

25. See Dan Glaister, "Fade Far Away, Dissolve . . . to Dylan," *The Guardian*, March 27, 1997, p. 3.

26. Paul Williams, *Bob Dylan 1960–73: The Early Years* (London: Omnibus Press, 1994), xii.

27. Leonard Cohen, *Leonard Cohen in His Own Words,* ed. Jim Devlin (London: Omnibus Press, 1998), 82.

28. Henrietta Yurchenco, "Folk-Rot: In Defence," *Sound and Fury* (April 1966). Reprinted in *The Bob Dylan Companion,* ed. Carl Benson (New York: Schirmer Books, 1998), 67, 69.

29. Adrian Rawlings, "What's Happening, Mr. Jones?," *Farrago*, April 29, 1966. Reprinted in Benson, *Bob Dylan Companion*, 73.

30. Suze Rotolo, cited in Robbie Woliver, *Hoot: A Twenty-five-Year History of the Greenwich Village Music Scene* (New York: St. Martin's Press, 1994), 76.

31. Andy Gill, *My Back Pages: Classic Bob Dylan 1962–69* (London: Carlton, 1998), 126.

32. Bob Dylan, interviewed by Robert Shelton, Denver, March 1966 (Robert Shelton Archive, Music Experience Project, Seattle).

33. Anthony Scaduto, *Bob Dylan* (London: Helter Skelter, 1996), 135.

34. David Sheppard, *Leonard Cohen* (London: Unanimous, 2000), 7.

35. David Bromige, "The Lean and Luscious," review of *The Spice-Box of Earth*, *Canadian Literature* (Fall 1961).

36. Sandra Diwa, "After the Wipe-Out, a Renewal," *The Ubyssey*, February 3, 1967.

37. Milton Wilson, "Letters in Canada: 1964 Poetry," in Gnarowski *The Artist and His Critics*, 21.

38. Stephen Scobie, *Leonard Cohen* (Vancouver: Douglas & McIntyre, 1978), 73.

39. Ira B. Nadel, *Various Positions: A Life of Leonard Cohen* (London: Bloomsbury, 1996), 87–88.

40. Letter from Cohen to Desmond Pacey, February 23, 1961 (Leonard Cohen Papers, box 11, file 14-1961, Thomas Fisher Library, University of Toronto).

41. Ed Kleiman, "Blossom Show," review of *The Favourite Game*, *The Tamarack Review* (Winter 1964).

42. Joan Irwin, "A Lust for Life," *The Tamarack Review* (Winter 1964).

43. Leonard Cohen, interview with Bruce Pollock, "The Obscure Case of Leonard Cohen and the Mysterious Mr. M," *After Dark: The National Magazine of Entertainment* (February 1977).

44. Leonard Cohen homepage, http://www.leonardcohen.com/.

45. Dennis Duffy, "Beautiful Beginners," *The Tamarack Review* (Summer 1966).
46. Desmond Pacey, "The Phenomenon of Leonard Cohen," *Canadian Literature* 34 (1967): 5.
47. George Bowering, TK.
48. Louis Dudek, "The Prophet as Celebrity," *McGill Reporter*, January 20, 1967.
49. Allen Ginsberg, "On the New Dylan," *Georgia Straight*, May 25, 1971.
50. Columbia Records Media Department, undated press release to coincide with the release of *Ten New Songs*.
51. Leonard Cohen, letter addressed to "People," Montreal, December 11, 1963. (Leonard Cohen Papers, box 11, file 14, Thomas Fisher Library, University of Toronto).
52. Letter from Cohen to Desmond Pacey, February 23, 1961. (Leonard Cohen Papers, box 11, file 14-1961, Thomas Fisher Library, University of Toronto).
53. Letter to the Canadian Broadcasting Corporation, June 12, 1963 (Leonard Cohen Papers, box 11, file 12, Thomas Fisher Library, University of Toronto).
54. Rasky, *Song of Leonard Cohen*, 31.
55. Scobie, *Leonard Cohen*, 5.
56. Diwa, TK.
57. Cohen does not use the Solanis example, but expresses his point of view in an interview with Diwa, "After the Wipeout."
58. Greil Marcus, *The Bob MacFadden Experience* (Cambridge, MA: Harvard University Press, 1995), 112.
59. Leonard Cohen, remembering his first meeting with Trocchi in *A Life in Pieces: Reflections on Alexander Trocchi*, ed. Allan Campbell and Tim Niel (Edinburgh: Rebel Inc., 1997), 131.
60. Irvin Welsh, "A Scottish George Best of Literature," in ibid., 17.
61. Alexander Trocchi, "Tapeworm," in ibid., 31.
62. Christopher Maurer, introduction to *Poet in New York*, by Federico García Lorca (Harmondsworth: Penguin, 1989), xi–xii.
63. Gary Geddes, review of *Death of a Lady's Man,* by Leonard Cohen, *The Globe and Mail*, September 30, 1978, 27.
64. Ibid.

$$\boxed{1}$$

THE POPULAR AS POLITICAL

I'm not angry. I'm a delightful sort of a person.
                                    —Bob Dylan, London, 1965[1]

I think my rise in the market place will be considered an interesting
curiosity, that's all.
                                    —Leonard Cohen, 1970[2]

In late 2001, within a few weeks of each other, sixty-year-old Bob
Dylan and sixty-seven-year-old Leonard Cohen released new CDs,
events significant enough to capture the covers of the major news
magazines. After recording careers that spanned five decades, both singer-
songwriters expressed notes of resignation: the world was no longer
such a hostile place in which to live, and the inner turmoil no longer
so tumultuous.

Cohen, the "Godfather of Gloom" and the "Prince of Darkness," had
emerged from the depression that enveloped him for most of his life. The
sadness remained, but the angst had dissipated. After years of searching
for his inner self, a certainty amid the comic tragedy of life, he concluded
that there is no fixed point to excavate; even inner feelings are transitory.[3]
There is a fatalism in Cohen's recording, *Ten New Songs,* that is perhaps
more disturbing than the fractured and chilling emotional landscapes of
his earlier years. In earlier efforts, there was always a sense that there
was something there to find, something that lay beneath the turmoil,
something that the poet could express. The quest for artistic truth, which
had taken him to the top of a mountain and subjected him to the rigors
of the disciplined life of a Buddhist monk, ultimately resulted in the

realization that the veil of ignorance is the only certainty that there is. Whatever plan may be unfolding, it is beyond our comprehension: "We don't write the play, we don't produce it, we don't direct it and we're not even actors in it."[4]

Dylan's CD, *Love and Theft,* was immediately hailed by critics as a classic. Its range of musical styles and variation in moods make it a much more complex and intricate collection than the somber *Time Out of Mind,* written after Dylan had suffered a serious heart infection. The mood ranges from the melancholy in "Mississippi" and "Sugar Baby" to the light and breezy, though often with sinister or macabre undertones, as in "Floater (Too Much to Ask)" and "Bye and Bye." There are wide cultural influences invoked in the songs, spanning Dylan's own maturation through varied points of reference, from *Alice in Wonderland* to *A Street Car Named Desire* in "Tweedle Dee and Tweedle Dum," to the blues of his youth and its more recent reincarnation, reflected in "High Water (for Charlie Patton)," with its references to Big Joe Turner, Robert Johnson's "Dust My Broom," and Clarence Ashley's "Coo Coo Bird." The political stance is not as overt as in his earlier albums, but we still find him alluding to familiar themes such as corrupt blood-sucking politicians ("Summer Days") and the obscenity of war ("Lonesome Day Blues").

The voices of the two icons in these later works may have dropped another octave and lost most of their range, but they have lost nothing of their expressiveness. On the cover of *Ten New Songs* Cohen (pictured with former backup singer Sharon Robinson, who earns cowriting credit on all the material here), looks suave, distinguished, and immaculately dressed, his lifestyle having taken no significant toll on his face. Dylan has affected the look of a Mississippi paddleboat gambler, the lines on his face deep, his eyes dull and sunken. He is the '60s dandy, looking like a new millennium cowboy.

Both writers, although resigned, still have their political points to make. Cohen, self-effacing, questioning his credentials and his resolve, ironically pleads "May the lights in the land of plenty / Shine on the truth some day" ("The Land of Plenty," *Ten New Songs*). On *Love and Theft* Dylan defiantly declares that the defeated will learn the beauty of peace and the proud will be subdued: "I'm going to spare the defeated, boys, I'm going to speak to the crowd / I'm going to teach peace to the conquered, I'm going to tame the proud" ("Lonesome Day Blues").[5]

Popular Culture and Politics

During the 1950s and early 1960s it was generally assumed that celebrities, although famous, wielded little political power. They constituted a powerless elite. However, in 1979 Richard Dyer contested this character-ization, arguing that the entertainment elite, particularly film stars, did exercise political power of an ideological kind, in the way that they communicated and bolstered certain values, especially when celebrities attached their names to particular causes.[6] In the music industry it is now not infrequent that stars, particularly the aristocracy of the pop world, espouse causes and promote activities publicizing and raising money for the alleviation of world poverty or for the eradication of AIDS. Individuals frequently define themselves in terms of particular issues: for example, Bob Geldolf with world poverty, Sting with saving the rain forests, and Bono with canceling third world debt. The 2003 Stop the Iraqi War march and rally in Hyde Park, London, included numerous celebrities, such as Kylie Minogue, Damon Albarn, Ms. Dynamite, and Bianca Jagger, as well as the playwright Harold Pinter.

In some sense all popular music is political, reflecting the dominant culture and norms of society, and even reacting against them emphasizes this dominance. For example, almost all love songs reinforce the view that heterosexual relationships are the norm. Songs expressing homosexual emotions or celebrating homosexual relations tend to be suggestive rather than explicit, such as the songs of the Village People. Songs that are more explicit or graphic in their depictions fall foul of the standards of public decency and tend to fail to gain airtime.

The projection of, or reaction against, the dominant culture may be characterized as the presentation of utopian or dystopian images that impress themselves upon an audience.[7] Utopian images include those critical of the current orthodoxy as well as those affirming it. The category accommodates such songs as Dylan's "Love Minus Zero/No Limit" and Cohen's "Suzanne," as well as "Masters of War" and "Democracy," both with strong critical edges, but with a vision of a higher form of society to be attained. Some songs, of course, can be both critical and affirmative by being appropriated by the very target against which they are directed. Woody Guthrie's "This Land Is Your Land" was originally composed as an antiestablishment, anti–big business song in defense of poor, hard-working, ordinary Americans, but it gradually became appropriated by that very establishment and turned into something like a national anthem inclusive of all Americans.

Dystopian imagery is more disturbing and pessimistic, playing on the senses by presenting a distorted and disjointed, often sinister and macabre, reality. This is certainly a category in terms of which such songs as Dylan's "Gates of Eden" and Cohen's "The Future" can be analyzed. It is a way in which songwriters, reacting against the system, reject the terms of reference of the dominant culture and project back upon it an alternative reality that it cannot accommodate, which may in addition be enhanced by theatricality, as, for example, in the Goth style and music of Marilyn Manson or the metal image of SlipKnot, with their characteristic grotesque masks.

At bottom most songs conjure a utopian or dystopian image, carrying with them direct or indirect ideological messages. The mid-1950s, when the Communist witch hunts led by U.S. Senator Joseph McCarthy had waned, was a time when on both sides of the Atlantic academics and statesmen were congratulating themselves on having achieved an age characterized by the end of ideology. Eminent academics such as Edward Shils and Seymour Martin Lipset contended that, whereas in the Soviet Union, people were consciously manipulated and socially engineered through the dissemination and propagation of an ideology that created and distorted reality, in the West ideological politics had come to an end because of the elimination of gross inequalities and the achievement of relative widespread affluence. There was, they argued, very little difference to be discerned between political parties, such as the Democrats and Republicans in the United States and the Labour and Conservative parties in Great Britain, on most social and political issues. The differences were simply a matter of degree. What was really being reflected in this argument was the implicit acceptance, indeed celebration, that the dominant culture had triumphed. Where it appeared to be under threat by the likes of rock-and-roll pioneers Jerry Lee Lewis, Bill Haley and His Comets, Elvis Presley, Little Richard, and Chuck Berry, concerted efforts were mobilized to discredit these purveyors of perversion and depravity.

Minority music, or the music of blacks, was absorbed by the dominant culture in America, which at first saw it as alien and other, and as a distinct threat, but then as a commodity that could be exploited. Black music in America was profitable because of the existence of a sizable market, and even major companies set up their own "race" labels directed exclusively at black culture. During the 1920s, with advances in recording technology, recording companies proliferated, and a wide range of esoteric localized music, such as that from the Appalachians, was preserved on such labels as Vocalion Race Records and Brunswick Race Records. This was not done as a magnanimous gesture to the diversity of American culture, but because it was possible to produce small runs and make a profit on the investment, while paying the artist a small flat fee and, if he or she was lucky, a minuscule royalty on sales. The availability and extent of this technology are portrayed in the film *Oh Brother, Where Art*

Thou? (2000), when the Soggy Bottom Boys cut "Man of Constant Sorrow" in a remote makeshift studio in the Deep South.

The Great Depression of the 1930s decimated the music industry, and most of the small independent companies went out of business. In 1933, for example, record sales were 7 percent of what they had been in 1929. The market revived during the late 1930s because of inexpensive 78 rpm pressings, but the localized and regionalized nature of the music was almost submerged. It was not until the 1950s, with the availability of new recording techniques, using tape instead of etching the music directly onto disk, that commercial recording by small independent companies once again proliferated. When Harry Smith compiled his *Anthology of American Folk Music* and released it on Moses Asch's Folkways label in 1952, it was assumed that the material didn't need a license, and royalties were not paid, either because the original company had gone out of business or because an existing company had deleted it from its catalog. Smith's idiosyncratic and eclectic collection was primarily an exercise in retrieval, but it was also revolutionary in ignoring the race divide. In the foreword to the handbook accompanying the *Anthology*, Smith acknowledges Okeh Records and record producer and engineer Ralph Peer's contribution to the advent of modern record making in taking portable recording equipment to Atlanta, but also credits Peer with inventing the term *race records,* by which they were still known by some manufacturers in 1952. The songs in Smith's anthology are organized thematically, and except for the odd photograph in the accompanying booklet produced by Smith, the race of the artist is not identified. Smith took some delight in knowing that he had sown confusion over whether particular singers were black or white. It took years, he said in 1968, before anyone realized that Mississippi John Hurt was not a hillbilly.[8]

Black music in America gained its mainstream respectability, despite generational protests, by being sung by white men and women. The context in which the songs were packaged and presented was a vast multicultural commercial enterprise whose concern was profit rather than taste, sales rather than race or the political content of the music, and entertainment rather than the message of a song. A huge music industry was the context within which the political gestures, whether explicitly or implicitly, conventional or countercultural, were made, while the companies orchestrated, merchandised, and sold the product. In this respect, even the subversive that became successful was compromised and invariably accused of selling out.

Another area of discontent that became coopted was the Beat movement. The radical point of what the Beats were trying to get across was lost on most people because the Beats themselves were absorbed in their own lifestyle and the means to their political goals figured more prominently than the ends. The sex, drugs, fast cars, and "happenings" gradually generated ridicule rather than admiration. The use of the term *beatnik* considerably defused the radical image of the Beats. The popular image of beatniks was of dirty, unshaven men in sandals playing bongo drums and smoking dope, accompanied by sexually promiscuous girls in tight-fitting leotards looking bored. Those people who left home and chose this alternative lifestyle were paradoxically disowned by Kerouac, who wanted to emphasize his working-class origins and the seriousness of his art. The conformity against which Kerouac, Ginsberg, and Burroughs raged ironically inspired thousands of young people to conform to the new radical orthodoxy. The Beats were themselves captives of the movement they served to ignite. Just as Karl Marx had denied that he was a Marxist, the Beats resented having their names used and exploited by the cult of the beatniks.

The prime example in the context of the folk revival that enabled Bob Dylan to launch his career was the popularity of hootenannies, gatherings of folksingers in which audiences often join in. Initially, as Dylan's own route testifies, the beatniks were not reaching out to a mass disaffected audience. The message that the beatniks projected in talking of travel, freedom, and transcending experiential and experimental barriers, though radical and almost forbidden, was vague and suggestive in its vision, intensely personalized and escapist. Only the periphery of the "silent generation" of apathetic college students of the 1950s turned to Beat, while gradually and accumulatively growing numbers turned to folk, with its emphasis on communal redemption and identifiable political ills with prescriptions for reform. The folk revival was constructive, whereas because the Beat movement was politically acute, in practice it seemed socially and personally destructive, and indeed was portrayed as such by the media that exploited the commercial potential of its subversiveness.

The folk revival offered constructive visions of communal defiance of social injustices. The road that the emerging politically conscious preferred was that of Woody Guthrie rather than Jack Kerouac. The folk inspiration was utopian and naive, in that it called upon city dwellers to look to the country for the wholesome values that should guide their conduct. During the 1940s and 1950s the likes of Cisco Houston, Pete Seeger, and Sonny Terry, as well as Woody Guthrie, inhabited Greenwich Village in New York City, infusing it with a populist, rather than elitist, intellectual touch. Seeger and his friends would hold Saturday morning activities in the Village for kids, teaching them songs and playing games. On Sundays in Washington

A 1959 beatnik film poster.

Square, the hub of the Village and thus the center of the avant-garde, people congregated to listen to singers and poets. It was in the post–World War II era that the hootenanny became a popular form of entertainment. It took various forms, from Sunday afternoon rent parties organized by Woody Guthrie and the Almanac Singers, including Seeger, to more formally organized gatherings at New York's Town Hall organized by Izzy Young's Folklore Center.

The term *hootenanny* became popular in Seattle in July 1940 after Terry and Berta Pettus of the (Seattle) *Washington New Dealer* organized a party with refreshments and entertainment, including singers chosen from the floor, calling it the Midsummer Hootenanny. The publication changed its name to *The New World* and continued to hold regular hootenannies. They were monthly, no format, fund-raising gatherings. Terry Pettus did not coin the term, however. When he grew up in southern Indiana, the term was commonly used for impromptu parties. In the autumn of 1955 issue of *Sing Out,* Pete Seeger wrote a piece on the origin of the term, attributing its use in New York to Woody Guthrie, who brought it with him from Seattle in the early 1940s.[10] Guthrie and the Almanac Singers rented a large house in the Village and had regular Sunday afternoon rent parties. The parties became so popular that they were moved to Town Hall and even Carnegie Hall. On Friday, October 5, 1962, for example, the Folklore Center organized a hootenanny at Town Hall billing Sandy Bull, Judy Collins, Bob Dylan, Lynn Gold, John Lee Hooker, and Ian and Sylvia as the main acts. A flyer advertised that "members of the audience will be selected to sing from the stage in this exciting event. Bring your guitars and banjos."

Hootenannies became so popular throughout the United States that the ABC television network started a regular Saturday evening show of the same name in the autumn of 1962. The legacy of blacklisting from the McCarthy era persisted even then. Pete Seeger and the Weavers, for example, were conspicuous by their absence from the shows. From the first broadcast opposition began to mount against the exclusion of what ABC originally called "inferior talent," a position that was quickly revised when the network demanded that Seeger and the Weavers sign a "loyalty oath affidavit." On September 28, 1963, the ABC network offices in New York were picketed by supporters of Seeger, and an accompanying press release declared that Seeger was not prepared to sign a loyalty agreement, having spent the previous seven years successfully fighting a court battle against the constitutionality of such oaths. Among the protesters were Judy Collins, Carolyn Hester, Joan Baez, Ramblin' Jack Elliott, and the Kingston Trio.

Hootenannies, then, although popular in the country under various names for an impromptu party with self-made entertainment, were primarily responsible in urban areas for creating the belief that folk music was for the people and by the people. The larger, more formally organized hoots, as they came to be called, engendered a great deal of criticism from within the folk community. The ABC show *Hootenanny,* as Robert Shelton recognized, generated a huge debate about politics and aesthetics, and was probably responsible for more controversy than any other show of the era. Shelton contends: "The 'hootenanny' craze spawned by the

FOLKLORE CENTER TRAVELING HOOTENANNY --

YES, ON FRIDAY NIGHT, OCTOBER 5TH 1962

WILL TAKE PLACE AT NYC'S TOWN HALL A

FOLKLORE CENTER TRAVELING HOOTENANNY

WITH:

    SANDY BULL

        JUDY COLLINS

            BOB DYLAN

   LYNN GOLD

      JOHN LEE HOOKER

         IAN & SYLVIA

SPECIAL HOOTENANNY! A special hootenanny will take place from
the stage of TOWN HALL. Members of the audience will be selected
to sing from the stage in this exciting event. Bring your guitars
and banjos.

TICKET INFORMATION: All seats are reserved; prices are -
$1.75 in the balcony, $2.50 in the orchestra &.$3.00 for
a few seats in the loge. Tickets can be purchased at the
Folklore Center, 110 MacDougal St. - GR7-5987, or at the
Town Hall box office after Labor Day.

MERRILL LYNCH, PIERCE, FENNER & BEANE, 70 Pine Street, New York 5, New York

Advertisement for a hootenanny with Bob Dylan and John Lee Hooker, October 5, 1962.

show was a study in the mechanics of American merchandising, fact-chasing and cashing in on what was topically popular."[11] The craze soon subsided, and serious folk followers were glad to see it go, with its strange mix of show business and folk music. Internal squabbling over the authenticity of folk music became characteristic of the leading figures in the folk revival, and Bob Dylan was himself a casualty of their censuring tendencies, first when he moved from the political to the personal in his songs, then when he switched from acoustic to electric guitar.

In this book the dominant political and social culture of the 1960s is predominantly the context against which the songs of Leonard Cohen and Bob Dylan are explored. There are political messages to many of the songs, whether in an explicit challenge to the status quo or in being inspired by particular injustices or momentous events. It has been commonly observed that the pop music of the early 1960s had become homogenized and bland, molded and packaged by the record companies, as the excitement and raw quality of the music derived from black culture was deemed to have mass appeal and sales potential. Just as chains of Mexican fast-food restaurants have manufactured a bland, almost spiceless Mexican menu that even children will eat, the music industry of the early 1960s transformed even the revolutionary sounds for mass consumption, which could bridge the generation gap in appealing to young and old. In the United States, Elvis Presley's early radicalism, reflected in such films as *Jailhouse Rock* (1957), and in Britain by Cliff Richard in *Expresso Bongo* (1960), became replaced by the more universally appealing image of the clean-cut boy next door, portrayed by Presley in *G.I. Blues* (1960) and by Richard in *Summer Holiday* (1963). From the atmosphere and mood of seediness beautifully portrayed in monochrome and subdued light, reflecting the genre of the new realism in both American and British films, we get a fantasy world of pastel shades and the innocence of youth, the ideal of the postwar consumer society. This attempt to commodify radicalism by subtracting what was radical is example of the dominant culture adapting and absorbing what was at first perceived as a challenge, and which later could be exploited to reinforce the dominant cultural values. It is against this homogenization and blandness in popular culture that the whole New York scene, to which the likes of Dylan, Cohen, and Andy Warhol's Velvet Underground, particularly John Cale, Lou Reed, and Nico, consciously rebelled.

Bob Dylan and Leonard Cohen are widely acknowledged as the great pop poets of the 1960s, transforming the popular song into a medium for questioning the personal, social, and political norms of their times. They emerged at a time when populist politics had come to the fore, but with features unique to the early 1960s. For the first time a very serious division was emerging between the values of the young and those of the older generation, so much so that the establishment voice that spoke for them was inauthentic, a voice that had no resonance in the soul of the disoriented, disillusioned, and directionless youth. So many of these young people described their adulation for Dylan and Cohen as the articulation or vocalization of what they were feeling but were unable to express: Dylan the anger, Cohen the angst and despondency. Bruce Springsteen, for example, heard "Like a Rolling Stone" at the age of fifteen and admired Dylan for having the "guts to take on the whole world and make me feel like I had to, too."[12] A German critic, speaking of Cohen, contended that "he is the incarnation of the unfulfilled wishes and unanswered questions of the young generation."[13]

The generation gap was the subject of a great deal of discussion, and what made it a unique phenomenon was that it was worldwide. The distinguished anthropologist Margaret Mead saw this as evidence that the young had truly become part of a world community, a cosmopolitan culture.[14] Mead had been a student of Franz Boas, an advocate of cultural determinism as opposed to biological determinism. Mead became famous for her study of Samoa. In opposition to the view that adolescent behavior and emotional turmoil were biologically programmed, she argued that teenagers in Samoa did not go through such an adolescent crisis, and therefore nurture, and not nature, was the determining factor in teenage behavior.[15] Mead's work was subsequently discredited because she had an inadequate grasp of the language and was underresearched and overgullible. Close scrutiny of court records showed that teenage delinquency in Samoa was indeed a cause for concern.[16]

In retrospect, it is significant that in Mead's argument for a worldwide culture of youth she eschewed particulars on the ground that such detail would hinder the search for an explanatory principle. As Richard Poirier noted, Mead hardly mentioned the fundamental issues and concerns that made the young rebellious and revolutionary, and instead pointed to the fact that the young all over the world owned transistor radios and tape recorders and were therefore able to share the world and make new contributions to it.[17] Mead argued that global communications and instanta- neous transmission of pictures make the same images available to all of us without editorial interference. Of course, such a view proved to be incredibly naive. The experience of the Vietnam War taught governments that in future conflicts the press would need to be much more carefully controlled, as was practiced in the Falklands crisis, the Gulf War, NATO's intervention in Kosovo, and the U.S. invasion of Iraq.

The 1960s was also the time when the invisible became visible and audible. Black culture interested and even fascinated young white youth, but it was an oppressed culture denied a place in middle American society. The civil rights movement constituted a threat to the American way of life comparable with the Civil War and the Great Depression. During the early 1960s the civil rights movement already had a semblance of organization. It is ironic that it was the black experience of the military into which they had at least notionally been integrated by the time of the

Korean War that inspired many blacks to join the civil rights movement and fight for civil equality outside of military life. Three organizations were firmly established. The National Association for the Advancement of Colored People (NAACP) had been formed in 1909 with the aim of fighting discrimination and segregation in America largely through the due process of law. The Congress of Racial Equality (CORE), founded in 1942, adopted the strategy of nonviolent tactics to highlight racial inequalities. Formed in the wake of the Montgomery, Alabama, bus boycott of 1955–1956, the Southern Christian Leadership Conference (SCLC), led by the Reverend Dr. Martin Luther King Jr., advocated a more militant stance, while continuing to espouse the principle of nonviolence. It was to some extent the frustration of the younger generation that demanded more rapid and palpable change that led to the gradual formation of a new and radically militant departure, the Student Non-Violent Coordinating Committee (SNCC), which was willing to use more confrontational tactics.[18] Bob Dylan's personal involvement with the civil rights movement predates its most radical phase. By the time he renounced his connection in 1965, having actually renounced his connection many times previously, the leadership and involvement of white middle-class liberal students and intellectuals was being resented and the integrationist stance associated with them rejected. The antiwar movement was beginning to deflect the attention of white supporters, and blacks gradually came to believe that they had a cause of their own to fight, and that many of their black leaders fell far short of their aspirations. The civil rights movement was significantly damaged nearly three years before the death of King, when looting, murder, and arson were the spectacle of the riots in the Watts section of Los Angeles in August 1965, the month that Dylan showcased his electric set at the Newport Folk Festival.

In 1966 SNCC took a dramatic turn. Its leader, John Lewis, espoused the ideals of nonviolence and the maintenance of alliances with white liberals as the best tactics for racial advancement. In its spring 1966 conference these ideals were rejected. The organization adopted the position that blacks must organize independently of whites to achieve liberation. John Lewis was replaced by Stokely Carmichael, one of the organizers of the Black Panther Party in Lowndes County, Alabama. In addition, SNCC produced a position paper defining and advocating Black Power. In that paper it stated: "If we are to proceed toward true liberation, we must cut ourselves off from white people. We must form our own institutions, credit unions, co-ops, political parties, write our own histories."[19] Out of this new radicalism came two strands of thinking and action, cultural nationalism and revolutionary nationalism. The cultural nationalists articulated the upward aspirations of many of the better-off blacks, using their African heritage as a mask for subscribing to capitalist economic ideals. Revolutionary nationalism represented the most oppressed and poverty-stricken blacks and advocated socialist revolution as the solution to the problem.[20] It was this revolutionary strand that precipitated the formation by Bobby Seale, Huey Newton, and Bobby Hutton of the Black Panther Party for Self-Defense in Oakland, California, in the autumn of 1966. Eldridge Cleaver became its minister of information and produced one of the most definitive theoretical statements of radical black liberation in a speech he gave on March 18, 1968, at the founding of the Peace and Freedom party. Cleaver argued:

> We start with the basic definition: that black people in America are a colonized people in every sense of the term and that white America is an organized Imperialist force holding black people in colonial bondage. From this definition our task becomes clearer: what we need is a revolution in the white mother country and national liberation for the black colony.[21]

Three weeks later, seventeen-year old Bobby Hutton was killed when police in Oakland ambushed him, Cleaver, and a number of Panther activists. With this surge of radicalism, the central place of folk music in the civil rights movement had become an irrelevance.

To compound matters, the almost pathological fear of communism, which had resulted in the witch hunts of the House Un-American Activities Committee in the late 1940s and early 1950s, had also brought the world to the brink of nuclear war and embroiled America in the Vietnam War. The threat of nuclear war drove an even deeper wedge between the establishment and the disillusioned youth culture. Politicians who could bring humanity to the edge of destruction could not be the authentic voice of the people, a feeling that was exacerbated by the widespread perceived futility of the Vietnam War. Civil disobedience became a mode of political action representative of such a significant minority of alienated youth that the authority and legitimacy of the American government were seriously undermined.

The movement against the Vietnam War thought of the conflict as immoral, irrational, and unjust. It was an aberration perpetrated by misguided politicians pandering to the pressure of the military-industrial complex. The movement saw its role as fundamentally educative. If it could disseminate the true facts by means of teach-ins, mass rallies, and lobbying

Congress, the nonviolent civil disobedience would awaken the conscience of the nation and its leaders. The authorities, however, responded to the marches and peaceful protests with voracious force in, for example, Los Angeles, San Francisco, and New York. The nonviolent tactics of peaceful protest came to be viewed as futile and were gradually replaced by violent revolutionary tactics. The understanding of the war as an irrational aberration also became transformed. The government lost credibility, and its justifications were distrusted. The Vietnam War became attached to a wider context of systematic American imperialism. The anti-Vietnam movement became not just antiwar but also antiimperialist. A statement on civil disobedience by the leaders of the Vietnam Day Committee dated May 22, 1965, asserted that protesters appealed to a higher law, the law that America invoked in Nuremberg after World War II to prosecute war criminals who acted in accordance with the laws of their own country, in order to resist American institutions that stifle the thought and poison the moral well-being of its citizens and offer no democratic redress in an electoral system that presented no alternatives. The statement warned that "our massive civil disobedience, aimed at blocking the war machine of the United States, will send shock waves from Maine to California, and from the United States to all parts of the world."[22]

The imperialist analysis was clearly articulated by Carl Oglesby, president of Students for a Democratic Society, in a speech delivered in November 1965 during the March on Washington, D.C., to end the war in Vietnam. He argued that it was no longer adequate to think of the war as the result of the actions of misguided evil monsters. It had to be seen as part of American liberal foreign policy since 1932. It was a policy of containment to protect the interests of America throughout the world. Revolution was to be prevented anywhere on the principle that if one Southeast Asian country succumbs to what Americans designate communism, they will all fall like a series of dominoes. Oglesby maintained that Americans, who constituted 5 percent of the world's population but consumed 50 percent of its resources, "take a richness that is in good part not our own, and . . . put it in our pockets, our garages, our split levels, our bellies, and our futures."[23] The dispatching of 22,000 American troops to the Dominican Republic in 1965 by President Lyndon Johnson clearly illustrated liberalism's illiberal foreign policy. Johnson unequivocally stated his motive: "We don't propose to sit here in our rocking chair with our hands folded and let the Communists set up any government in the Western Hemisphere."[24] This anti-Communist ideology also impelled Johnson fundamentally to change the nature of American involvement in Vietnam. What President John Kennedy had called "their war" in 1963, Johnson made "our war" in 1965 by sending American bombers to North Vietnam and combat units for the first time to the South, initiating a war that was to last longer than any in American history and resulting in more American deaths in combat than at any time with the exception of the Civil War and the two world wars, the cost of which was second only to World War II.[25]

It is important to emphasize that Dylan's involvement with civil rights and antiwar protesters predates the shift to radical politics and widespread civil disobedience. Dylan was very much associated with the protest, or topical, songs of the folk music movement of the early 1960s. This movement was broadly left wing and, among its purist members, taking a counterculture stance, mocked other forms of popular music because of its commercialism. It was strongly oriented against what President Dwight Eisenhower called in a speech in 1961 the "military-industrial complex," which in itself constituted a powerful pressure group for prosecuting war. Eisenhower warned against the immense power of the military-industrial complex, which proved to be one of the most prophetic statements a U.S. president ever made. Three days later, Kennedy made his inaugural speech in which he emphasized the collective ethos: "Ask not what your country can do for you—ask what you can do for your country."

Kennedy's election to office did nothing to assuage the fears of threat that so exercised minds during the Eisenhower years, that is, the possibility of nuclear war. In 1961, with the resumption of Russian atmospheric testing of nuclear weapons, Americans feared the consequences of fallout and strontium 90 poisoning, and looked to fallout shelters as a possible defense. The Ban the Bomb movement in Great Britain was slow to take hold in the United States, where only pockets of resistance to the dominant culture could be discerned in the radicalness of the Beat Generation. Pete Seeger, on his return from Britain after encountering the extent of civil unrest against the threat of nuclear war, lamented the fact that the voice of American radicalism, even in song, was not being heard.

The subsequent reflection of contemporary social and political issues in the lyrics of folk songs, along with a heightened awareness that the whole folk song tradition harbored subversive elements, generated as strong a condemnation from conservative forces, as Elvis Presley and Jerry Lee Lewis had done in the 1950s. In September 1963, at the height of the folk revival and the popularity of the hootenanny, the U.S. Senate debated a call from the Fire and Police Research Association of Los Angeles for the House Un-American Activities Committee (HUAC) to investigate Communist influence in folk music. The call was prompted by the conclusion that the Soviet Union, in pursuance of its goal of world domination, was using the folk movement as an instrument to subvert the youth of America. Its method was dialectical, alluding to a key Marxist concept, and cybernetic, alluding to the nascent powers of persuasion in the advancement of computer technology.

This call came at a time when the reputation of Congress was being impugned by criticism of the overzealous and often unjust activities of HUAC. Senator Keating of New York, with a good degree of satire and tongue in cheek, reported that there is no smoke without fire, and seeing the humor in the situation, suggested that that was probably why the Fire and Police Research Association was involved. The senator related its evidence of songs in which people were incited to disregard embargoes and concluded that if widely sung now, the embargo against Cuba could be undermined. In addition, in such songs as "Darwin Cory" and "Copper Kettle," which Dylan was later to record for *Self Portrait* (1970) in what is widely deemed to be his postprotest phase, excise duty on liquor is widely being evaded. Indeed, the family in "Copper Kettle" has not paid any whiskey tax since 1792. Even more sinister is the Negro spirituals that preached pacifism and disarmament: "Gonna lay down my sword and shield / Down by the river-side / And study war no more." The Fire and Police Research Association concluded that the subversive implication of the song was that West Point and other military academies be closed to prevent the study of war and to facilitate Soviet domination.

Obviously concerned that the Senate would become a laughing stock if it recommended the investigation of folk music, Keating asked the rhetorical question, that on top of all the senators, congressmen, and presidents who have been accused of being Communists are we to add, "merciful heavens, American folk music. And who knows what lies ahead?" Keating's views were echoed by other senators, one of whom maintained that any attempt to suppress such expression would smack of the Soviet totalitarian suppression of impressionist artists and jazz musicians.[26]

This, of course, needs to be placed in context. The call from the Fire and Police Research Association of Los Angeles came three months after a huge outcry in the press and on television stations surrounding the suppression of Bob Dylan's song "Talkin' John Birch Paranoid Blues." Dylan had been scheduled to sing it on the *Ed Sullivan Show,* May 12, 1963. CBS network honchos feared that the lyrics might prompt a lawsuit and put pressure on the young singer to substitute a different song. Instead, he walked out, gaining much more publicity for his views on right-wing myopia in relation to communism than had he sung the song. Dylan himself complained to the Federal Communications Commission, accusing WCBS-TV of exercising "a form of censorship and economic tyranny."[27]

A couple of months after the Senate debate, Dylan performed the song at Carnegie Hall, introducing it by saying, "There ain't nothin' wrong with this song."[28] Its sentiments were, in fact, in line with some of the more enlightened members of the Senate who would have been totally in sympathy with the song's ridiculing of Communist paranoia: "Now Eisenhower, he's a Russian spy / Lincoln, Jefferson, and that Roosevelt guy." The Red Scare was echoed in Britain by the more sensationalist of the popular Sunday newspapers, claiming that the contemporary worldwide movement in folk music masked the clandestine tactics of the Kremlin to poison and subvert young minds. Derek Johnson, in the *New Musical Express* in November 1963 dismissed with contempt these hysterical and paranoid allegations.

The CBS incident was indicative of a wider problem, and that was the dependence of television and radio on sponsors and advertising. In a 1961 documentary, quoting Edmund Burke's famous phrase "All that is necessary for the triumph of evil is for good men to do nothing," host Howard K. Smith prophesied race riots in Birmingham, Alabama. CBS forced Smith to resign. The desire to avoid offending anyone on television stifled even legitimate protest. In post-1945 America, there have been two strands in the extreme right, the one upholding the Bible and the other the Constitution. Robert Welch of the John Birch Society was far more vociferous in the 1960s in rejecting the aspects of the democratic process than, for example, Father Charles E. Coughlin in the 1930s, in his opposition to President Franklin D. Roosevelt and support of the economically outcast against the banks, or Senator Joseph McCarthy in the 1950s, who concentrated his anti-Communist attack on the symbols of upper-class society, being careful, for example, not to antagonize the unions.

The John Birch Society with its economic conservativism appealed very much to the upper strata of society and advocated restricting the suffrage. The three right-wing movements epitomized by Welch, Coughlin, and McCarthy shared common elements: they were isolationist and intensely nationalist, they all stressed both the internal and external dangers of communism, and they were willing to disregard due process when confronting the problems of internal communism. Members of the John Birch Society, for example, were reluctant to extend civil liberties to Communists, atheists, and pacifists, and likely to deny the right of public meeting to those opposing the American form of government. Many advocated censuring the "crime comic book" as an undesirable influence upon the young. A poll in California in 1963 indicated that Republicans rather than Democrats, those living in Southern California, those better

educated and in a higher economic category, and those who were fundamentalist in religion, concerned about communism, and committed to
economic conservatism were more likely to support the society than those
who had a different socioeconomic profile. These members of the radical
right, although paranoid, were relatively sophisticated in their discrimina-
tions and tended to abstain from expressing anti-Semitic views or those
associated with other forms of traditional bigotry. Their attack on religion
was upon the National Council of Churches, with its liberal-leaning, high-
status Protestant affiliates. Welch, in fact, tried to limit his followers to
attacking communism and those sectors of the political elite that he thought
most susceptible to it, that is, the intellectuals who influence political
organizations.[29] They were strongly opposed to the civil rights movement
and the intellectuals who led it, and by implication disagreed with the
proposed level of government intervention to improve the plight of blacks.
In fact, Welch thought that Eisenhower was part of the Communist
conspiracy. He wondered why Eisenhower had helped destroy McCarthy,
placated the Korean Communists, refused help to anti-Communist forces
in Indochina, Berlin, and Hungary, and extended "socialist" policies initiated
by liberal Democrats. Welch developed a sophisticated conspiracy theory
that was global in nature and historically concerted. The John Birch Society
was not a party and did not seek mass membership. It regarded itself as
a striking force. Given the economic profile of its supporters, who were,
it must be added, a tiny minority of the population, CBS did not want
to offend a potential source of income. "Talkin' John Birch Paranoid Blues"
had, however, in a slightly different version, been sung by the Chad Mitchell
Trio the day before on *Hootenanny*, on the ABC television network.[30]

Harriet Van Horne, in a piece dated May 15, 1963, in the *New York
Telegram and Sun*, accused CBS of having little moral fiber in effectively
condoning an organization that had been denounced by the three major
faiths in America, by the responsible press, by the attorney general of the
United States, and even by President Eisenhower. Horne highlighted a
vacuum that in many ways the folk movement filled, supplying the critical
edge that the networks were unwilling to develop. Horne argued: "There
seems to be no zest for major battles at any network. Worse, there is no
moral passion, no deeply felt need to educate the public to show 'the
simple who believeth every word' where the philosophy of Robert Welch
may be in error."

By the mid-1960s, Dylan had rejected the more overtly political
protest songs—having never claimed to be a protest singer—and the folk
movement of which he was hailed as one of its greatest leaders. Although
the civil rights movement was the context of his political finger-pointing

songs, he declared that he was not part of any movement and that he was not going to be constrained by its rules.[31] His songs then developed what was already emerging in the earlier albums, a more personal and less communal expression of his own emotions, whether in love songs, or surrealist imagery, or sheer poetry set to music. Cohen, while becoming part of the same folk music tradition, never wrote topical or protest songs, but his songs are highly political in their imagery of the modern world. He explores the depths of human experience and alienation. Donald Henahan, the cultural editor of the *New York Times,* in comparing Dylan and Cohen, captures the essence of the different characters of their music: "Whereas Mr. Dylan is alienated from society and mad about it, Mr. Cohen is alienated and merely sad about it."[32] To put it differently, in the early years Dylan was the manifestation of popular resistance, the exemplar for an alienated youth to emulate. In contrast, Cohen differentiates himself: "If you were going to talk about the political aspect of my music I would say that it is the music of personal resistance."[33]

From an early point in their careers Dylan and Cohen shared the same contradiction: they resented excessive intrusion into their personal lives, expressing a deep cynicism of the adulation and sainthood they had achieved, while simultaneously cultivating it for all they were worth. Their cynicism bordered on public arrogance and is manifest in their early dealings with the press, as well as in documentaries in which they self-consciously present personas that are evasive, ambivalent, defiant, arrogant, and egotistic. These features are evident in Dylan's *Don't Look Back* (1966) and Cohen's *Ladies and Gentlemen, It's Leonard Cohen* (1965). Both use cynicism about their egos as a method of self-defense, preserving something of their private life and maintaining their integrity. That they were able to play games with the press that took their outrageousness at face value and maintain credibility with their audience is a sign of the extent to which the establishment, along with the media, was completely out of touch with the emergent and defiant youth culture.

Even though both have continued to enjoy considerable success, it is their early albums, Bob Dylan's up to 1968 and Leonard Cohen's up to 1971, that continue to define them and against which everything else they do is judged. On the occasion of Dylan's sixtieth birthday, for example, Ian MacDonald in *Uncut* magazine suggested that the years of drug abuse, withdrawal from methamphetamine, and the consequent damage meant that Dylan was never again able to scale the heights of the artistry he achieved in those early years.[34] In the collector's edition of *Q Dylan,* John Harris maintains that between 1962 and 1966 Dylan marked the world's consciousness "as much as any musician ever has."[35] In 1984 Dylan lamented that "I look at those songs and wonder where they came from, and how they came. I couldn't do them now, and I don't even try."[36] Robert Sandall suggested that nothing Cohen had done since *The Songs of Leonard Cohen* (1968) had made the same impact. He argued that the 1988 album *I'm Your Man* showed that the dark, depressive poetry benefited from an inventive arrangement.[37] *Cohen's Greatest Hits* (1975), a selection of songs from the early albums, was voted in 1998 top of the all-time "gravest hits," or music to get depressed by, despite the much less manic-depressive material of his later years.[38] Even the Columbia Records Media Department press release accompanying the release of *Ten New Songs* played on this reputation by calling Cohen "the master of mortification" and the "sentry of solitude."

The music industry is exactly that, an industry aggressively seeking profit from a lucrative market share, and as Tom Petty graphically remarked, it doesn't give a damn about the music and is motivated by profit and nothing else. In the 1987 film *Hearts of Fire,* Dylan plays a rock star who has seen better times, and is cynical and embittered about the experience. In one scene Dylan, whose dignity is so affronted by the corruption of the music industry, smashes up a hotel room in an uncontrollable rage.[39] The impact of the point is lost when the event is so common and attributed to far less well intended motivations.

The labels are commercial enterprises competing for a share of the lucrative market, prepared to invest heavily in those they see as potential profit boosters. The United States constitutes over 30 percent of the world market, generating over $10 billion in sales annually. It is no wonder that all successful artists attempt to make it in America. In comparison, British sales constitute some 10 percent of the world market. Britain's participation in the global popular music market did not come about until the 1960s, with the phenomenal success of the Beatles and the British invasion.

In 1991 Tony Powell, the managing director of MCA Records, announced that record companies now see themselves as entertainment companies concerned with projecting global personalities through multimedia formats. The quest today is for entertainment icons who can be plugged into the vast network of media communications globally developed.[40] Both Cohen and Dylan predate the globalization of pop and were to some extent vehicles of it. They had become legendary before the transformation of the industry, which allowed them a certain degree of self-indulgence, Dylan more so than Cohen, in constantly surprising his audience with new, sometimes unwelcome, shifts in style.

Cohen's relationship with CBS/Sony has been cordial, but he has often found it difficult to disguise his obvious irritation at attempts to force his music into categories and conform to sounds that are not his, and with what he considers the low-key marketing of his work. In an interview he gave prior to the release of his first album in 1968, Cohen complained of how his lack of familiarity with recording studios encouraged engineers and musicians to manipulate him and tell him how to make music. It was, he complained, a constant struggle to prevent them from putting him into their categories. Yet by the time he recorded *Songs from a Room* (1969) he had accepted responsibility for being unaware of "the techniques of collective enterprise."[41] He never felt that he had an appropriate degree of control until he learned to play the keyboard and became better able to convey to those around him the sort of sound he wanted to create. *I'm Your Man* (1988) was the result of this process and became the record that relaunched, even rescued, his career.

Cohen certainly occupies a specialist market in which the heaviest demand is in Europe, especially France and Scandinavia. His sales are not modest. In the CD era alone he has sold around thirteen million copies, and his most popular offering, *I'm Your Man,* sold almost two million. Whenever Cohen speaks of his relationship with his record company it is in a mixture of tones, feigned gratitude, and light sarcasm. In the *Billboard* interview of November 1998, Cohen remarked that "I have always been touched by the modesty of their interest in my work. I do feel patriotic, because, you know, in conjunction with the [Central Intelligence Agency], they have released my records as part of a covert operation." He was particularly hurt by the decision of Walter Yetnikoff, one of Columbia Records' executives, not to release *Various Positions* (1985) in the United States. Nevertheless, he readily acknowledged the fact that the executives at Columbia were hardly likely to recommend to Sony that they "commit the resources of the hit making machine" to a record whose potential was ten times less in sales than one of their big acts. Cohen resignedly conceded that although the company could do more to promote and sell his records in the United States, there was no reason to since putting their weight behind another, more popular act would yield it greater profits.[42] Dylan was in a stronger position with Columbia and Sony. Having felt that his initial deal was exploitative, he never again allowed Columbia to dictate terms.

Like Cohen, Dylan's fortunes have fluctuated over the years. In the early 1990s his artistic well appeared to have dried up. Whereas there had been droughts previously, when, for example, he released *Self Portrait,* ironically comprised of covers of well-known songs across a wide, span of genres, the two acoustic albums of the early 1990s—*Good as I Been to You* (1992) and *World Gone Wrong* (1993)—comprising uninspiring versions of blues songs that were with him in the early days in Greenwich Village, were hailed as Dylan's swan song. He confounded the critics once again by releasing *Time Out of Mind* (1997), an album reflecting his near-death experience and conveying beautifully the maudlin, the resignation, and the fear of growing older and facing up to death. It was a huge commercial success, and he won a Grammy for it in 1998. He topped this achievement by winning an Oscar for "Things Have Changed," which he wrote for the film *Wonder Boys* (2000).

Endnotes

1. Quoted in *Bob Dylan in His Own Words,* ed. Christian Williams (London: Omnibus Press, 1993), 19.
2. Quoted in *Leonard Cohen in His Own Words,* ed. Jim Devlin (London: Omnibus, 1998), 25.
3. Alan Franks, "Love's Hard Man," *London Times Magazine,* October 13, 2001, 16.
4. Quoted in Doug Saunders, "State of Grace," *Globe and Mail,* September 1, 2001.
5. Cohen has commented about this album: "I love everything that Dylan does and I love to hear the old guys lay it out. *Love and Theft* produces tremendous energy." Leonard Cohen, CBS Web site chat, October 16, 2001.
6. Richard Dyer, *Stars* (London: British Film Institute, 1979).
7. Jason Toynbee, *Making Popular Music: Musicians, Creativity and Institutions* (London: Arnold, 2000), xi.
8. See Greil Marcus, *Invisible Republic: Bob Dylan's Basement Tapes* (London: Picador, 1998), 104. Marcus wrote the liner notes for *The Basement Tapes.* Smith compiled a fourth volume of the *Anthology* but didn't get around to releasing it in his lifetime. One reason he gave was that he wanted to present a comprehensive content analysis of the songs but had lost interest. The Harry Smith Archives and Revenant Records released volume 4 (RNV 211) in 2000 with a short book. Harry Smith's reasons for not releasing the fourth volume are given on page 32 of this book. I would like to thank Joe Evans for bringing this to my attention.
9. See Matt Theado, "The Beats in New York City," in *The Beats: A Literary Reference,* ed. Matt Theado (New York: Carroll & Graf, 2003), 17–18.
10. For details of the origins of the term *hootenanny,* I am grateful to Robert Shelton's research held in the Liverpool University Archive, Institute for Popular Music.
11. Robert Shelton, "Something Happened in America," 17 (Manuscript held in the Robert Shelton Archive, Liverpool University Archive, Institute for Popular Music).
12. Speech by Bruce Springsteen on Bob Dylan's induction to the Rock and Roll Hall of Fame, January 20, 1988, in *Wanted Man: In Search of Bob Dylan,* ed. John Bauldie (New York: Citadel Press, 1991), 179.
13. Cited in Harry Rasky, *The Song of Leonard Cohen: Portrait of a Poet, a Friendship and a Film* (Oakville, Ontario: Mosaic Press, 2001), 24.
14. Margaret Mead, *Culture and Commitment: A Study of the Generation Gap* (New York: Doubleday, for the Museum of Natural History, 1970).
15. Margaret Mead, *The Coming of Age in Samoa* (London: Penguin, 1943).
16. Derek Freeman was responsible for the systematic refutation of her thesis, *Margaret Mead and Samoa: The Making and Unmaking of an Anthropological Myth* (Canberra: Australian National University Press, 1983).
17. Richard Poirier, "Rock of Ages," in *The Performing Self* (London: Chatto & Windus, 1973), 183.

18. Daniel J. Gonczy, "The Folk Music of the 1960s: Its Rise and Fall," *Popular Music and Society* 10 (1985). Reprinted in Elizabeth Thompson and David Gutman, eds., *The Dylan Companion* (New York: Da Capo Press, 2001), 7.
19. Reprinted in Bruce Franklin, *From the Movement toward Revolution* (New York: Van Nostrand Reinhold, 1971), 73–74.
20. Ibid., 71.
21. Eldridge Cleaver, "Revolution in the Mother Country and National Liberation in the Black Colony," reprinted in ibid., 76.
22. Reprinted in ibid., 46.
23. Reprinted in ibid., 43.
24. Cited in Arthur M. Schlesinger Jr., *The Imperial Presidency* (London: Deutsch, 1974), 178.
25. Ibid., 178.
26. "Mine Enemy the Folk Singer," *Congressional Record* 154, September 26, 1963, 17290–17292.
27. Letter dated, May 16, 1963 (copy in the Robert Shelton Archive, Institute for Popular Music, Liverpool University).
28. Howard Souness, *Down the Highway: The Life of Bob Dylan* (London: Doubleday, 2001), 13–14.
29. For a good overview, see Seymour Martin Lipset, *Three Decades of the Radical Right: Coughlinites, McCarthyites and Birchers*, in *The Radical Right*, ed. Daniel Bell (New York: Anchor Doubleday, 1964). See also Seymour Martin Lipset and Earl Raab, *The Politics of Unreason* (London: Heinemann, 1971).
30. Val Adams, "Satire on Birch Society Barred from Ed Sullivan TV Show," in *Bob Dylan: The Early Years, a Retrospective,* ed. Craig McGregor (New York: Da Capo Press, 1990), 36.
31. Nat Hentoff, "The Crackin', Shakin', Breakin' Sounds," *The New Yorker,* October 1964. Reprinted in McGregor, *Bob Dylan,* 59.
32. Cited in Rasky, *Song of Leonard Cohen,* 19; and Ira B. Nadel, *Various Positions: A Life of Leonard Cohen* (London: Bloomsbury, 1996), 159.
33. Rasky, *Song of Leonard Cohen,* 118.
34. Ian MacDonald, "Wild Mercury: A Tale of Two Dylans," *Uncut, Dylan 60th Birthday Special* (June 2001).
35. John Harris, "In Praise of Bob Dylan," *Q Dylan* (2000): 11.
36. Cited in MacDonald, "Wild Mercury," 63.
37. Robert Sandall, "Crucial Cuts," *London Sunday Times,* November 2, 1997, Culture section, 20.
38. Emily Sheffield, "Cohen Tops Misery Charts," *The Guardian,* February 4, 1998, 3.
39. Tim Riley, *Hard Rain: A Dylan Commentary* (New York: Da Capo Press, 1999), 275–276.
40. Keith Negus, *Producing Pop: Culture and Conflict in the Popular Music Industry* (London: Arnold, 1992), 1.
41. Michael Harris, "Leonard Cohen: The Poet as Hero: 2," *Saturday Night* (June 1969): 26. Reprinted in *Leonard Cohen: The Artist and His Critics,* ed. Michael Gnarowski (Toronto: McGraw-Hill, 1976), 46.
42. Leonard Cohen, interviewed by Susan Nunziata, *Billboard,* November 28, 1998.

2

FROM FOLK ROOTS TO NEW ROUTES

> So Washington Square was a place where people you knew or
> met congregated every Sunday and it was like a world of music.
> —Bob Dylan, talking about New York, 1978[1]

Both Cohen and Dylan were perceived to have rebelled against the
culture that initially embraced them. Part of this rebellion entailed
becoming fully submerged in the burgeoning drug culture of New
York. Dylan's rebellion was more overt against the folk music/protest
movement of the 1960s. As one of the leaders of the folk music revival
of the early 1960s, he composed a number of the anthems that epitomized
the era. On his arrival in New York, he was immediately accepted into
the counterculture of the folk/beatnik/coffeehouse social milieu of Greenwich Village.

Since the nineteenth century, Greenwich Village in New York City
has held an attraction for writers, artists, and musicians because of its
unique character as a town within a city, where the grid system of midtown
Manhattan breaks down into interesting and enticing winding side streets.
Edith Wharton, Edgar Allan Poe, and Mark Twain, among the notables,
had inhabited the Village, and one of Henry James's most famous novels,
Washington Square (1881), records his observations of the Village and its
center of activity.

In the immediate post–World War II period, Pete Seeger lived in a
small house next to the Provincetown Playhouse on MacDougal Street
and started a music publishing venture with folksinger-songwriter Oscar
Brand called People's Songs, the aim of which was to make available the
new material that was being written, and not to have to rely on collections

of antiquarian folk songs. Folk music firmly insinuated itself into Greenwich Village in 1950, when Allan Block opened his sandal shop on West Fourth Street. The store became a meeting place for those interested in folk culture, including Cisco Houston, Leadbelly (real name Huddie Ledbetter), Josh White, Will Geer, and Woody Guthrie. It was also in 1950 that the magazine *Sing Out!* first appeared. It was edited from 1951 to 1967 by Irwin Silber, who was to become influential in the Newport Folk Festival. *Sing Out!* replaced *People's Songs* as a vehicle for left-wing songwriters. It tried to strike a balance between publishing new material and preserving traditional songs. Many people were nervous about being associated with the new publication because of the anti-Left atmosphere pervaded by the Korean War, Senator Joseph McCarthy, and the cold war.

At this time Greenwich Village was a well-established working-class area of downtown New York, with a large Italian and Irish population, and a plethora of cafes and bars catering to them. There were many factories adjacent to the housing, and the cafe owners made their money from workers on their way home. When the factories were demolished, the cafe owners had to try to recoup their losses and often turned to live entertainment. This was the origin of Mike Porco's business at 11 West Third Street. The name of the cafe, Gerdes (often spelled Gerde's), was retained by Porco, a Calabrian immigrant, from the previous owner, William Gerde, who sold the premises to Porco, his brother John, and his cousin Joe Bastone. They even took the name with them when they relocated to 11 West Fourth Street in the late 1950s, where it continued under the same management until 1969. Various entertainers, such as Lenny Bruce, Thelonious Monk, and Phyllis Diller, worked the clubs and cafes around the Village.

In reaction to the austere conservatism of the Eisenhower years, a new generation of antiestablishment poets emerged both on the East and West Coasts. The Beat poets were tolerated but were not part of this community. The self-styled Beat Generation adopted the Village as their own and hung around the cafes, where they exchanged poems and ideas. The term *Beat Generation* was used derisively by mainstream critics, as the names of so many art movements have been (for example, the Impressionists and Fauves). Allen Ginsberg has suggested that the term was coined by Jack Kerouac and John Clellon Holmes in 1948, but in fact they had heard it from Herbert Huncke, a friend of Kerouac and a Times Square drug addict and hipster. Kerouac didn't purposely name his generation but sought instead to unname it by using the term *beat*. Huncke extended its use into "hip" street language, but it came to have a very wide range of reference, from downbeat to upbeat to deadbeat. Ginsberg argues that the Beat Generation artistic movement had an immense influence on all forms of liberation, from oppression, both sexual and racial, to censorship. It also contributed to a greater acceptance of drug use and influenced the evolution of rhythm and blues into the high art form of rock and roll in the work of Bob Dylan and the Beatles. Among other things the Beat Generation was environmentally conscious and opposed the military-industrial complex.[2] Beat poetry was the poetry of the street, taking everyday objects, using slang language, and weaving words into free-style verse. What the Beats produced was a confrontational realism.

At the same time as Lawrence Ferlinghetti, working with Kenneth Rexroth, was presenting live jazz and poetry performances in the basement of City Lights in San Francisco in the mid-1950s, Kerouac was fusing jazz and poetry in the Circle in the Square Theatre in Greenwich Village and reading his works at the Village Vanguard, usually drunk on Thunderbird. Jazz, in Kerouac's view, was not incidental to the Beat Generation, but central. When asked why, Kerouac answered:

> Jazz is very complicated. It's just as complicated as Bach. The chords, the structures, the harmony and everything. And then it has a tremendous beat. You know, tremendous drummers. They can drive it. It has just a tremendous drive. It can drive you right out of yourself.[3]

Coffeehouses proliferated in the Village and were animated by the sound of chanted poems and scented by the sweet smell of marijuana burning. The Cedar Tavern was a popular congregating point for artists such as Larry Rivers and Robert Rauschenberg, whose poetic comrades included Frank O'Hara, Kenneth Koch, John Ashbery, and Ted Berrigan, later known as the New York school.[4] In the late 1950s public poetry reading sessions were common, and the likes of the young Leonard Cohen, while at Columbia University, and Richie Havens, as a nineteen-year-old, would listen to Ferlinghetti, Kerouac, Ginsberg, and Ted Jones.

The White Horse was another popular venue on Hudson Street. It was an old English-style pub, a favorite haunt of Dylan Thomas and actor Richard Burton when they were in New York. It had a party atmosphere, where Irish singing groups such as the Clancy Brothers and Tommy Makem and writers Mike Harrington and James Baldwin, along with the extrovert Richard Farina, would entertain with wildly exaggerated yarns. Farina, who married folksinger Carolyn Hester, after being introduced to her in the White Horse by Robert Shelton, would emphasize Irish ancestry as he recited poems or read stories with exaggerated, sweeping gestures. Bob Dylan described him as "a silent-moving-picture-actor."[5] The White

Horse was also a place Dylan frequented, often with Shelton. Dylan knew Farina from the White Horse and came to know him more intimately during a brief stay in London, as well as out in Carmel, California, when Mimi Baez, Joan Baez's younger sister, and Farina lived close to Joan. Dylan once described Farina as the king of bullshitters with nothing to say. He thought that Farina had become too uptight and took his music too lightly. Dylan didn't like any of Farina's songs because they were all "shucks."[6]

By 1959 many of the Beats had migrated to the West Coast, and the folk revival was well and truly taking off. San Francisco was a particularly attractive destination for many of the poets, such as Ferlinghetti, who had started up the City Lights bookstore in 1953 after moving out west in 1950, as well as artists such as Wallace Berman, David Meltzer, and Robert Alexander. The attraction was that San Francisco was cosmopolitan and more tolerant of alternative lifestyles during the constraining and constricting McCarthy years. It was very European in appearance, with Italian cafes, Victorian architecture, and compact, pedestrian-friendly streets.

Topical songs became a popular form of expression in Greenwich Village, and *Sing Out!* was not able to keep up with the demand for space and came to focus on the songs of movements rather than individual songwriters. *Broadside* came to fill the gap as a topical song magazine featuring the work of the new generation of finger-pointers. The folkies and Beats, although often associated, were mutually antagonistic, without being hostile. When Beats got up to read or chant a poem, sometimes to free-form jazz guitar, the folkies would groan, and when a folksinger filled the gap between two poets with songs of poverty, deprivation, and injustice, calling upon the workers to unite in unions, the Beats would cringe.

The Beats responded to the nuclear era with deep angst and personal introspection, and experimented not only with hard liquor but, in true Rimbaud style, with hard drugs that pushed them to the extremes of experience. They were famous not only for their poetry but also for their lifestyle, which was often self-destructive. Marianne Faithfull recalls that when she went to Paris in 1964 Ginsberg, Gregory Corso, and Ferlinghetti shared the same room in the Hotel Louisiana as she and her new husband, John Dunbar. They ranted about homosexuality, Rimbaud, and Ethel and Julius Rosenberg while vomiting on the floor and spilling rosé all over the place. Breakfast for Corso consisted of mixing up a Brompton cocktail—an equal blend of morphine and cocaine—then passing out on the floor.

The Beats glamorized drugs in a way that neither Bob Dylan nor Leonard Cohen ever did, even though both notoriously experimented with numerous banned substances. Take, for example, Alexander Trocchi, the Glaswegian Beat, who spent time in New York and who Cohen met in Montreal. Trocchi used drugs to reach the limits of consciousness and saw it as his public duty to introduce everyone else to the experience. At the time Cohen met him, Trocchi was working in New York with a group of writers and publishers thought by the "provincials" in Montreal to be at the cutting edge of literature and poetry. Cohen had read *Cain's Book* and was familiar with Trocchi's messianic view of drugs, which was not unusual among the Beat poets and philosophers, who thought that this tainted and smudged reality could be penetrated and a more authentic existence apprehended, embraced, and lived. Cohen thought him not unlike William Burroughs and Allen Ginsberg, who believed that our perceptions of reality had to be radically altered. These were not new ideas and had been thoroughly explored in England for centuries, for example, by De Quincey and in France by Céline and Rimbaud. Cohen's *The Favourite Game* was compared favorably with the prose of the Beats by the Shelley scholar Kenneth H. Cameron. Cohen's novel, he thought, had a subtle strong flow, and a solid structure that was deceptive. This set Cohen apart from the Beats such as Kerouac, who sporadically wrote well but lacked movement.[8]

On one occasion, Trocchi fixed himself on opium in Cohen's Montreal apartment on Mountain Street and gave him the residue that lined the rim of the pot used to dissolve it. Being inexperienced in hard drugs, Cohen digested the dangerously high-residue dosage. In the middle of traffic he suddenly went blind, panicked, and collapsed. On recovering, Cohen concurred with what was a general impression, that Trocchi's company was high risk. Writing from Quebec in 1961, Cohen expressed relief at just ridding himself of Trocchi on a ship bound for England. He commented that Trocchi was a tremendous responsibility and wanted you to feel, and that was his motivation for fixing himself in public: "He's a public junky."[9] Although this was Cohen's private view, he wrote a poem about Trocchi that valorized the author for living on the edge and risking his life, convinced of his own mission.

> You don a false nose
> line up twice for the Demerol dole;
> you step out of a tourist group
> shoot yourself on the steps of the White House,
> you try to shoot the big arms

of the Lincoln Memorial;
through the flaw in their lead houses
you spy on scientists,
stumble on a cure for scabies;
you drop pamphlets from a stolen jet.

("Alexander Trocchi, Public Junkie, *Prié pour Nous," Flowers for Hitler*)

Subsequently, Cohen's view of the Beat glamorization of drugs was that it was a dangerous experiment that had disastrous consequences, but that for some it may have served a purpose, and that for a few it led to some revelations. Dylan, too, was an admirer of Beat poetry. He had been introduced to it in Minneapolis through one of his teachers, Dave Morton, who sang at the Ten O'Clock Scholar. Dylan looked back on those days with affection when he said that there was a great deal of unrest in the air, reinforced by the recitation of poems by Kerouac, Corso, Ginsberg, and Ferlinghetti. The atmosphere was like that of a calm before the storm. Lawrence Ferlinghetti read at The Band's farewell concert, in which Dylan performed, immortalized in the film *The Last Waltz* (1978). Ginsberg was part of Dylan's entourage in the mid-60s and performed in the 1975 Rolling Thunder Revue, which included Dylan backed by Joan Baez and other friends. Ginsberg, although central to the Beat scene, was regarded as something of an anomaly in comparison with Burroughs, Corso, and Trocchi. When Cohen met Ginsberg in Athens in 1961 he thought him a nice, quiet, clean-shaven Jewish boy who had fallen in with bad company, namely, the beatniks.[10] Marianne Faithfull knew him quite well and thought him genial and out of his depth with the rock-and-roll circus onto which he had latched.[11] Ginsberg's manner, however, disguises a courageousness that cannot be underestimated: the publication of *Howl* got him caught up in an obscenity trial; for criticizing Cuban leader Fidel Castro's denunciation of homosexuality, he was deported from Cuba; on being elected May King in Prague, he was detained by the Czech authorities; and he tried to halt a train carrying nuclear waste by sitting on a railway track in Colorado. In other words, like Trocchi, Ginsberg was committed and wanted to change the world, and he used his poetry as an instrument. He was a master of stunts and came to be something of a parody of himself, which he seemed to recognize in his own self-deprecating way, especially in "Ode to Failure."[12]

While Jim Morrison, Tim Hardin, and other performers of the time were sucked into the elusive quest for a more authentic reality through drugs, Dylan distanced himself from the whole glamorization of the drug culture associated with the Beats.[13]

Dylan and Ginsberg in North Beach, San Francisco, 1965 (Photographer: Larry Keenan).

Besides the charge of commercialism against Bob Dylan, one equally applicable to Joan Baez, Peter, Paul, and Mary, the Clancy Brothers, the Kingston Trio, the Chad Mitchell Trio, Harry Belafonte, and the Weavers, Dylan's transition to a more poetic style of composition away from the popularist emphasis may have tapped into the latent hostility of the folkies toward the Beat poets. Dylan's adoption of the persona of poet, as well as his befriending of Ginsberg, would not have endeared him to the finger-pointers of Greenwich Village. Immediately prior to the infamous electric set at the 1965 Newport Folk Festival, Dylan was in London with Ginsberg, who appears in the D. A. Pennebaker film *Don't Look Back* (1967), lurking in the background of the opening sequences as Bob Dylan nonchalantly flips flash cards with key words from "Subterranean Homesick Blues." Even the title of the song betrays the Beat connection. Jack Kerouac had

Magazine cover exposing the supposed excesses of the Beat culture.

written the book *The Subterraneans* (1958), and Ranald MacDougall had gentrified it for the screen in 1960.

The social consciousness of the folkies made it anathema to them to identify with the Beat culture, whose members were popularly portrayed as psychopathic deviants, misfits, and weirdos in whose company no one's daughter was safe. For example, in Hollywood films such as Charles Haas's *The Beat Generation* (1959), a rapist masquerades as a beatnik, and in Roger Corman's *A Bucket of Blood* (1959), a coffeehouse waiter who becomes a murderer pretends to be a Beat sculptor. In the 1959 British film *Beat Girl* (aka *Wild for Kicks*), directed by Edmond T. Gréville, the poster shows a semidressed girl dancing, with a moody Adam Faith in the foreground appearing in his first film. The film tells the story of a middle-class girl who rebels by sinking into the seedy world of the beatniks.

When Dylan, the country boy became the urban dandy, he sided with the bohemian culture of angst, hopelessness, and despair, of which the folkies disapproved because of their fundamentally different, altogether more optimistic outlook. Even though the subject matter was injustice in all its guises, for the folkies, the point of exposing these injustices was to rectify them. There was, in fact, a point toward the end of the famous Baez-Dylan tour, before their departure for London in 1965, when Joan Baez realized that Dylan had lost his belief that he and others in the folk community could transform the world: his attitude had changed from being angry at the injustices in society and wanting to transform the world to a despairing resignation at the futility of trying to change the degradation around him.

The folk revival of the late '50s and early '60s sat uneasily for a while with the jazz and Beat followers, who looked disdainfully at the popularist and self-righteous tendencies of Pete Seeger and Irwin Silber. Dave Van Ronk, whose arrangement of "House of the Rising Sun" appears on Dylan's first album, moved into folk even though his first love was jazz. Jazz was moving out of the Village along with the Beats. Jazz had an air of intellectualism about it that no longer carried with it an automatic challenge to academic authority. It had become highbrow and elevated in people's minds to an advanced form of serious music. In San Francisco, Greenwich Village, and Cambridge, Massachusetts, intellectuals found in folk music an abundance of anti-intellectualism to challenge academic authority.[14]

Gerdes Folk City, the most famous of the Village clubs, began life as The Fifth Peg and was the initiative of Izzy Young, the owner of the Folklore Center at 110 MacDougal Street, near Washington Square, which he opened in 1957. Israel Young was a promoter of numerous concerts, including Bob Dylan's first New York concert. At first, he was a great enthusiast of Dylan, but he later became one of Dylan's most vociferous detractors and accused Dylan of selling out to commercialism. Izzy and his business associate, Tom Prendergast, approached the Italian restaurateur and cafe owner Mike Porco and suggested to him the idea of a regular folk club. They said that they would cover the folksingers' fees and publicity, while Porco would keep all the bar profits. Regulars who drank at Gerdes would be allowed in free of charge. There was no reverence afforded the singers, and they often had to compete for the attention of the audience. Regular drinkers were irritated by rousing choruses when they were about to emphasize a point, and singers and folkies would get irate about raucous laughter during a sad lament.

During the day, Gerdes catered to the culinary needs of New York University students around Washington Square. In the evening, it would accommodate a mix of Irish and Italian workers looking for a drink and the "intellectual" folkies encountering and mixing with the people about whom they sang.

Gerdes was the first of the venues that enabled folk music to emerge from the cafes and flourish in a context of drinking. Unlike other small cafes and bars, such as the Why Not, the Basement, and the Slam, that did not pay acts, but instead passed a basket around for contributions, Gerdes paid the performers and gave a degree of independence and pride to them. An informal class stratification took place whereby regular folk-singers paid to perform resented being spoken about in the same terms as "basket house" entertainers. Dave Van Ronk, for example, took umbrage when the cover of his first album displayed an old-fashioned espresso machine, "because to be identified as a coffee-house folk singer was considered so *infra dignitatem* as to almost be slander."[15] Peter Tork played the basket house circuit for about two and half years from the winter of 1961 before finding fame with the Monkees. Coffeehouses were notoriously bad employers, treating folksingers often with contempt. The Cafe Wha was singled out as the focus of a protest because of its management practices. For twelve or fourteen hours a day it would pay solo acts $5 and groups $3 per person. The entertainers were demeaned by soliciting contributions from the audience, claiming that such tips were their only means of support. The money in fact went into the pockets of the owners, who paid the regular starvation wage irrespective of the collection. The Coffee House Entertainers Benevolent Association, led by Van Ronk and including Tom Paxton and Peter, Paul, and Mary's Noel Paul Stookey on the executive committee, campaigned for fair minimum wages across the board.

The Fifth Peg venture between Izzy Young and Mike Porco was often fraught because Izzy, barely getting by on the door take, wanted a percentage of the bar take, which Porco claimed was already too close to the margin. Porco, much to Young's anger and to the consternation of many performers, eased Young out and hired Charlie Rothschild to take care of the bookings. Izzy Young copyrighted the name The Fifth Peg, and Mike Porco was forced to find a new name. Taking suggestions, he finally settled on Gerdes Folk City. Carolyn Hester fronted the first show on May 30, 1960. Porco himself knew nothing about folk music; for him, it was purely a business venture. Izzy's friends who hung out at the Folklore Center on MacDougal Street boycotted the club for a while, but in reality they could not afford to turn down paying gigs. Dave Van Ronk, for example, reluctantly returned and continued to frequent the Folklore Center. Izzy was not the sort of man to hold it against anyone, and there were no recriminations.

Flyer for Bob Dylan's appearance at Gerdes Folk City, April 24 to May 6, 1962.

A wide range of acts were booked, usually for a week at a time. Porco always pleaded poverty, so if he wanted the Clancy Brothers, he would book two of them, knowing that the other two would come along anyway. The music ranged from bluegrass to blues and folk, and at first it relied on many established names, such as Cisco Houston, Reverend Gary Davis, John Lee Hooker, Odetta, and Ramblin' Jack Elliott, the son of a New York surgeon who adopted the Woody Guthrie image and tailored it to his own style.

Hootenanny nights on Mondays, at one time Tuesdays, gave new performers their first chance to get up and sing, but they also attracted established and seasoned singers who were unlikely to be working so early in the week. There was no admission price on these hoot nights, just a $1 or so cover charge toward a first drink to ensure no free riders. A roster was drawn up, at one time by lot, and singers would be allocated their spots. When the hoots became popular, singers would wait downstairs in a cellar room for their turn, swapping songs, guitar techniques, and stories.

Gerdes was the place where acts like José Feliciano and Peter, Paul, and Mary (Al Grossman's manufactured folk group, who took Dylan's "Blowin' in the Wind" to the top of the charts long before Dylan was known) got their first break. It was an extremely important venue for folk artists because it offered an opportunity for greater exposure. Robert

THE FOLKLORE CENTER

Presents

BOB DYLAN

IN HIS FIRST NEW YORK CONCERT

SAT NOV 4, 1961   8:40pm

CARNEGIE CHAPTER HALL

154 WEST 57th STREET   NEW YORK CITY

All seats $2.00

Tickets available at: The Folklore Center
110 MacDougal Street
GR 7 - 5987   New York City 12, New York

Advertisement for Bob Dylan's first New York concert, November 4, 1961.

Shelton, the music critic for the *New York Times*, spent a lot of time at the club and frequently reviewed the acts, making him the target for teasing by his colleagues, who wondered out loud why their music correspondent preferred a sleazy nightclub to the opera house.

Izzy Young was persuaded by Grossman, Dylan's manager, to stage Dylan's New York debut concert at Chapter Hall, a smaller concert space in prestigious Carnegie Hall in midtown Manhattan. It was a few days after Shelton's *New York Times* review of Dylan's appearance at Gerdes Folk City, opening for the Greenbriar Boys, that Young decided to take the risk. The embarrassingly low turnout of fifty-three people on Saturday, November 4, 1961, was a considerable contrast with the success of Joan Baez, who the following week had sold out the 1,700-seat Town Hall on Forty-third Street. Both of Baez's albums were already considerable commercial successes before Dylan started recording his first, and he was relatively unknown outside the Village. Village people rarely traveled uptown to music venues. They may have gone around the corner to the Gaslight or to Gerdes, but Carnegie Hall was off the map.

Today you take a subway from midtown Manhattan to downtown, alighting at Christopher Street and Sheridan Square on Seventh Avenue. On Sixth Avenue the subway stops at West Fourth Street, where Dylan rented a one-bedroom apartment at 161 West Fourth Street for $80 a month. Many of the cafes and bars remain, but the folksingers have been replaced by rock bands. Blues and jazz are still featured prominently in the night life of the Village. The Folklore Center at 110 MacDougal Street and Gerdes Folk City at 11 West Fourth Street are gone. The Kettle of Fish, where everyone hung out to unwind and exchange stories and songs, has moved from MacDougal Street, more or less intact, to 57 Stonewall Place, two doors up from 55 Bar, established in 1919 and catering to jazz and blues enthusiasts. Cafe Wha on MacDougal Street, where the current owners claim Dylan played his first live Village date on an open mike night, now has resident bands.[16] The Bitter End on Bleecker Street, established in 1961, continues as a live venue and is frequented by the famous, including Dylan, Ron Wood, Keith Richards, and Rod Stewart.

Dylan, after meeting Woody Guthrie, quickly became friendly with Woody's pals, Ramblin' Jack Elliott, Pete Seeger, and Cisco Houston, all of whom taught him songs and guitar styles in the course of spending time together. He was also invited to play harmonica on a number of recordings in 1961, including a session with the established black blues singers Big Joe Williams and Victoria Spivey, which was quite an achievement for a young, inexperienced white boy. While playing harmonica on a recording session for Carolyn Hester, Dylan met the legendary record producer and talent scout John Hammond Sr., whose eye he had already caught, but was now able to cement Hammond's interest with Shelton's glowing review of Dylan's September 26 performance at Gerdes Folk City, which appeared on the day of the recording session, September 29, 1961. Hammond signed him to a Columbia Records contract, and Dylan recorded his first album at the end of 1961. His popularity and reputation were much broader than the traditional audience for folk music. Peter, Paul, and Mary's version of Dylan's "Blowin' in the Wind," for example, gained him wide recognition. Dylan was central to the whole folk movement as a political force for change, but he could not have become so successful if he were merely a Guthrie clone. While his persona was Guthrie-esque, his depth of musical experience made him an interpreter rather than an imitator. He combined the styles of Guthrie and country legend Hank Williams, and added the harmonica inflections of bluesman Jesse Fuller.

The American, particularly New York, folk scene was almost policed by a well-meaning, well-intentioned, but nevertheless oppressive and intrusive political correctness enforced by those associated with *Sing Out!* magazine, such as Irwin Silber and Pete Seeger. Founded in May 1950, *Sing Out!* built upon what was left of *People's Songs* and a collective that called itself People's Artists. People's Artists undertook a whole range of activities on behalf of its members. It was a booking agency that promoted concerts and published and recorded music. Those associated with it were performing artists interested in promoting trade unionism, civil rights, and peace. It was a particularly useful organization in the 1950s in securing work for members who had been blacklisted in the McCarthy witch hunts. One of its main purposes was to promote an alternative culture. *Sing Out!* saw itself very much as living up to these concerns and ideals.

The folk culture in both America and Britain was heavily influenced, even orchestrated, by overt and covert political and cultural conventions and taboos. Ewan MacColl, the name Jimmie Miller adopted, presumably, for greater folk authenticity, and Bert Lloyd were at the forefront of the folk revival in Britain in the 1950s and '60s, espousing a purity that amounted to a strict code of conduct in the "singers' clubs" that had sprung up around the country. MacColl was in fact completely dismissive of Dylan, calling him a "mediocre talent."[17] In an interview for *Melody Maker* in September 1965, MacColl attacked Dylan for being someone who accepted the world for what it is, and for not wanting to change it. His poetry, MacColl said contemptuously, was derivative and old hat.

By the early 1960s a younger generation of more adventurous players, inspired by British folk-blues guitarist Davey Graham, fused different styles of music in Britain into a contemporary genre that gradually became more acceptable around the metropolitan folk clubs. In the United States, too, there were conventions governing what could and could not be sung by whom and in what context. There was a tension between authenticity and innovation. The purists couldn't accept any deviation from original recordings, the constant reliving of the past in the present, whereas Dylan's approach was to absorb and use that past heritage to advance and develop his own style. Folksinger Eric von Schmidt recalls that when he first met Dylan in 1962, the era of the singer-songwriter had not yet dawned, and most folkies were still suffering from the syndrome of "it can't really be folk music if you wrote it."[18] Dylan appealed to the "progressives," who were more interested in whether a song was good rather than in its origin on an obscure mountain range in Alabama. In the first of his columns, and in the first issue of *Hootenanny* (Autumn 1963), Robert Shelton's short-lived folk music magazine, Dylan hit out at the hair splitting in which folk enthusiasts appeared to revel. He maintained that it was unhealthy to let music run your life to that extent. He exhorted his readers to beware of those who stultify the medium by having to categorize it into neat little boxes. The accompanying notes to Dylan's album *Biograph* (1985) echo the same sentiments and convey his impression of the folk music scene around 1961. He accused it of being a pathetically rigid establishment that strictly demarcated what was appropriate: English ballads didn't mix with Texas cowboy songs, nor Southern mountain blues with Southern mountain ballads or city blues. Dylan was central to the American folk revival, but no one could have envisaged in 1961 that folk music would become so central a part of popular music by the mid-1960s. There were some perceptive commentators, however, who had an inkling of its potential beyond an antiquarian curiosity in preserving a past culture. In reviewing Dylan's visit to London to appear in the BBC play called *Madhouse on Castle Street,* R. Gilbert tentatively suggested that despite the skepticism of British record company producers, as an outside bet folk music was in the running to become the next boom in popular music.[19]

There was certainly an ambivalence in Dylan's protest singer persona. His songs were adopted by those who were firmly in the business of political protest and saw themselves in the vanguard of the civil rights movement. Although he was labeled by both his fellow Greenwich Village workers in song and the newspapers as self-consciously politically charged and a leader of youth culture, Dylan himself was less happy with the label. In the same month, August 1963, such music papers as the *New Musical Express* placed him firmly in the American protest movement, while the *National Observer,* reviewing the Newport Folk Festival, quoted Dylan as saying that he was neither an authentic folksinger nor a writer of protest songs: "[I] just have thoughts in my head, and I write them. I'm not trying to lead any causes for anyone else."

By 1964 Dylan showed more emphatic signs of being uncomfortable at the forefront of the protest movement. His *Another Side of Bob Dylan* (1964) was more introspective than the first three albums—much more personal—and implicitly intimated that he was not prepared to be tied down by the constraints that others put upon him. "It Ain't Me, Babe" symbolically represents his unease with being so inextricably linked to the movement, which was sanctimonious, not only in its self-congratulatory stand on social issues, but also in its rejection of contemporary popular music. Dylan sings "Go lightly from my window. Leave at your own chosen speed. I'm not the one you want, babe. I am not the one you need." Nat Hentoff, who was present at the recording session, quoted Dylan in the *New Yorker* magazine as saying: "Now, a lot of people are doing finger-pointing songs. You know—pointing to all the things that are wrong. Me, I don't want to write *for* people anymore."[20] The most clear, yet thinly veiled, rejection of the movement and the way that he had felt used by it was "My Back Pages." In it Dylan is critical of his own self-assuredness and naivete. He is angry with himself and with those who encouraged him to see everything in terms of black and white, and for becoming his own worst enemy, the self-ordained professor and preacher of liberty. Each verse ends with the revelation that with relinquishing the burden of self-righteous indignation came the shedding of years: "Ah, but I was so much older then, I'm younger than that now."

At the time of recording *Another Side of Bob Dylan,* Dylan explained why he moved toward a different mode of expression. In 1964, he was still mythologizing his own past, but he was intermittently much more open than in the interviews that became indicative of him, a game he played with interviewers, giving answers that were surreal or not answers at all. He said that in reflecting on all the people who were pointing fingers at the Bomb (meaning nuclear annihilation) he came to realize that the Bomb was not the problem. The problem was that so few people were free to express themselves. In Dylan's view, most people were completely constrained by their situations and represented an interest that simply added to the confusion of opinions out there. Too many people had a vested interest in the way things were. The implication was that the folk "establishment," which soon reacted in the way he intimated, was similarly constrained, and the people who comprised it were not free to express themselves outside of a given set of parameters.[21]

Another Side of Bob Dylan was criticized by many of the Greenwich Village crowd for its apparent lack of political commitment. In the November 1964 issue of *Sing Out!,* the editor, Irwin Silber, wrote "An Open Letter to Bob Dylan," voicing his concerns and those of "many other good friends of yours as well. . . . " The letter was both condescending and sanctimonious in tone, warning Dylan that his recent performance at the Newport Folk Festival had underlined the impression that, surrounded as he was by an entourage of sycophants he had distanced himself from the reality that his audience faced every day. The songs, Silber complained, had become too introspective, maudlin, even cruel, directed not at the audience in front of him, but to a few cronies behind.[22] *Another Side of Bob Dylan* did not sell as well as his previous two albums, and in fact failed to enter the American top forty. He had certainly lost some of his folk audience, and instead of reverting to style in order to recapture them, he not only created a new form in poetic imagery, but also sought to develop a completely new sound, and a new image.

Just as he chose the 1964 Newport Folk Festival to showcase *Another Side of Bob Dylan*, after which Silber wrote his scathing open letter, Dylan next chose the 1965 festival symbolically to renounce the past and herald a new departure in folk-rock. Given the fact that his previous departure had been received by Silber, but not by the audience, so badly, he must have been well aware that his new songs, particularly his electric set, would outrage the management. To the sound of booing and hissing, Bob Dylan played an electric set with some members of the Paul Butterfield

Blues Band and Al Kooper. The three songs they performed were "Maggie's Farm," "Like a Rolling Stone," and an early version of "It Takes a Lot to Laugh, It Takes a Train to Cry." To have gone electric was equivalent to selling out to commercialism and to the establishment. "Positively 4th Street," the single that immediately followed "Like a Rolling Stone" and recorded four days after the 1965 Newport Folk Festival, has widely been interpreted as a bitter attack on Dylan's former friends in the folk world. At the time, he was living on West Fourth Street in Greenwich Village. This is an issue over which Dylan fans differ, and it has also been suggested that the song refers to Fourth Street in Minneapolis, where he went to the university there and dropped out.

It is the music that Dylan recorded between 1965 and 1968 that makes his claim to be a poet much more strongly than the earlier protest material. This poetry is full of social, political, and psychological imagery that probes the private recesses and the unexplored cavities of the mind, but it is not protest music as it was conventionally understood by "topical" singers. It is to a large extent a journey of self-exploration. Dylan renounced protest songs and dissociated himself from the folk movement. He was not asking anyone to follow him; indeed, he abjured the very idea of following leaders, a point he made in "Subterranean Homesick Blues" and in one of the lucid moments of the famous 1966 *Playboy* interview: "My motto is, never follow anything."[23]

This new phase is best represented on *Bringing It All Back Home* (1965), *Highway 61 Revisited* (1965), *Blonde on Blonde* (1966), and *The Basement Tapes,* the latter recorded in 1967 but not released until 1975. Here capitalism and racism are no longer the specters, injustices are no longer the focus as they had been in his self-righteous phase; instead, the absurdities, ironies, and contradictions of the technocratic society, in all of their grotesqueness and hopelessness, are the subject. His topics range from the lover who ends up peeking through a keyhole down upon his knees ("She Belongs to Me"); to the young person who is put on the day shift after twenty years of schooling ("Subterranean Homesick Blues"); from the idea that failure is a form of success ("Love Minus Zero/No Limit") to the assertion that money doesn't talk, but instead swears ("It's Alright, Ma (I'm Only Bleeding)"); from the wish to be on an Australian mountain range just because it has to be different from where he was ("Outlaw Blues") and out of the "twisted reach of crazy sorrow" ("Mr. Tambourine Man") to the gates of Eden, outside of which there are no truths ("Gates of Eden"). The songs paint a landscape in which we all sit stranded but won't admit it to each other or to ourselves ("Visions of Johanna"); in which freaks are the norm, where sanity and insanity are indistinguishable, and where the familiar appears in unfamiliar guises—Shakespeare in an alleyway with a French girl ("Stuck Inside of Mobile with the Memphis Blues Again"), flesh-colored Christs that glow in the dark ("It's Alright, Ma"), a mule wearing jewels and binoculars around its neck ("Visions of Johanna"), and Einstein disguised as Robin Hood ("Desolation Row").

The songs express the futility and illusions of the American dream, presenting disturbing images of a reality that lay beneath the appearances. That reality was itself an escape into alternative illusions; the certainty of temporal salvation through self-righteous innocence; the breaking of the chains of conventionalism merely to become imprisoned by hedonistic pleasure seeking, precipitated by a drug culture that cultivated dependence in the name of freedom, and liberation of the mind through enslavement of the body. Paradise in New York or Los Angeles ironically became more of an illusion than the great American dream itself because the new Jerusalem was induced hallucinogenically; it was not about self-knowledge, but self-delusion—escapism and fantasy. Flower power, although an escape from the city, was nevertheless escapism, the delusion of saving the world by retreating into a dream world, the culmination of this myth being the legendary Woodstock festival, the shrine of the 1960s. The festival was in fact about 30 miles from Woodstock, New York, where Dylan lived, but he refused to be part of it. Having rejected the protest culture that he served to consolidate, he rejected the subculture that his poetic imagery created. The young who embraced flower power were, in his view, just fantasizing, and taking too much acid, the result of disillusionment induced by cultural and mass overload.[24]

The rediscovery of the dream would come, not by severing oneself from the culture one despised, but by rediscovering tradition through a new communion with nature: the countryside became the promised land, and the city the site of a new biblical Exodus from Egyptian enslavement. Dylan's *John Wesley Harding* (1968) constituted a nascent vision of the true path to salvation, self-discovery, and understanding, not in dependence on a drug culture, but in cultivating the spiritual dimension of the soul through religious redemption. Dylan himself described it as the first album of biblical rock. It was, he said, "a fearful album—dealing with the Devil in a fearful way."[25] It was an album that confronted fear, sin, and false conceptions of freedom through allegorical stories. "As I Went Out One Morning," for example, portrays the fairest damsel the singer had ever seen—conjuring up the imagery of ancient chivalry—wandering around in chains, in stark contrast to the sense of freedom evoked by reference to the air around Tom Paine. Paine, of course, was the famous defender of natural rights and of the American and French revolutions, who was the symbol and embodiment of the subjected versus the state for the civil rights movement. The song is sung in the first person and is an allegory on the first temptation of Christ.[26] The singer realizes that the beautiful maiden means him harm, and rejects her by saying, "Depart from me this moment," the equivalent of "Get thee behind me, Satan." The damsel is a metaphor for the civil rights movement, portraying itself as innocent and pure, which on the inside was misguided and manipulated by self-interested satanic orchestrators who sought to capture and use Dylan for their own purposes. It is Tom Paine who rescues the singer, implying that the symbol of the movement was himself above it, and could not be perverted by it.

Andy Gill, commenting on the album and sleeve photograph, makes the interesting remark that even though Dylan seems to be wearing the same suede jacket as he wore on the cover of *Blonde on Blonde*, "there was none of that album's air of stifling urban decadence. Instead a rural breeze whispered through its lonely margins."[27]

Endnotes

1. Quoted in *Bob Dylan in His Own Words,* ed. Christian Williams (London: Omnibus, 1993), 10.
2. Allen Ginsberg, prologue to *Beat Culture and the New America 1950–1965,* produced by the Whitney Museum of Modern Art (New York: Whitney Museum, in association with Flammarion, 1996), 17–19. John Clellon Holmes, one of the Beats, chronicled the Beat Generation in *Nothing More to Declare* (1967).
3. Interview by Mike Wallace with Jack Kerouac, *New York Post,* January 21, 1958, in *The Beats: A Literary Reference,* ed. Matt Theado (New York: Carroll & Graf, 2003), 118.
4. Robbie Woliver, *Hoot: A Twenty-five-Year History of the Greenwich Village Music Scene* (New York: St. Martin's Press, 1994), 8. This book was first published in 1986 by Pantheon Books as *Bringing It All Back Home.*
5. Bob Dylan, interviewed by Robert Shelton, Denver, March 1966 (Robert Shelton Archive, Experience Music Project, Seattle).
6. Bob Dylan, interviewed by Robert Shelton on a flight from Lincoln, Nebraska, to Denver, March 1966 (Robert Shelton Archive, Experience Music Project, Seattle).
7. Marianne Faithfull, *Faithfull: An Autobiography* (New York: Cooper Square Press, 2000; first published 1994), 61.
8. Leonard Cohen, letter to his sister Esther, September 17, 1963 (Leonard Cohen Papers, box 11, file 13, Thomas Fisher Library, University of Toronto).
9. Leonard Cohen, letter dated Quebec, '61 and addressed "Dear Bob" (Leonard Cohen Papers, box 11, file 4, Thomas Fisher Library, University of Toronto).
10. Leonard Cohen, letter to his sister Esther, September 18, 1961 (Leonard Cohen Papers, Thomas Fisher Library, University of Toronto).
11. Faithfull, *An Autobiography,* 42–48.
12. Allen Ginsberg, *Collected Poems* (London: Viking, 1985).
13. See Robert Shelton, *No Direction Home* (New York: Da Capo Press, 1997; first published 1986), 16–17.
14. David Hadju, *Positively Fourth Street* (London: Bloomsbury, 2001), 16.

15. Dave Van Ronk, cited in Woliver, *Hoot,* 135.

16. Dylan played for a couple of months around Times Square before going down to the Village and working in basket houses. The first place he played in the Village was The Commons on MacDougal Street, near Minetta Lane. It was, however, Gerdes Folk City that gave him his real break.

17. John Harris, "In Praise of Bob Dylan," *Q Dylan* (October 2000): 11.

18. Quoted in Isaiah Trost, "Beyond Bleecker: A Boston Folkie Recalls His Friendship with Dylan," *Guitar World Acoustic* 31 (1999): 89.

19. R. Gilbert, "Tomorrow's Top Twenty?" *Scene* January 26, 1963. Reprinted in *The Bob Dylan Companion,* ed. Carl Benson (New York: Schirmer Books, 1998), 15.

20. Cited in Paul Williams, *Bob Dylan: Performing Artist 1960–1973* (London: Omnibus, 1994), 110.

21. See "The Dylan Interviews Revisited," *Folk News* (May 1978): 12.

22. Irwin Silber, "An Open Letter to Bob Dylan," *Sing Out!* 14(5) (1964). Reprinted in Benson, *Bob Dylan Companion,* 28.

23. Quoted in Nat Hentoff, "The *Playboy* Interview: Bob Dylan." Reprinted in *Bob Dylan: The Early Years, a Retrospective,* ed. Craig McGregor (New York: Da Capo Press, 1990; first published 1972).

24. Jim Jerome, "Bob Dylan: A Myth Materialises with a New Protest Record and a New Tour," *People,* November 10, 1975. Reprinted in Benson, *Bob Dylan Companion,* 131.

25. Ian MacDonald, "Wild Mercury: A Tale of Two Dylans," *Uncut* (June 2001): 63.

26. We will see later that Dylan was the recipient of the Tom Paine Award, December 13, 1963. His acceptance speech offended many at the Emergency Civil Liberties Committee reception. In his letter of explanation, Dylan wrote: "It is a beautiful award. There is a kindness in Mr. Paine's face and there is almost a sadness in his smile. His trials show thru his eyes. I know really not much about him; somehow I would like to sing for him. There is a gentleness to his way" (Robert Shelton Archives, Institute for Popular Music, Liverpool University).

27. Andy Gill, *My Back Pages: Classic Bob Dylan 1962–69* (London: Carlton, 1998), 126.

3

THE CHANGING MAN

Everybody works in the shadow of what they've previously done.
But you have to overcome that.

—Bob Dylan, 1989[1]

Franz Kafka's short story "The Metamorphosis" depicts a young travel-ing salesman, Gregor Samsa, who awakens one morning transformed into a repulsive insect. While Dylan's transformations were never as drastic or instantaneous, to many who witnessed them they were, metaphorically speaking, equally as horrendous. The young rock-and-roll aspirant, who first adopted the voice of Hank Williams and the persona of James Dean, invented his first pseudonym, Elston Gunn, in 1958, wanted to be like Little Richard, moved from Hibbing, Minnesota, to Minneapolis, played with Bobby Vee as Gunn, denied his family and Jewish religion, manufactured for himself a past, claimed in New York that he was an orphan from New Mexico, moved through country blues to the social consciousness of Woody Guthrie, created a style and voice of his own, gained fame with his protest songs, became disillusioned with the assorted movements of the '60s, experimented with country music, became a born-again Christian in the late '70s and did quasi-religious albums in the early '80s, began the retrospective Never-Ending Tour in the late '80s, with live concerts on and off into the late '90s, rediscovered his folk roots in the '90s, and renewed himself to claim the title of *grand homme* of folk-rock.

In Minneapolis he had changed his given name from Robert Allen Zimmerman to Bob Dylan, which some say was initially Dillon after Marshall Dillon in the popular TV western *Gunsmoke*. Bob Dylan had, of

69

course, heard about the poet Dylan Thomas, but he always denies that he made a conscious decision to take the Welshman's name. Obviously irritated by the constant identification, Dylan said in 1965: "I've done more for Dylan Thomas than he's ever done for me."[2] In fact, he wasn't particularly fond of Dylan Thomas's poetry. Bob Dylan didn't try to set Thomas's poems to music, nor did he try to emulate his style. He thought the words were good, but too flowery, and concluded, "Who needs it?"[3]

Even in his early days in Minneapolis Bob Dylan's propensity to be the "Changing Man" was unambiguously identified. Dylan himself has commented upon his low boredom threshold, and in conjunction with his capacity, and rapacity, for learning, he was able to absorb new influences in a matter of weeks. Paul Nelson, the cofounder, with Jon Pankake, of *The Little Sandy Review*, which espoused folk music values above political opinions, was impressed by the rapid and ceaseless transformations that Dylan effected. They were not just transformations in music and style: "Every few weeks, Bob would become a different person with a different style."[4] In fact, when Dylan went to New York and began to write topical songs, he was accused by his friends and associates in Minneapolis, such as Tony Glover, of selling out to popularism by moving away from the authentic folk and blues idiom he had so adeptly adopted and transformed. *The Little Sandy Review* was Dylan's most vehement critic, and in the program notes for the 1963 Newport Folk Festival, edited by Robert Shelton under the pseudonym of Stacey Williams, Dylan justified himself in about 150 lines of free verse. In conciliatory tones he asserted that the old songs that Glover sang, those that were not overtly political and simply reflected a traditional way of life, fundamentally presupposed clear-cut demarcations, black and white, fascist and antifascist, exploiters and ex-ploited, but now the world was much more complex, the foundations of society had been shaken by new threats. That is why, Dylan argued, he had to sing songs that reflected the contemporary "scared raped world." He was not rejecting apolitical songs. Their value to him was that they demonstrated that the lyrics of a song could express something human.

After achieving fame and notoriety for taking on the significant social and political issues for a new generation, Dylan became more introspective in expressing the emotion of his own personal relationships, particularly with his girlfriend, Suze Rotolo, and later his wife, Sara Lownds (also spelled Lowndes).[5] He moved on to a completely new style and image, had a motorcycle accident in 1966, and became a family man in Woodstock. Releases during this period included the country-style *Nashville Skyline*, *Self Portrait*, and *Dylan*. Dylan underwent yet another transformation in 1974, one that so fundamentally changed him that his wife, Sara, was unable to recognize him as the same man—he had become a stranger. He had spent two months under the tutelage of Norman Raeburn, a seventy-three-year-old Jewish Russian émigré, who taught art classes but didn't merely improve technique; instead, he imparted a way of looking at things and of thinking about ultimate realities, particularly those induced by self-reflectiveness.

After his motorcycle accident, Dylan no longer felt that he had the ability to compose in the manner of *Highway 61 Revisited.* He had forgotten how to write unconsciously and strove to recapture consciously what his unconscious once produced. It was the reincarnation of his songwriting ability for which Raeburn was responsible. Dylan said of Raeburn, "He put my mind and my eye together, in a way that allowed me to do consciously what I unconsciously felt."[6] The result was the celebrated album *Blood on the Tracks,* the first album, Dylan claimed, in which he was able consciously to take a focus and so intensify it, like a magnifying glass in the sun. That focus was the concept of no time, in which the past, present, and future were all present at one time and in one place. Dylan himself described it this way: "You've got yesterday, today and tomorrow all in the same room, and there's very little that you can't imagine happening."[7] This self-consciousness about the illusion of time, Dylan contended, was most fully manifest in *Street Legal* and found visual expression in the film *Renaldo and Clara* (1978), for which he did the soundtrack.

The aesthetic and musical path that Dylan treads is not unique in American history, and in fact represents a long-standing identifiable phenomenon, the marrying of Anglo and African American in rock and roll. Dylan is heir to the dual legacy of romanticism, Ralph Waldo Emerson's mythological figures of the Wild West, and Walter Pater's mythology of aestheticism. Rock and roll represents what Perry Meisel describes as the crossing over of the cowboy's realism and the dandy's aestheticism, or country and city, in the fusion of romanticism and the blues. The process is one of chiasmus and not linear progression. Chiasmus is a process of mirror inversion where the second element in a body of music or of language turns back upon and over the first. Meisel argues that Afro-America resists or turns back American romanticism's presumed movement from the East to the West, the supposed path of freedom itself, and transforms the idea of freedom, in the words of "I Shall Be Released" by bringing the "West back to the East."[8]

Dylan combined the country with the urban, the folk of Woody Guthrie and the blues of Muddy Waters and John Lee Hooker, and with his cowboy boots and Carnaby Street suits and silk shirts and scarves he crossed over from the cowboy to the dandy. Indeed. When Dylan first arrived in New York, he consciously exploited the city cowboy image, making hick hip and reaching out to the same radical, disaffected audience Woody Guthrie had found at the end of his career in New York. Ramblin' Jack Elliott had taken on the Guthrie mantle, and Dylan extended the art form of wise country hick. In an interview with Robert Shelton, Dylan said: "I KNEW THAT WOODY DID THIS KIND OF THING AND WOODY WAS FAMOUS, and I used it."[9] Arlo Guthrie, Woody's son, although brought up in New York, similarly affected this style, coining the label "The Last of the Brooklyn Cowboys" for Ramblin' Jack Elliott, but later using it as a self-description in the title of his album of the same name.[10]

As we will see, Dylan is the archetypical "changing man," and what his move from acoustic to electric in the '60s represented was not a renunciation of folk music, but the rejection of a dream, the dream that the folk revivalists lived in their heads. It was the idealization of the country over the city. It was a denial of the belief that the urban chaos, degeneration, and loss of direction could be retrieved by recovering the strange, weird, wonderful, and authentic world of real America, relatively uncorrupted and still with solid community values, as it projected itself through Harry Smith's *Anthology of American Folk Music*. In other words, it was a self-conscious celebration of the country over the city, or good, honest labor over capital. Dylan's electric turn and the adoption of the style of the Carnaby Street dandy was, in Greil Marcus's words, the affirmation of "the claims of the city over the country, capital over labor— and also the claims of the white artist over the black Folk, selfishness over compassion, rapacity over need, the thrill of the moment over the trials of endurance, the hustler over the worker, the thief over the orphan."[11]

Whereas rock and roll is seen as the crossing over and bringing together of the traditions of country and blues, Dylan constantly reenacts the journey, reliving the process time and time again, reemerging as the folk popularist on *John Wesley Harding*, the country crooner on *Nashville Skyline* through to *Dylan* (1973), the renaissance of classic Dylan partially hinted at in *Planet Waves* (1974) and tapering off on *Street Legal* (1978), leading into the born-again Christian phase of *Slow Train Coming* (1979) and *Shot of Love* (1981). *Infidels* (1983) was Dylan's first commercial venture beyond born-again Christianity, and out of the same sessions, but not included on the album, was his tribute to Blind Willie McTell. The rock phase was resurrected with the uninspiring *Empire Burlesque* (1985) and *Knocked Out Loaded* (1986), but turning back on himself again in *Oh Mercy* (1989), with a complete back flip to his country blues and folk phase in *Good as I Been to You* (1992) and *World Gone Wrong* (1993). *Time Out of Mind* (1997) re-creates some of the somberness and eeriness of *World Gone Wrong,* but also resurrects the morbid fascination with death that so characterized his first album, which faked the world weariness of an aging man worn down and worn out. In *Time Out of Mind* we get the real thing.

Every change in Dylan's music and style brought its critics; only the shrillness of the outcry varied. The man who, despite his endearing charm and boyishness and, in the perception of some, a psyche of a little boy lost who needed protecting, was perceived by many of his acquaintances, in both Minnesota and New York, to be a user motivated largely by self-interest, calculating in his friendships, driven by an instrumental rationality designed to maximize his gain. Like the philosopher Thomas Hobbes's depiction of life as an unending race seeking one satisfaction after another, finding contentment in none, Dylan's character exhibited a restlessness that prevented him from either enjoying or resting content with his attainments. He was deeply distrustful of people, believing that he himself was not the user but the used. In 1986 Dylan presented himself as detached from the public persona of Bob Dylan, claiming that he was only that person when he wanted to be, and for the rest of the time he was himself. For twenty-five years the very embodiment of his imagination had stalked the world stage, and like an actor rehearsing and performing new parts, he worked from a script created by his other self.

Like Joseph K. from Kafka's *The Trial,* who awoke, as Gregor Samsa did in "The Metamorphosis," to find himself overtaken by a completely unanticipated twist of fate, Dylan pursued the fame but was totally unprepared for the responsibility that his unique role had brought with it. Unlike the rock-and-roll rebels Bill Haley, Elvis Presley, Little Richard, and Chuck Berry, whom he so greatly admired, and the characters played by James Dean in *Rebel Without a Cause* (1955) and by Marlon Brando in *The Wild One* (1954), Dylan was the rebel *with* a cause. Rebels portrayed by young angst-ridden actors such as Brando represented an "attitude" and postured against conformity. In *The Wild One,* Brando is asked by a girl what he is rebelling against, and answers, "What have you got?" Dylan was terribly affected by Dean's death, more so than by that of Buddy Holly, who had played Hibbing, Minnesota, a few days before his death in a plane crash. Dylan's obsession with death in the blues songs he sang may have been inspired by this romanticism of the artist cut down in his prime. Dylan saw *Rebel Without a Cause* a dozen times or more, read books about Dean voraciously, and collected photographs of him. His parents thought that he may have been influenced to get his first motorcycle, a Harley-Davidson, by James Dean.[12]

73

Dylan had a voice as well as an attitude, and was hailed as a spokesman for a generation of disaffected youth—a leader. As early as his first major concert at New York's Town Hall on April 12, 1963, people were talking about him, expressing what they felt but were unable to articulate.[13] Todd Gitlin wrote that "Dylan sang for us . . . we got in the habit of where he was taking us next."[14] He gave inspiration not only to his audience but also to fellow performers. Joan Baez, for example, although politically conscious and a political activist, had never sung protest or topical songs before Bob Dylan wrote them. In her view, before Dylan came along, topical songs were crudely finger-pointing and crass. He made it possible to make a political statement subtly. It was to Baez that he expressed his fear of being held responsible for the hopes of his generation. At a concert with her in 1965, the audience called out for "Masters of War" and "With God on Our Side." After the show he said to her, "Hey, man, I heard those kids, I heard them, right? I can't be responsible for those kids' lives."[15] This was not a new unease. On a return trip to Minneapolis in August 1962, Dylan was already expressing frustration about writing political songs for other people to the neglect of songs about himself. In 1963 Baez and Dylan were hailed as heroes at the Newport Folk Festival, where the "hip, wandering Minnesotan" songwriter disavowed any intention to lead his generation. Whereas Baez began to devote more time to political causes, especially disarmament, Dylan accepted no invitations to appear at rallies or protests after the March on Washington in the summer of 1963.

His record label, however, had other plans. Even in 1965 CBS, capitalizing on the chart success of the single "Subterranean Homesick Blues," advertised his back catalog of four albums by "the New CULT Leader DYLAN," all in the top twenty album chart. Despite Dylan's disavowal of the title, he could not abdicate the crown. In March 1966 he was still being viewed in the same terms: "TEENAGERS RECOGNIZE in Dylan one of their own, a spokesman for their rejection of the adult world."[16] He simply could not absolve himself of the responsibility for his generation. Again in 1978 he said unequivocally: "I'm not the spokesman for anybody's generation. Far from it. In fact, I want to emphatically deny being the spokesman for our generation. Fame is just having your name known by a lot of strangers."[17]

Perhaps of more significance was his feeling that the leaders of the civil rights movement lectured him about his responsibilities and even thought that they had some say in what he should include in his songs. He felt that he was being censored and that his freedom of expression was being violated. Even his friends were critical of his rejection of the overtly political and his desire for a mass audience. Phil Ochs warned that in losing his anchorage in politics, Dylan would be swallowed up by the very audience he craved.[18] Ochs, Tom Paxton, and Baez all continued to combine their music with political activism, and along with Country Joe McDonald and David Ackles, constituted the most powerful collective voice in the anti-Vietnam movement, while Dylan remained detached, almost reclusive, looking to religion for salvation and redemption. However, each of the "purists" who criticized him also moved to the more commercial end of the spectrum in acquiring electric backing and embarking upon big-venue tours, writing and performing songs with an eye for the market rather than the political. Ochs remained more faithful to his political commitments, but he was profoundly disturbed by the retreat into a drug culture that so many youths saw as the escape route from the evils he articulated. He eventually became completely disillusioned, ceased to write after his ironically titled *Greatest Hits,* and adopted a new identity at New York's Chelsea Hotel in 1975. He called himself John Train and became self-absorbed, abusive, and out of control on drink and drugs. He committed suicide a few years later at the home of his sister in New York.

Why could someone, such as Dylan, then Cohen, suddenly become a cultural icon? After all, popular culture and the counterculture it generated in the 1950s and early 1960s were relatively bland, certainly not something endowed with artistic merit, and not something that was wholly respectable. Despite the fact that Dylan was accused of selling out in 1966, he could not have become as popular as he was then if it had not been for a transformation in the way that record companies turned their signings into commercial products. The commercial potential of Bob Dylan could be harnessed without having to force him to conform to the uniform blandness it had begun to generate. In so far as there were now causes to which to become attached, civil rights, anti–Vietnam War, and nuclear disarmament, Dylan was associated with them.

Auteur Theory and Popular Culture

Both Dylan and Leonard Cohen benefited from the tendency among critics and audiences to think of the producers of popular culture as creative artists or authors. This was particularly true in the case of movies. The emergence of this phenomenon in the early 1960s was called "the auteur theory," introduced into America by Andrew Sarris.[19] It had long been the case that European filmmakers such as Sergei Eisenstein and Jean Renoir were afforded classic status because of their ability to control or influence all aspects of a film's production. The director was seen to be the author of a *work*. In general, the commercialism of the Hollywood studio system and the extent of control exerted tended to detract American filmmakers from being viewed as authors, and their films were pejoratively labeled low culture. As Stephen Scobie argues, there were two developments in the late 1950s that led to a reevaluation of the American film. First was the quality of films produced in Europe that justifiably claimed for their makers the accolade of author on the grounds of their artistic merit. Their work was so revered that they could be referred to by their surnames alone—Bergman, Fellini, and Antonioni. Above all it was the French New Wave, or *nouvelle vague* directors—Claude Chabrol, Alain Resnais, François Truffaut, and Jean-Luc Godard—who elevated the status of director to artist. It was they who were responsible for the second factor that contributed to the making respectable of popular culture, the *politique des auteurs*. They not only endowed kudos of author upon the obvious continental European directors, but also upon the likes of Alfred Hitchcock, Howard Hawks, John Ford, and Nicholas Ray.

There is no doubt that with structuralism and poststructuralism in film studies, auteur theory soon became passé. The irony is that it took hold in American film criticism at a time when European critics were rebelling against it following French theorist Roland Barthes's famous argument of 1968 proclaiming the death of the author during a time of widespread revolutionary student protest, particularly in France.

Although the auteur theory was not self-consciously applied to popular music, a similar phenomenon arose. The typical stars of the 1950s were famous for putting their own particular imprint or style on a song but not for writing it. Elvis Presley, Bobby Darin, Tony Bennett, Pat Boone, Dean Martin, and a host of others were not expected to write their own songs—there was a songwriting industry to do that for them. However, the elevation of the performer to the status of artist became manifest in the new cultural icon of the singer-songwriter. Scobie maintains that "pop music became respectable in exactly the same way that movies had, since there was now a place for the traditional centre of serious artistic activity: the Author."[20] The argument is perhaps overstated. There were, of course, many popular music performers who wrote their own material, among them Little Richard, Chuck Berry, Buddy Holly, J. P. Richardson aka the Big Bopper, Paul Anka, the Everly Brothers, and Jerry Lee Lewis. It was not just the fact of being a singer-songwriter, but the fact that there was a qualitative difference between the new singer-songwriter and the old, to some extent facilitated by the broadening of the subject matter of the song—the espousal of a cause or the expression of an emotion different from love. The folk music revival, with its emphasis on tradition, kept alive by Moses Asch, who founded the Folkway label, and the systematic attempts to preserve the rich heritage of music that was rapidly fading into the hinterland of neglect, such as the immensely esoteric and eccentric collection put together by Harry Smith, gave an air of respectability to this form of popularist music that popular music had not yet attained. The folk revivalists, as Robert Shelton recognized, were effectively saying that there was a way out of the modern urban malaise by a voyage of self-discovery through the relatively uncomplicated, unpretentious, beautiful, and simple lifestyles of country people.[21]

The folk music revival, however, was backward looking, and what was needed was not only singer-songwriters (there were plenty of those around) but also ones of genius who could distinguish themselves from their contemporaries. Whereas John Lennon and Paul McCartney opened the way for singer-songwriters to be recognized as artists in their own right, it was Bob Dylan who elevated this art form to new heights. The fusion of both his folk and rock-and-roll roots, with powerful lyrics and disturbing images, propelled him to the status of poetic icon, whose example a whole generation of singer-songwriters wanted self-consciously to emulate, among them Leonard Cohen. Indeed, Cohen once thought of himself as Dylan's ancestor: "It wasn't his originality which first impressed me, but his familiarity. He was like a person out of my books, singing to the real guitar. Dylan was always what I had meant by the poet—someone about whom the word was never used."[22]

Dylan made it possible for his Greenwich Village contemporaries suddenly to become commercial successes, and for popular music with meaning to become a respectable art form. This, nevertheless, was a phenomenon that Louis Dudek, Cohen's teacher, found wholly regrettable because it elevated the popular entertainer, such as the Beatles and Bob Dylan, to the status of serious artist and degraded the promising serious artist, such as Cohen, to the level of popular entertainer.[23]

The art of the singer-songwriter placed emphasis on performance. Both Dylan and Cohen, although not noted for spectacular stage acts, were nevertheless meticulous performers and were careful to cultivate and develop stage personas. Both performers created and re-created themselves, responsive to the contexts and passage of time. One of the most widely read books of cultural criticism focusing on the 1960s is Richard Poirier's *The Performing Self* (1971). Poirier argues that the self is a socially constructed convenient fiction, an invented persona related to the purposes we pursue. The invention, and indeed reinvention, of the self takes place primarily in performance, which is an act of self-discovery, self-perception, and self-gratification. It is the direction of one's energy toward self-understanding and the exploration of human potential. As Scobie suggests, Poirier is not much concerned with the responsiveness of critics or of audiences.[24]

A more sophisticated discussion of self-disclosure and self-enactment in conduct in general is to be found in Michael Oakeshott's *On Human Conduct* (1975). Oakeshott is concerned, not only with the choice of actions, but also with the motives that the person chooses in performing them. In conduct we disclose what we desire in the actions we choose to perform. This Oakeshott calls self-disclosure. In addition, we enact, invent, and live a character in developing specific motives and virtues in the performance of actions. This is not simply a distinction between act and motive, between what a person chooses to do and the character that influences those choices. An act is not something simply chosen, it is the result of an understanding that could have been different. Acts, then, are not given but contingent upon our understandings. Acts are contingent responses to understood situations that may be modified, compromised, or thwarted by other persons. This is because actions performed in relation to other persons depend on their responses and are therefore inescapably infected with contingency.[25]

From Playing the Fool to Playing It Cool

Much has been written about Dylan's performance style in the early years, about his self-enactment and self-disclosure. He was not merely a blues and protest singer, but also an entertainer who relied on humor and used props as part of his performance. The hat, which he wears on the cover of the first album, provided a focus as he moved it around his head and curved his body in Chaplinesque routines. He communicated with the audience, was self-deprecating, and often conveyed messages through the medium of the talking blues song—the punch line of the joke comes at the end of the verse followed by a blast on the harmonica, a short comment, and then another blast. His stage persona was that of the sympathizer with the working man, the articulator of social injustices, dressed in blue jeans and denim or check cotton shirt.

When he added a Fender Stratocaster to his acoustic Gibson, he made more than a musical statement. He changed his whole style. The frenetic lifestyle he adopted was fueled by elaborate cocktails of drugs, and reports abound about how he had to be assisted on and off the stage at venues, and in many cases the sheer amazement that he could perform at all under the circumstances. This, of course, was not unique to Dylan; it was part of the style of the counterculture. Cohen similarly was almost comatose in many of his live appearances. LSD, speed, and Mandrax were integral to his life. In his 1972 tour of Europe with his band, the Army, he acquired the name of Captain Mandrax and had difficulty in finding the pitch of his songs and of maintaining their tempo.[26] He is famously said to have collapsed in the street after taking opium with the infamous Alexander Trocchi.

Almost every era has a focal physical center. In the 1890s it had been gay Paris; the 1920s, decadent Berlin; the 1940s, glamorous Hollywood; and the 1950s, *la dolce vita* Rome. It was London in the Swinging '60s. New York may have been the center of avant-garde art, film, and experimental music, but London was the center of fashion and popular music. Dylan dressed expensively in the height of '60s fashions.

Dylan had gone to London for almost three months from the middle of December 1962 at the instigation of Al Grossman, who had managed to persuade the BBC to fly the young folksinger over to appear in an undistinguished television play, *Madhouse on Castle Street*. During his time in London Dylan acquainted himself with the London folk scene. He became friendly with Martin Carthy, whom he met at the Troubadour, and who at that time epitomized traditional English folk music. Carthy later became one of the leading expositors of the fusion of English traditional folk with rock music in the band Steeleye Span. Some of the tunes that Dylan learned from Carthy, such as "Lord Franklin" and "Scarborough Fair," surface on *The Freewheelin' Bob Dylan,* with contemporary words and themes in the form of "Bob Dylan's Dream" and "Girl from the North Country," respectively.

Dylan returned to London again in 1964, playing various venues, including the Festival Hall. During the interim his popularity had grown immensely, partly because "Blowin' in the Wind" had been a huge hit for Peter, Paul, and Mary, and CBS had begun seriously to market him, realizing his potential not only as a singer but also as a songwriter whose songs were widely being covered. Dylan was competing in a market dominated by the Beatles and the Mersey Sound and the Rolling Stones, who led the way for the Animals, the Yardbirds, and Pretty Things in rhythm and blues. The early Beatles and the rhythm and blues bands were actually reviving a good deal of American 1950s music, which had now been eclipsed by a blander, all-American, "safe" pop culture. Dylan himself was attuned to the fact that it was still possible to make money out of playing the old kind of music he used to play. These were the days when commercialism demanded artistic compromises, such as the Rolling Stones changing the words of "Let's Spend the Night Together" to "Let's spend some time together" for the *Ed Sullivan Show,* and when such gestures as refusing to appear during the finale on the revolving stage at the London Palladium could shock a nation. The Animals recorded two of Dylan's songs, "Baby, Let Me Follow You Down," changed to "Baby, Let Me Take You Home" for English consumption, and his version of "House of the Rising Sun" (Dylan had used Dave Van Ronk's arrangement), the central character of which underwent a sex change in order not to offend sensibilities and radio stations. It was the Animals' recordings of his songs that led Dylan to see the possibilities of fusing the horizons of folk and rock. Indeed, in his 1965–1966 world tour he included an upbeat version of "Baby, Let Me Follow You Down" in the electric set.

When Dylan returned to London for a brief tour in early May 1965, he was already well into the process of transforming himself, a process that has never stopped. The photographer Daniel Kramer, who spent much of 1964 and 1965 with Dylan, commented that not only the songs but Dylan's whole appearance changed that year: "He was new all the time."[27] He dressed in fashionably sharp leather jackets, had discarded the workshirt, wore dark glasses, and had begun to cultivate the curly, tasseled, electric-shock hairstyle that came to epitomize him. He also brought with him a filmmaker, D. A. Pennebaker, who captured, in Dylan's words, a "one-sided" portrait of the artist, mostly in hotel rooms, backstage, and at press conferences. In Pennebaker's documentary, *Don't Look Back,* Alan Price, who by now had left the Animals, figures prominently in the crowd that surrounds Dylan and memorably opens a bottle of Newcastle Brown Ale on the edge of an expensive piano. Dylan had a reputation at this time for being cutting and cruel. In the film, Britain's answer to Dylan, Donovan, is disparaged by an agent in words, but Dylan does it more subtly by example. Donovan sings a few bars of his banal "To Sing for You," and Dylan says, "Hey, that's good, man," then visibly deflates and assassinates him with a rendition of "It's All Over Now, Baby Blue," which was yet to be released. Paul McCartney, to give another example, was eager to impress Dylan at the Savoy Hotel and played an acetate of a song that he had been working on. Eager with anticipation, he looked at Dylan, who simply got up and walked out of the room without comment, completely deflating McCartney's self-esteem.[28]

Dylan had recorded the songs for *Bringing It All Back Home* in January 1965, but it was not released in Britain until the completion of his short tour at the end of May. This was the album that signified the transition to folk-rock, and also the transition in style. The cover features a stylishly dressed Dylan in the foreground, and behind him an elegant brunette in a red dress (Al Grossman's wife). Between her and an ornately carved mantelpiece is a partially visible album sleeve of *Another Side of Bob Dylan,* indicating that that part of his life had now receded into the past. He had not yet publicly gone electric, and even though the Pennebaker tribute opens with the promotional film for the electric "Subterranean Homesick Blues," the tour was acoustic. (Ironically, the type of songs from which Dylan had been trying to distance himself for well over a year had become commercially successful and coincided with the tour.) His first U.K. single, "The Times They Are A-Changin'," entered the charts in April 1965, and *The Freewheelin' Bob Dylan,* although released for some time, suddenly went to number one in the album charts, which had been dominated by the Beatles and the Rolling Stones since 1963. In addition, the albums *The Times They Are A-Changin'* and *Another Side of Bob Dylan* were in the U.K. top twenty albums chart. In the year since he played the Festival Hall, Bob Dylan had become a star in Britain. Now everyone who was anyone, including the Beatles and the Rolling Stones, regularly visited him at his luxury Savoy Hotel suite.

Initially, the music industry and the media had reinvented the Beatles by jettisoning the "greaser" motorbiker image of their Hamburg/Cavern days, portraying them as the clean-cut lads from Liverpool in designer suits with no collars, in contrast with the wild boys of rhythm and blues, the Rolling Stones. The breakthrough that Dylan had made in redefining the subject of the popular song also released the Beatles from the constraints of their earlier compositions, and paved the way for Mick Jagger and Keith Richards to inject a degree of imagery and narrative into their songs, beyond such commercially oriented compositions as "That Girl Belongs to Yesterday," a hit of Gene Pitney, and "As Tears Go By," the vehicle of Marianne Faithfull's passage to fame. While the Rolling Stones gained a reputation for being the greatest rock performers, they never attained the consistency of vision, musical inventiveness, and lyrical adeptness of Lennon and McCartney. The combination of composition, lyricism, style, and performance was something that the Beatles exhibited in abundance, and was equaled only by Bob Dylan, who, as a solo performer, backed by musicians whose very name conjured anonymity, The Band, eclipsed any individual in the collective known as the Beatles. Both the Beatles and Bob Dylan, and also to a lesser extent the Rolling Stones, possessed the quality of being ahead of their audiences, never becoming their creature, and always reaching for new frontiers of music to allow the audience to glimpse.

From the time Dylan landed in London, he was subjected to a merciless round of press interviews, at which he became more and more obtuse, visibly irritated by the banality of the questions, and only occasionally playing it straight when interviewed by the "serious" music press or the odd student newspaper when the line of questioning interested him. Two days after the conclusion of the tour, he arranged a recording session with one of the most well-respected British blues bands, John Mayall's Blues Breakers, but nothing came out of it due to overindulgence in drink and drugs. After a break in France and Portugal, where he contracted food poisoning, Dylan recorded two thirty-five-minute live acoustic shows for the BBC. They were to mark the end of his wholly acoustic sets.

Dylan had become famous as an acoustic player, and folk music had been elevated from the cafes and bars to the theaters and concert halls. So why didn't he capitalize on this success, produce more of the same, and promote the material by touring? The answer is complex. The success, in fact, was almost a complete surprise to him, and his appearance in Britain, after he had recorded "Subterranean Homesick Blues," which, although electric, was itself a finger-pointing song, generated interest in his earlier acoustic material. Artistically, however, he felt that he had reached a plateau, and the musical form with which he was working had become an expressive straitjacket. Singing the songs for which he was now famous produced a predictable enthusiastic audience reaction, but the performance was no longer a challenge, and the songs no longer indicative of, nor capable of expressing, the range and intensity of the new poetic influences on him.

A case could plausibly be made to suggest that in the light of poor sales for *Another Side of Bob Dylan,* and scathing criticism from his associates in Greenwich Village, he felt that he had to reach out to a new audience. In other words, his lack of success had already instilled in him the necessity for change before he unexpectedly took off in Britain. This may have been a factor, but I think that there are probably more fundamental psychological reasons best explained in a famous passage on the master/slave relationship in G. W. F. Hegel's *Elements of the Philosophy of Right.* We hear a great deal today from feminists and multiculturalists about the struggle for recognition, but it was Hegel who most articulately explained its philosophical importance. It is through the process of the struggle for recognition that we become conscious of who we are and how we differ from others. The irony of the master/slave relation is that the slave gets more out of it than the master. In subjecting the slave to himself, the master does not attain recognition, because he does not respect the person who recognizes him. The master does not achieve recognition, because the slave is a dependant rather than a free, autonomous, self-conscious will, and his recognition is therefore worthless. Dylan admired and socialized with Ginsberg, the Beatles, and the Rolling Stones, but he didn't think that he had produced the poetry or the music that could command their respect. The adulation of his audience, then, was not the recognition he was seeking. He wanted to produce poetry that could be compared at the level of expression with the French Symbolists, the German Expressionists, and the American Beats, but he also wanted a sound that went beyond rhythm and blues, and he felt that he had achieved both in "Like a Rolling Stone."

When he returned to the United States, having shed Joan Baez and acquired Sara Lownds, he completed "Like a Rolling Stone," which for him marked a new and stimulating creative phase in expressive writing, and recorded it using Mike Bloomfield on guitar and Al Kooper on organ. This song proved for Dylan that he did not need to go outside of the medium of song in order to express what he was feeling. He had spent months writing poetry, plays, and freestyle verse, and was increasingly frustrated by his inability to make his book *Tarantula* into something with which he could identify. In writing "Like a Rolling Stone," he found that he could just let his thoughts take over and "vomit" onto the page. Distilling the lyrics of "Like a Rolling Stone" from twenty pages of a free-flowing stream of consciousness, he was able to transform the popular song, disregard the conventional constraints dictated by radio airtime, and create one of the most liberating songs of the genre.

After recording "Like a Rolling Stone," he then spent a month at his new home in Woodstock, New York, near his manager, Al Grossman, and devoted himself to writing new songs for *Highway 61 Revisited*. This creative process was interrupted by his first major commitment after the British tour, the Newport Folk Festival. He not only had new songs, but also a new image, which was a development of the style he affected in Britain, where he had tasted for the first time the type of adulation and frenzied star worship not normally enjoyed by folksingers.

Having got used to the luxury of the Savoy in London, Dylan booked into a luxurious hotel just out of town, distancing himself somewhat from the communal spirit of the festival. He turned up at the festival with Al Kooper and Bob Neuwirth in clothing completely incongruous with the setting. The sunglasses and smart jackets he had worn in London now became developed into a fashion statement. All three shed their blue jeans and wore puff-sleeved dueling shirts and black trousers. For the workshop performance, Dylan wore a black leather jacket and dress shirt, and for the mainstage show, he wore a green shirt with large white polka dots.

On the whole of the tour that followed he wore mod-cut suits, polka dot shirts, and pointed "winkle picker" shoes with Cuban heels. He hung out with the giants of rock and roll, the Beatles and the Rolling Stones. Both bands had visited him at the Savoy Hotel in May 1965, and at the end of the year, during their American tour, Dylan visited the Stones in their New York hotel and a few days later met up with them at one of the in clubs in town, the Phone Booth. Brian Jones had plans to spend Christmas with Dylan at the end of the tour. All five Rolling Stones were at Dylan's Royal Albert Hall concert on May 26, 1966.[29] *Highway 61 Revisited* was released at the end of August 1965, a couple of months after the Newport Folk Festival, and marked the clearest public statement of the completed transition from playing the fool to playing it cool. Dylan is holding a pair of sunglasses in his hand, wearing a blue-and-pink, abstract, leaf-patterned open silk shirt, revealing a white Triumph motorcycle T-shirt. As Andy Gill comments: "If there was a cooler person on the planet—Beatles and Stones included—no one had told Bob Dylan."[30] Marianne Faithfull, who visited him at the Savoy in 1965, described him as "the hippest person on earth . . . my Existential hero, the gangling Rimbaud of rock."[31]

Back to the Booing

A great deal of mythology has arisen around the reception of the "new" Dylan. It is generally maintained that the booing, slow hand clapping, and catcalls were the reaction of folk purists, or what Dave Van Ronk called "the folk fascists,"[32] who resented Dylan for "selling out" to commercialism. I think those who indicted Dylan on charges of commercialism were in fact not against his popularity, but against his move away from "authenticity." Folk music was already immensely popular. During the early 1950s, for example, the Weavers, which included Pete Seeger, projected folk music into the mainstream of popular music with such commercially successful hits as "On Top of Old Smoky," "Wimoweh," and Leadbelly's "Good Night, Irene." Leadbelly's original words, which carry dark sexual undertones, were modified for a mass audience, as, for instance, was his "My Girl" by the Four Pennies over a decade later, when they called it "Black Girl" and eliminated the sinister theme. In fact, Lee Hays, a founding member of the Weavers, saw little wrong with commercialism: "Why not be good and commercial?" he once asked.[33] Seeger's commercial success, which made his record company and him huge profits, came to an end because of his political stance. He was blacklisted in 1952 for his association with communism in the company of Leadbelly, Woody Guthrie, and the folklorist Alan Lomax. Radio stations, major recording labels, and concert halls closed their doors to them.[34] Seeger continued to perform in schools, community centers, and small clubs, hoping to sow the seeds of egalitarianism by encouraging people to play the music for themselves. He inspired Dave Guard to play the banjo, which he later played in the Kingston Trio. The Kingston Trio sold over a million copies of a traditional somber and poignant civil war song, "Tom Dooley," making it one of the top ten singles of 1958.

What was really at issue in relation to Bob Dylan was not only commercial success, because there were indeed many followers of folk who believed that the fewer the people who listened to the authentic voice of the rural peoples, the better it must be, but more importantly the perceived abandoning of one's political principles in order to achieve success. After all, Pete Seeger, Woody Guthrie, Harry Belafonte, Joan Baez, and Peter, Paul, and Mary were household names before Dylan recorded his first album. None of these commercially successful performers abandoned their radical politics. Peter, Paul, and Mary (singers Peter Yarrow, Noel Paul Stookey, and Mary Ellin Travers), Al Grossman's orchestrated attempt to capitalize on the success of the Kingston Trio, were strongly identified with left-wing politics, making it clear that there was a strong link between their music and their social philosophy. Peter, Paul, and Mary were evident in all the important civil rights marches. For example, they were part of the 1963 March on Washington and the Selma and Montgomery, Alabama, marches, as well as a host of others, despite the fact that they realized that being overtly political could lose them the Southern market. They consciously decided that the issue of human rights was more important to them than Southern sales.[35] They were also aware of the influence they exerted, to the point of overinflating Peter Yarrow's ego.

There would be some, of course, who abjured commercialism of any kind, whether Dylan remained true to his political stance or not. Among these was his then girlfriend, Suze Rotolo, who thought that playing Carnegie Hall, and being part of the Columbia machine, was selling out to the establishment, something that Dylan had always fought against.[36]

The evidence shows that throughout the extensive round of touring by Bob Dylan beginning July 24, 1965, at the Newport Folk Festival, and continuing through the United States, Canada, Australia, Scandinavia, Britain, and Paris, and ending in two concerts at London's Albert Hall on May 26 and 27, 1966, elements of the audience did react badly to the electric set, which filled the whole second half of each show. It would be naive and simplistic, however, to impute the same intention to everyone, or indeed to imply that this was something new in Dylan's experience.

Dylan had engendered indifference and hostility right from the very start. When he played in 1959 at the Ten O'Clock Scholar in Minneapolis, his singing was so off-key and tuneless that he drove customers away. Although he insisted on singing, the proprietor often had to ask him to stop.[37] Bonnie Beecher, the subject of "Girl from the North Country," recalls how Dylan would mortify and embarrass her in front of her friends by playing the piano and harmonica, neither of which he had mastered, and by refusing to play the guitar and songs that he could perform adeptly. Her friends would call people around to hear him on the promise that "you're not going to believe this."[38]

Dylan had, in fact, been an inconsistent performer throughout his career. He had also always been a confrontational performer, deliberately trying to provoke a reaction. Folksingers frequently performed while intoxicated, or the worse for wear on drugs, and audiences at clubs tended to accept this lack of professionalism as a sign that the performer was not pandering to commercialism. At larger, less intimate venues it was not always appreciated. Dylan's charismatic stage persona often transfigured audiences, but at other times his performance could be indifferent, completely lacking commitment and enthusiasm. When he sang with others, it was frequently a matter of chance whether they hit the same note at the same time, and the harmonies were not infrequently inharmonious. The live recordings from the Newport Folk Festival at which Dylan sings with Joan Baez and assembled singers are technically a travesty, but because of the power of the songs themselves, they received a warm reception.

Dylan's relationship with Baez furthered his career in that his guest appearances singing duets, which he did not reciprocate in his 1965 tour of Britain, exposed him to much larger audiences than he could command on his own. Her sweet, melodic, note-perfect, almost operatic voice jarred with his rasping, limited range, and unconventional delivery. The version of "With God on My Side," sung to the tune of Dominic Behan's "The Patriot Game," which Dylan and Baez sang together at Newport in 1964, is almost unbearable to hear. If he is making any attempt to synchronize his voice with hers, he does a marvelous job of disguising it. John Bauldie's notes to the CBS official bootleg series, volumes 1–3, comment that when Baez and Dylan sang "Mama, You Been on My Mind," they would "almost always ham the song up unmercifully." Baez herself commented that when she had him on stage as a guest, many people who were unfamiliar with him would get infuriated and even boo. In early October 1963, at the

Hollywood Bowl in Los Angeles, he was heckled and booed for spoiling the pure Baez set.

Even the content of his topical songs were bound to infuriate more conservative elements, but they also upset his friends back in Minnesota, who thought he was merely jumping on the band wagon of protest songs and selling out more authentic American folk blues. At the first Columbia Records convention in 1963, Dylan sang "With God on Our Side" and "Only a Pawn in Their Game." The Southern delegates were outraged and staged a walkout. When people expected him to sing protest songs, he changed direction. At the 1964 Newport Folk Festival, he appeared at the "Topical Song Workshop" and instead of singing protest songs, he sang "It Ain't Me, Babe" and "Mr. Tambourine Man" but nevertheless received a warm reception. During the 1965 tour of Britain, he had been provocative and obtuse with the press, but musically he was still doing the acoustic set, and he was treated like a star. At the end of this tour, he seriously thought of giving up songwriting and singing and instead devote his attention to writing poetry and novels (he was in fact working on his book *Tarantula*). The reason was that the audience reaction was predictable. In other words, he did not feel that he was challenging or shocking the audience despite the fact that he was now a hugely commercial success.

The question still remains to be answered, why did people boo at Bob Dylan concerts during and after the Newport Folk Festival? Blues was just as much a part of the Newport Folk Festival as folk. Indeed, Paul Butterfield's Blues Band, including Mike Bloomfield, played in the afternoon before accompanying Dylan in the evening. Dylan had also used electric backing during some sessions for *The Freewheelin' Bob Dylan* and released a single called "Mixed Up Confusion," which was quickly withdrawn and which had a four-piece rock band backing. On the B side was "Corrina, Corrina," a traditional song that Muddy Waters had also sung. It is the only accompanied track on *The Freewheelin' Bob Dylan*. Electric guitars weren't, then, necessarily commercial.

Dylan was not the first to fuse folk with blues or rock and roll. At the 1964 Newport Folk Festival, where Dylan not only showcased his personally oriented songs but also gave a lackluster performance that irritated those who supported him as being completely unprofessional, Muddy Waters brought an electric band on stage, having developed his city blues in Chicago, and Johnny Cash took a new direction in orienting himself toward Nashville. Richard Farina, who consciously set poetry to music before Dylan began describing himself as a poet, included two tracks on an album he did with his wife, Mimi Baez, which had Bruce Langhorne playing a raunchy and raw electric guitar in the autumn of 1964. The album was *Celebrations for a Grey Day* (1965). In fact, Richard and Mimi planned to include electric backing at the Newport Folk Festival on the afternoon that Dylan played the fateful set. The band was to include Mike Bloomfield and Bruce Langhorne for the finale of the set in which the two electric songs from *Celebrations for a Grey Day* would figure, along with a new hard-rocking song "Hard-Loving Loser." Farina's plans were thwarted by the weather. The heavy rain constituted a danger to the live cables linking up the amplifiers and sound system. They nevertheless played acoustically and had a party on the stage, with spectators dancing in the rain. Dylan was there under the bleachers and thought that the man had gone insane.[39]

Farina persuaded Joan Baez to go electric, and he produced the album, which she never released, after the untimely death of her brother-in-law in a motorcycle accident. Baez's criticisms of Bob Dylan were not because, in going electric, he had sold out, but in abandoning his overt political stance he had betrayed himself and the cause. The message one gets from Dylan in 1965, Baez remarked, was, "Let's all go home and smoke pot, because there is nothing else to do. . . . We might as well go down smoking."[40]

Dylan's move from acoustic to electric, or from cowboy to dandy and from country to city, Meisel contends, "is so superb an example of our paradigm that its importance to our story cannot be overestimated."[41] *Bringing It All Back Home* (1965) is the exemplar of crossing from the country to the city. As if in defiance of the move, side two of the album crosses back over again from electric to acoustic, from the city to the country, from the dandy to the cowboy. As Meisel quite rightly contends, and as we have seen, "the pattern of reversal is, as it turns out, not unfamiliar, in either Dylan's earlier work or his later."[42] By the time of the Newport Folk Festival, *Bringing It All Back Home* had already been released, with the electric backing on one side, and "Subterranean Homesick Blues" was a top forty hit single in the United States. CBS also released "Like a Rolling Stone" the week before the festival, which took place on July 24 and 25, 1965.

What made Dylan's use of the electric guitar and backing so provocative and offensive? There were, of course, the purists, who would object to electrification because of its commercialism, and there was no getting away from it: Dylan was now commercially successful and had changed his image accordingly.

The sheer volume of Dylan's delivery was one of the crucial factors in audience reaction and needs to be put in context. A typical tour would include the headliner and up to three or four top-name supporting acts.

Take as examples the Rolling Stones 1965 spring tour and the Rolling Stones 1966 tour of the United Kingdom. The former featured the Konrads, Dave Berry and the Cruisers, the Checkmates (without Emile Ford of "What Do You Want to Make Those Eyes at Me For" fame), and Goldie and the Gingerbreads. The 1966 tour featured Ike and Tina Turner, the Yardbirds, and Peter Jay and the Jaywalkers, who had just had an instrumental hit with "Totem Pole." The show was compared to British blues singer Long John Baldry. Venues would have their own sound systems, sometimes supplemented with a couple of small cabinet column speakers at the side of the stage, and in the middle a set of drums and three 100-watt amplifiers would look lost on the sparsely populated stage. For the support acts, you could generally guarantee that the sound would be at a reasonable volume and without distortion. Even the Yardbirds, with Jimmy Page and Jeff Beck, renowned for their "loud" guitar playing, didn't create a deafening wall of sound (but nevertheless managed to drown out Keith Relf's voice). When the Rolling Stones appeared, they would not have extra towers of equipment, yet all that could be heard of their set was the first few bars of each song, with the rest drowned out by screaming fans.

Contemporary commercial folk music was doing quite well in the charts in Britain in 1966. Dylan, Donovan, Baez, and the Seekers were commercially successful. What distinguished Dylan from other performers of his generation was that he was the feature of the whole show, and the volume of his music was louder than anything anyone had heard before. His tour took its own sound system with them, a practice that was not to become standard until a couple of years later. They took with them tons of equipment, including huge column cabinet speakers that filled the stage.[43] C. P. Lee describes the equipment in his recent book:

> The gear that Dylan's roadies were hauling around the world was state of the art American technology costing over $30,000 [a veritable king's ransom at today's prices]. It was huge. There were big black bin speakers piled on top of one another at each side of the band. There were box shaped foldback monitors positioned all over the stage, some angled directly at Dylan. On the sides were arrows pointing up and the words, 'handle with care' stencilled on them. Microphones, cables, guitar amps, organ amp, all being pumped through the PA at 1000 watts.[44]

In Manchester, the management had to remove seats already sold in order to accommodate the unprecedented volume of equipment.

The situation is, then, much more complicated than the question of Dylan going electric. The volume in itself was a problem, accentuated by the contrast with an acoustic set. Complaints about the volume and distortion of sound followed Dylan from the 1965 Newport Folk Festival to the culmination of the world tour in the two Albert Hall concerts in London on May 26 and 27, 1966.

At Newport, for example, the three-song set was appalling. On the one hand, it was underrehearsed and had been put together overnight. Opinions vary as to the sound quality and mixing. It was the playing that left a lot to be desired. The music was loud, the sound surged, the organ was barely audible, and the vocals were lost in the background because Dylan turned away from the microphone. Dylan himself, always ready to attribute conspiratorial motives to others, claimed that those who knew what he was going to play at Newport twisted the sound in a deliberate attempt to sabotage him.[45] Much of the heckling related to the technical issues of balance, calling for the vocals to be turned up and to make the organ audible. Even the production manager, who was, contrary to the general view of the set, quite pleased with the balance, commented that by the "standards of the day it was the loudest thing that anybody had ever heard."[46] The band was unable to sustain the beat on "Like a Rolling Stone" and at times almost completely lost the plot. There were indeed people who called out for the old songs, and who can blame them when the new ones were so poorly executed, with the only saving grace being their raw energy, which, anyhow, cut no ice with the purists. When the band left the stage, the people felt shortchanged. They had come to see Dylan, and he did only three songs. There were catcalls, howls, and insults expressing their disquiet at such a short set. Dylan came back on alone (the band had exhausted their repertoire) and sang two acoustic songs, "It's All Over Now, Baby Blue" and "Mr. Tambourine Man."

Three weeks later, on August 28 at the Forest Hills Music Festival in New York City, Dylan showcased the electric set that, with a few changes, would characterize his live set throughout his world tour over the following nine months, and the reaction he received was also to prove the hallmark of the tour. His new lineup was Al Kooper, Harvey Brooks, and two members of the Canadian band the Hawks, Robbie Robertson and Levon Helm. After the Hollywood Bowl concert a few days later, Kooper and Brooks pulled out of the scheduled world tour to begin in September. It is at this point that Dylan recruited the rest of the Hawks and rehearsed with them in Canada. Levon Helm pulled out at the end of November, worn down by the heckling and booing, and was replaced with session drummer Bobby Gregg, who in turn was replaced by Sandy Konikoff before Mickey Jones joined in April 1966 for the European leg of the tour. When they played Honolulu on April 9, again, the sheer volume of the performance was central to the criticism. The reviewer Bruce Cook claimed that Dylan "can make more noise than The Beatles, Byrds and Animals put together."[47]

Throughout the tour Dylan and The Band seemed to take an inordinate time tuning between songs, generating slow hand clapping and shouts to turn down the volume. These breaks also allowed the purists to heckle and call Dylan a traitor. After being called Judas at the Manchester show (a wounding, cruel remark with unintended depth of intensity when thrown at a Jew), a visibly shaken Dylan, after a few seconds' delay and not being able to summon any witticism to shrug it off, responded with the words "I don't believe you" and after another pause, "You're a liar." He and the group then broke into "Like a Rolling Stone," and Dylan turned to the others and said, "Play it fucking loud." John Cordwell, who famously shook Dylan at the Manchester Free Trade Hall by shouting "Judas!" during the electric part of the set, explained his outburst as a reaction not only to the denial of the folk movement, which was such a force for change, but also to the utter contempt with which Dylan treated his audience: "Dylan was our 'voice'."[48] The sound quality in the hall was dreadful, nothing like the recording taken from the sound desk, but worst of all was the on-stage posturing and the inability of the audience to hear the words.

The next time that The Band and Dylan officially played live together was at the Isle of Wight in 1969, to a bemused but more appreciative audience, somewhat startled by the "Great White Wonder."[49] Dylan chose The Band when he decided to go on the road again in 1974 for the first time since 1966. They had played two unannounced concerts together at St. Louis and the Brooklyn Academy of Music in New York. The Band was now extremely well established in its own right, and people wondered why they would want to risk being in Dylan's shadow. The Band played quite a few numbers without Dylan, but there were always people in the crowd shouting for him. Robbie Robertson said that they expected that, and in fact a few voices calling for Dylan were nothing compared with the howls and boos they received eight years before.[50]

This, of course, wasn't the last time that Dylan faced such hostility, and the frequency with which he elicited it seems to indicate something of a psychological need to stand up with the courage of his convictions and to convert everyone else to them. The most explicit manifestation of this phenomenon was his conversion to Christian fundamentalism, after which he preached a peculiar type of evangelicalism emphasizing the wrath of God, the presence of the Antichrist, the imminence of Armageddon, and the Second Coming of Christ. As a baptized member of the Vineyard

A Bob Dylan "Saved" sticker.

Fellowship in California, he took his religious convictions on the road in late 1979 and early 1980. In Hartford, Connecticut, he launched into a tirade about the "ungodly vice" of homosexuality that was sweeping San Francisco. He seems to have thrived on the negativity of audiences, gaining strength from the challenge to which he had to rise. At the same concert, referring to the hostility that he encountered in playing songs like "Maggie's Farm" and "Subterranean Homesick Blues" in 1965, Dylan told the audience: "I was always prepared for adversity. I was always prepared back then, and now I'm even more prepared."[51] At the two-week opening engagement of the tour in San Francisco's Warfield Theatre, Dylan sang only his new religious songs, prompting placard protests outside the theater, one of which read "Jesus Loves Your Old Songs, Too." This hostility to his conversion to fundamentalist Christianity was at least as shocking as his decision to go electric, and the protests continued. A group of people called Stepchild, for example, printed stickers to adhere to the cover of Dylan's next Christian album, *Saved*. The sticker read: "WARNING: This Bob Dylan Album 'SAVED' is the worst Bob Dylan album ever released. Don't buy it unless you already have every other Bob Dylan album."

The Element of Surprise

I am not attempting here to write a history of Dylan's changes, merely to highlight the fact that the changes are constantly taking place and, like Capability Brown's garden landscapes, always include the element of surprise, making him one of the most enigmatic performers on the contemporary music scene. When he returned to recording after his 1966 motorcyle accident, the change in his musical style was almost as surprising and shocking as his electric turn. Dylan's musical return marked yet another transformation. The urban decadence of *Blonde on Blonde* was replaced with the homely authenticity of the country. The songs were as imaginative but set in a narrative form celebrating the style and atmosphere of the legend and heritage of inherited stories, delivered to a backing now stripped of heavy rock guitars, which are replaced by low-key bass, drums, and guitar. It is quite a remarkable statement and as equally radical a renunciation of the leadership role he had abjured in the transition from protest to poetry. Prior to his motorcycle accident, Dylan had become a leader of a different type, in style and in musical direction. He was responsible for the imaginative musical metamorphoses of the Beatles in *Sgt. Pepper's Lonely Hearts Club Band* (1967) and the Rolling Stones in *Her Majesty's Satanic Request*. Suddenly the leader was no longer out in front on the same trail. He had switched horses and taken a different route. It showed an immense self-confidence in himself and in his music to cut himself so completely free from the ultra-cool, urban decadent style that he had created.

His most serious incarnation after his long exile, with intermittent appearances such as the Isle of Wight, was the Rolling Thunder Revue, which appeared to be a conscious synthesis of both the cowboy and the dandy, combining songs and people from his early days in Greenwich Village, including the finger-pointing material, with his avant-garde phase, and with the neo-country-and-western period of *Nashville Skyline,* en route taking in *Blood on the Tracks* and the imminent album *Desire.* For the Rolling Thunder Revue venture, Dylan returned to Greenwich Village, the site of a very different scene from the days of his departure. By the late '60s and early '70s, the folk scene in the Village had gone the way of jazz. When serious drugs permeated the coffeehouses and bars, the folksingers became unreliable and found it difficult to get work. Loudon Wainwright worked in the Village from about 1968 and found that everyone had gone to Woodstock. It was because James Taylor had brought folk music back into vogue that Wainwright got a record deal and brought out his first album in 1970.[52] Dylan's return in 1975 attracted better performers back to the Village and to the clubs that were until then just about surviving: Gerdes Folk City, the Kettle of Fish, the Dug Out, and the Other End.

Dylan's return caused quite a stir, as he was seen, often on his own, leaving his loft on Houston Street and frequenting some of his old haunts. He was to be seen at the newly reopened Other End. On July 4, 1975, he was persuaded to join his friend Bob Neuwirth on stage at the Other End in a jam session. Dylan sang only harmony that night, but during the subsequent week many of the musicians that were to accompany him on the tour appeared around the Village, including Rob Stoner, Steve Soles, Mick Ronson, and Ramblin' Jack Elliott. The revue was launched on Mike Porco's birthday, October 23, 1975, at Gerdes Folk City, and it was to be the first time that Allen Ginsberg had ever read there. The previous evening many of them had gone to see and jam with David Blue at the Other End. The tour itself was literally a revival of the '60s folk ideal, captured on film in *Renaldo and Clara* and edited into a semifictitious and semidocumentary form (the film was later lambasted as pretentious and incoherent by the critics and even by the singers and actors who appeared in it). The musical experience, for delighted audiences, was almost the opposite of the celluloid nightmare. The tour was not only an ensemble of Dylan's early days in the Village but also a conscious attempt to revive the "familial spirit" of an earlier generation that inspired him, the Almanac Singers, including Woody Guthrie and Pete Seeger.[53]

Bob Gruen, a reviewer of the tour that followed, testified to the ever-changing image: "You need more than a weatherman to know which way Bob Dylan blows."[54] The tour made its way across the United States, taking the public by surprise in playing small venues at short notice, with up to fifteen musicians and performers in various combinations. It seemed to be a deliberate gesture to shun the wave of publicity and emotion that accompanied Dylan's 1974 tour with The Band, which visited stadiums throughout the country, giving millions of fans the opportunity to see Dylan in the first advertised concerts since the 1969 Isle of Wight appearance. The Rolling Thunder Revue was shrouded in mystery. Not even the musicians were aware of the itinerary, and no date was fixed more than five shows ahead in order to minimize ticket touting and box office hysteria. Dylan himself was billed equally with the other stars in the revue, implying a conscious rejection of his superstardom image, just as he had rejected the role of leader. However, he was very much the leader of the show, which included a film crew that was to shoot *Renaldo and Clara*, in which the characters were played by the stars of the revue, including Joan Baez and Dylan's wife, Sara.

Poster for the Rolling Thunder Revue.

Dylan's autumn tour of the United States in 2002 augured another change in direction. Playing a considerable part of the set standing at an electric piano, he indulged in an unlikely string of covers that were more faithful to the originals than he was to his own songs. In 1999 he had surprised audiences by including in his repertoire religious standards such as "Hallelujah, I'm Ready to Go," "Somebody Touched Me," "Pass Me Not, O Gentle Savior," and "Rock of Ages." In the 2002 tour he regularly performed rock classics, such as Don Henley's "End of Innocence" and Neil Young's "Old Man." He also paid homage to Warren Zevon by including various songs by Zevon, such as "Boom Boom Mancini," "Mutineer," and "Accidentally Like a Martyr." Dylan included these songs in all his shows because Zevon had disclosed in the summer of 2002 that he was terminally ill with cancer. His show at Madison Square Garden on November 13, 2002, had added poignancy in that Dylan dedicated the finale to George Harrison, "a good buddy of mine," by singing a faithful version of "Something." Dylan's voice softened and was noticeably more melodic during this tribute. Harrison had died of cancer in December 2001, and Dylan was unable to be at the memorial concert for him.

Endnotes

1. Quoted in *Bob Dylan in His Own Words,* ed. Christian Williams (London: Omnibus, 1993), 27.
2. Ibid., 15.
3. Bob Dylan, interviewed by Robert Shelton on a flight from Lincoln, Nebraska, to Denver, March 1966 (Robert Shelton Archive, Experience Music Project, Seattle).
4. Cited in Robert Shelton, *No Direction Home* (New York: Da Capo Press, 1997, first published in 1986), 73.
5. Sara, whose real name was Shirley Noznisky, was a friend of Al Grossman's wife, Sally, through whom she met Dylan. She had been married to the fashion photographer Hans Lownds, and after their separation lived in the Chelsea Hotel with her daughter, Maria. She and Dylan married in 1965 and divorced in 1978.
6. Bert Cartwright, "The Mysterious Norman Raeburn," in *Wanted Man: In Search of Bob Dylan,* ed. John Bauldie (New York: Citadel Press, 1991), 87.
7. Ibid., 88.
8. Perry Meisel, *The Cowboy and the Dandy: Crossing Over from Romanticism to Rock and Roll* (New York: Oxford University Press, 1999), 8–9.
9. Bob Dylan, interviewed by Robert Shelton on a plane from Lincoln, Nebraska, to Denver, March 1966 (Robert Shelton Archive, Music Experience Project, Seattle).
10. Tom Smucker, "Arlo Guthrie and the Communist Mystical Tradition," *Voice,* August 29, 1976, 38.
11. Greil Marcus, *Invisible Republic* (London: Picador, 1997), 30.
12. Interview conducted by Robert Shelton with Bob Dylan's parents, Hibbing, Minnesota, May 1968 (Shelton Archives, Experience Music Project, Seattle).
13. Anthony Scaduto, *Bob Dylan* (London: Helter Skelter, 1996), 137.
14. Todd Gitlin, *The Sixties: Years of Hope* (New York: Bantam, 1987), 197.

15. Scaduto, *Bob Dylan*, 196.
16. Ralph J. Gleason, "The Children's Crusade," *Ramparts* (March 1966): 31.
17. Cited in Scott M. Marshall (with Marcia Ford), *Restless Pilgrim: The Spiritual Journey of Bob Dylan* (Lake Mary, FL: Relevant Books, 2002), 12.
18. Phil Ochs, *The War Is Over* (New York: Barricade Music, 1965).
19. Andrew Sarris, "Notes on the Auteur Theory in 1962," in *Film Theory and Criticism: Introductory Readings*, ed. Gerald Mast and Marshall Cohen (Oxford: Oxford University Press, 1985).
20. Stephen Scobie, "Racing the Midnight Train: Leonard Cohen in Performance," *Canadian Literature* 152–153 (1997): 56.
21. Shelton, *No Direction Home*.
22. Richard Goldstein, "Beautiful Creep," *Village Voice*, December 28, 1967, 20. Reprinted in *Leonard Cohen: The Artist and His Critics*, ed. Michael Gnarowski (Toronto: McGraw-Hill, 1976), 43–44.
23. Louis Dudek made his comments in "The Prophet as Celebrity," *McGill Reporter*, 20 (January 1967).
24. Richard Poirier, *The Performing Self: Compositions and Decompositions in the Languages of Contemporary Life* (New York: Oxford University Press, 1971). See also Scobie, "Racing the Midnight Train," 58.
25. Michael Oakeshott, *On Human Conduct* (Oxford: Clarendon Press, 1975), 70–73. See also Terry Nardin, *The Philosophy of Oakeshott* (College Park, PA: Pennsylvania State University Press, 2001), 192–193.
26. John Walsh, "Research, You Understand . . . Leonard Cohen," *Mojo* (September 1994): 60.
27. Cited in Andy Gill, "Judas Christ Superstar," *Mojo* (November 1998): 39.
28. See, Marianne Faithfull and David Dalton, *Faithfull: An Autobiography* (New York: Cooper Square Press, 2000; first published in 1994), 55.
29. See the official fan magazine *The Rolling Stones Book*, nos. 19, 20, and 25 (London: Beat Publications, 1965–1966).
30. Gill, "Judas Christ Superstar," 42.
31. Faithfull with Dalton, *Faithfull*, 40.
32. Dave Van Ronk, "Talkin' New York," *Guitar World Acoustic* 31 (Summer 1991): 36.
33. Cited in Shelton, *No Direction Home*, 88.
34. See David Hadju, *Positively Fourth Street* (London: Bloomsbury, 2001), 7.
35. Mary Travers, cited in Robbie Woliver, *Hoot: A Twenty-five-Year History of the Greenwich Village Music Scene* (New York: St. Martin's Press, 1994), 58.
36. Suze Rotolo, cited in ibid., 85.
37. Scaduto, *Bob Dylan*, 28.
38. "The Girl from the North Country: Jaharana Romney Interviewed by Marcus Wittman," in *Wanted Man: In Search of Bob Dylan,* ed. John Bauldie (New York: Citadel Underground, 1991), 18–25.
39. Bob Dylan, interviewed by Robert Shelton on a plane from Lincoln, Nebraska, to Denver, March 1966 (Robert Shelton Archive, Music Experience Project, Seattle).
40. Cited in Hadju, *Positively Fourth Street*, 236.
41. Miesel, *The Cowboy and the Dandy*, 122.
42. Ibid.
43. See Tony Glover's notes to volume 4 in the bootleg series *Bob Dylan Live 1966: The Royal Albert Hall Concert* (Columbia Records, 1998).
44. C. P. Lee, *Like the Night: Bob Dylan and the Road to the Manchester Free Trade Hall* (London: Helter Skelter, 1998), 47.
45. Nora Ephron and Susan Edmiston, "Bob Dylan Interview." Reprinted in *Bob Dylan: The Early Years, a Retrospective,* ed. Craig McGregor (New York: Da Capo Press, 1990), 87.
46. Joe Boyd, the production manager at the festival, had pressed for the hiring of Paul Rothchild who produced the Paul Butterfield Band, and later the Doors and Janis Joplin. Boyd described the production by Rothchild in glowing terms: "As a result, you didn't have some square

sound guy fumbling around, you had powerfully, ballsy-mixed, expertly done rock'n'roll." "Newport '65," Joe Boyd, interview by Jonathan Morley, August 31, 1988, reprinted in *Wanted Man: In Search of Bob Dylan*, ed. John Bauldie (New York: Citadel Press, 1991), 64.

47. Cited by Lee, *Like the Night*, 72.

48. Ian MacDonald, "Wilde Mercury: A Tale of Two Dylans," *Uncut* (June 2001): 40.

49. "Great White Wonder" refers to the white suit Dylan wore at the Isle of Wight festival and also to the title of a bootleg album—*The Little White Wonder*. Prior to the reunion in 1969, Dylan had played at the tribute to Woody Guthrie at Carnegie Hall in 1968.

50. Ben Fong-Torres, "Dylan Opens to a Hero's Welcome," in *Knocking on Dylan's Door,* by the authors of *Rolling Stone* (London: Dempsey/Cassell, 1975), 32.

51. See Clinton Heylin, "Saved! Bob Dylan's Conversion to Christianity," in Bauldie, *Wanted Man*, 132.

52. Woliver, *Hoot,* 173.

53. Tim Riley, *Hard Rain: A Dylan Commentary* (New York: Da Capo Press, 1999), 252.

54. Bob Gruen, "King and Queen Back in Triumph," *Melody Maker*, November 14, 1975.

4

LADIES AND GENTLEMEN, MR. LEONARD COHEN

> I've had people tell me that my records have made their lives not worth living.[1]

> I loved Dylan's stuff as soon as I heard it. I was living, in a certain sense, in the same kind of universe that he was living in, and that when I heard him, I recognized his genius, but I also recognized a certain brotherhood in his work. And we have since become . . . acquaintances, I might even say friends. There is some kind of communion between us.
>
> —Leonard Cohen

ohen's early interest in music came after the big band era, but just before the rise of a youth culture and the invention of the teenager. He enjoyed the music of Frank Sinatra, Tony Bennett, Frankie Laine, and Johnny Ray, and later became passionate about Hank Williams and Ray Charles. Ray Charles, for example, achieved worldwide success in 1960 with the Hoagy Carmichael song "Georgia on My Mind" and classics such as "Take These Chains from My Heart" and "Hit the Road, Jack." He recorded two volumes of country-and-western-influenced material that became extremely popular. These albums, *Modern Sounds in Country and Western Music, Volumes One and Two* (1962), were among Cohen's record collection, and played over and over again while he worked on his poems and prose.

These musical influences surface most distinctively on *Death of a Ladies' Man*, the album overproduced by Phil Spector, and which lack of success inspired CBS America to become distinctly cool toward Cohen until the huge popularity of *I'm Your Man* in Europe in 1988. The song inspired by

Leonard Cohen and girl.

Nico on *Death of a Ladies' Man*, "Memories" is played in the style of Frankie Laine, with loud, wailing saxophones in the foreground and the voice receding into the distance, and opens with the line "Frankie Laine was singing 'Jezebel.' "

When Cohen was young, he played guitar and clarinet and also took piano lessons. The first live performance Cohen attended, in 1949, was of Josh White, who was associated with the leftist folk movement of New York, but who later lost a lot of credibility because of his testimony against Communist folksingers in the McCarthy witch hunts. At the age of fifteen, Cohen was more thoroughly introduced to the world of protest music by Irving Morton,[2] a folksinger and left-wing agitator who, at a Jewish community camp, Camp Sunshine, in 1950, taught Cohen and other campers traditional songs from John Lomax's *The People's Songbook,* which included songs from Woody Guthrie and Josh White. (One of the compilers of the book was Pete Seeger.) Cohen later acknowledged the influence of these songs by including several of them on his first live album, *Leonard Cohen: Live Songs* (1973). At the time that he was introduced to the songbook, Cohen was learning Spanish guitar and reading the poems of Federico García Lorca. The songbook included songs of Spanish oppression and resistance, which had an inspiring effect on Cohen, who was at that time, following the death of his father, his mother's remarriage to Harry Ostrow, exhibiting early signs of the depression that was to plague him throughout his life.

Ed McCurdy in Montreal, the Weavers, Pete Seeger, and the work of John and Alan Lomax were making popularist music more widely known. The emphasis on "the people" in these songs gave the whole genre a left-wing slant. "The people" themselves were to be the salvation of society, delivering it from all its evils. It was perhaps a naive but laudatory faith in the power of democracy. *The People's Songbook* included antifascist songs and French and Spanish Republican Army partisan songs. The book taught Cohen that music was a medium through which freedom, resistance, and political protest could be conveyed, reflecting both social and personal optimism. Evenings later spent in Montreal cafes and bars and in friends' houses, playing these songs and composing a few of his own, helped shape Cohen's style. It was through folk music that he discovered what a lyric was, and he was inspired to undertake a more formal study of poetry at McGill University and later at Columbia University.

Poetry and Jazz

Cohen developed his public persona primarily through poetry recitals, often with fellow Canadian poets Louis Dudek, Irving Layton, and A. M. Klein. In addition to these, the Canadian Broadcasting Corporation brought together poets A. J. Smith and F. R. Scott for the film *Six Montreal Poets* (1957), which followed the poetry tour and interviewed Cohen along the way. Cohen read eight poems from his *Let Us Compare Mythologies,* which was first published in 1956.

Cohen also chanted poetry to the accompaniment of his own guitar improvisation and occasionally to jazz music. His first readings to jazz accompaniment were in 1957 (some sources say 1958) in Birdland, a poor imitation of the original New York club, above Dunn's Restaurant and Emporium on Sainte-Catherine's Street, Montreal. Cohen would improvise, while Bill Barwick's Trio or Maury Kaye and his jazz group played. Cohen also worked with a jazz guitarist from Winnipeg named Lenny Breau, for example, when they played Manitoba in 1964.

Cohen had heard Jack Kerouac's jazz poetry readings at the Village Vanguard while he was a student at Columbia University. It took guts for Cohen to stand up in a seedy nightclub—where most of the clientele had

Poster for Leonard Cohen poetry and jazz, 1964 (original held in the Thomas Fisher Rare Book Library, University of Toronto).

come to see the girly floor show the Tappettes, in which the buxom dancers undressed to the legally permissible limit—and chant poetry to jazz accompaniment. One account relates how, early in the evening, Maury Kaye's band would play more conventional popular tunes in keeping with the floor show. When the excitement died down around midnight, Cohen, dressed in black and illuminated by a single spotlight, would appear. To the audience's astonishment and their exclamations of "What the fuck!" he would start reciting poetry.[3] On occasion Cohen was joined by other poets, including Layton, Dudek, and Daryl Hine.

A $2,000 Canadian Arts Council grant enabled Cohen to go to London in the late 1950s, before it became the "swinging" place to be. There he started to write a novel, *The Favourite Game* (then titled *Beauty at Close Quarters*), which he completed on the Greek island of Hydra, where he had bought a house for $1,500. He returned to Montreal in 1959 for a brief period to earn some money at poetry readings, including one in New York with Layton and his former teacher, F. R. Scott.

In 1961, at the age of twenty-six, he published his second collection of poems, *The Spice-Box of Earth*. His popularity became such that the National Film Board of Canada made a documentary, directed by Donald Brittain and Don Owen, with Cohen as the centerpiece. The film *Ladies and Gentlemen . . . Mr. Leonard Cohen* (1965) captured the poet as performer, humorist, and personality. In it Cohen delivers a carefully prepared, immaculately timed comic routine in which he pauses strategically for laughs.

Cohen's next collection was the much more deliberately provocative and offensive. *Flowers for Hitler,* originally titled *Opium for Hitler,* which was published in 1964. The poems reflected the themes of his adopted island of Hydra, history, and politics.

Like Dylan, Cohen has projected a public image that has changed over the years, but not as persistently and radically as Dylan's. The answers he gave to serious questions in interviews were often irreverent, flippant, and mostly tongue in cheek. Privately, however, he was very shy and insecure, uncertain of his talents and his prospects of success. Cohen's papers in Toronto University show that he was much more self-disclosing than Dylan. Cohen is self-effacing, disarmingly honest in talking about his lack of success with publishers. In his private correspondence he doesn't try to present himself as other than what he is. The letters reveal that while he was writing what was to be described as "pure filth," *Beautiful Losers,* he was at heart a good Jewish boy, writing to his mother and sister Esther frequently. The struggling artist relied heavily on the support of both, receiving the odd cash contribution and loan when times were hard.

Many of his relatives visited him on Hydra, including his mother, Marsha, his cousin Alan, and his uncle Edgar.

While on Hydra, Cohen worked intensively and obsessively on his second novel, *Beautiful Losers*, published in 1966, which outraged some critics and sent others into raptures. In Canada it was almost wholly vilified. *Maclean's Review* characterized it as reducing "sex to something at once more elemental and sick, more psychotic than pornographic." Robert Fulford, in the *Toronto Daily Star*, thought it "the most revolting book ever written in Canada." Outside Canada Robert Arn, writing in *Cambridge Review*, described the book as a "tirade of obscene poetry." Its message, according to Arn, was little more than that we live in strange and disturbing times, the originality of which consisted in the fact that it is "expressed with such relentless insistence in terms of the genitals."[4]

In the United States, critics were kinder. *Beautiful Losers* was better received in the *New York Times Book Review* and the *New York Review of Books*. In the former, for example, despite the fact that "constipated, masturbated, fantasy-sated, our hero promises the experienced reader of anguished monologues another ride through another hell," the critic acknowledged that there are "bursts of expository eloquence."[5] It is a novel, another critic commented, that delighted in blood and buggery in a way reminiscent of William Burroughs.[6] *Beautiful Losers* was eventually translated into twenty languages and sold over three million copies, after selling only a few thousand copies before Cohen became famous for his singing and songwriting. In the same year he published the collection *Parasites of Heaven* (1966).

After being well received as both a poet and an author, Cohen made his way to New York and became part of the folk music culture, which had changed considerably since Dylan's entry into it. Cohen had listened to country music on the Armed Forces Radio broadcasts in Greece while writing *Beautiful Losers* and had written some early versions of songs. It was Nashville that beckoned to him, but on the way he became interested in a new phenomenon in music, Bob Dylan. In a self-deprecating way, Cohen once described to a friend the qualities he possessed that enhanced his own chances of success: "I've got three things going for me. I have a terrible voice, can't even carry a tune. Also I'm very small, emaciated, with a residue of acne. And I'm demonstrably Jewish (Dylan is not). The only thing going against me is that I play the guitar too well."[7] For a year or so Cohen simultaneously pursued his musical and poetry reading careers. Invitations to his manager, Mary Martin, continued to flood in for his appearance at poetry festivals and for his contribution to panels discussing the state of modern poetry, even after his musical success.

In New York, Cohen associated with Phil Ochs, Pete Seeger, and Joan Baez and made his debut at a Judy Collins anti–Vietnam War benefit concert in April 1967. When he first met Collins in 1966 to play her his songs, at Mary Martin's instigation, Cohen struck her as "very shy and nervous," especially about singing in public.[8] He had been introduced to Collins by Martin, Al Grossman's Canadian assistant, who was also responsible for getting the Hawks to play backup for Dylan. Collins immediately thought Cohen's songs were beautiful but believed there was nothing in his repertoire for her. She asked him to let her know when he had something else in which she might be interested. Cohen went back to Montreal to finish *Parasites of Heaven* and there put the finishing touches on a song that he had been working on for some time. He knew the lyrics were powerful, capturing the mood of the Montreal waterfront and the righteous beauty of Suzanne Vaillancourt, the wife of Cohen's friend Armand Vaillancourt.

Meanwhile, Cohen's fame in Canada as a novelist and poet worked to his advantage as a singer in so far as he was permitted a little self-indulgence. He first sang on television on the CBC show *Take Thirty* in 1967. The producers had never heard Cohen sing but took the risk in order to get an interview with the poet. For the show, he wore an immaculately tailored gray flannel suit and sang a twenty-minute version of "The Stranger Song," which was considerably shortened for broadcasting. Cohen's publicity for poetry reading recitals, such as the one he gave with Irving Layton in New York in February 1966, describes him at the time as also being a "song-writer."

"Suzanne" was the song that launched Cohen's musical career. Judy Collins released it on her successful album *In My Life* in November 1966, and Noel Harrison took it to the charts in 1967. Collins's follow-up LP, *Wildflowers,* reached number five in the charts in November 1967 and included three Cohen compositions: "Sisters of Mercy," "Priests," and "Hey, That's No Way to Say Goodbye." Collins's next album, *Who Knows Where the Time Goes* (1968), included two Cohen songs, "Story of Isaac" and "Bird on the Wire," both of which were featured on Cohen's second album, *Songs from a Room* (1969). (His first, *Songs of Leonard Cohen,* was released in December 1967.)

Even though Cohen has never written a conventional protest song, he has nevertheless included some in his repertoire over the years. In his 1972 tour of Europe, for example, he included the anticapitalist song "Banks of Marble," which Pete Seeger made popular, an Irish Republican song, "Kevin Barry," and the American labor movement and civil rights song "We Shall Not Be Moved."

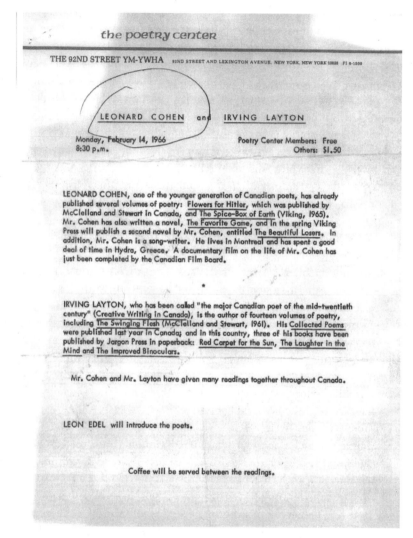

the poetry center

THE 92ND STREET YM-YWHA   92ND STREET AND LEXINGTON AVENUE, NEW YORK, NEW YORK 10028   FI 9-1500

LEONARD COHEN and IRVING LAYTON

Monday, February 14, 1966   Poetry Center Members: Free
8:30 p.m.   Others: $1.50

LEONARD COHEN, one of the younger generation of Canadian poets, has already
published several volumes of poetry: Flowers for Hitler, which was published by
McClelland and Stewart in Canada, and The Spice-Box of Earth (Viking, 1965).
Mr. Cohen has also written a novel, The Favorite Game, and In the spring Viking
Press will publish a second novel by Mr. Cohen, entitled The Beautiful Losers. In
addition, Mr. Cohen is a song-writer. He lives in Montreal and has spent a good
deal of time in Hydra, Greece. A documentary film on the life of Mr. Cohen has
just been completed by the Canadian Film Board.

*

IRVING LAYTON, who has been called "the major Canadian poet of the mid-twentieth
century" (Creative Writing in Canada), is the author of fourteen volumes of poetry,
including The Swinging Flesh (McClelland and Stewart, 1961). His Collected Poems
were published last year in Canada; and in this country, three of his books have been
published by Jargon Press in paperback: Red Carpet for the Sun, The Laughter in the
Mind and The Improved Binoculars.

Mr. Cohen and Mr. Layton have given many readings together throughout Canada.

LEON EDEL will introduce the poets.

Coffee will be served between the readings.

Flyer for a Layton and Cohen poetry reading in New York, 1966.

Although Cohen was often linked with the New York folk music
scene, he was nevertheless distanced from it in a number of ways. He
was much older than the new generation of folksingers when he released
his first album. At thirty-three, he was positively ancient. He had a
university education and wore expensive suits. But above all he was not
as overtly politically left wing as the movement in general. He was more
comfortable with the avant-garde New York cultural scene surrounding

Leonard Cohen at the 1970 Isle of Wight Festival (Glenn A. Baker Archives/Redferns).

Andy Warhol and the Chelsea Hotel. He was also much more self-absorbed than many of the young folksingers. He was only half joking when he said that after seeing Nico, the singer with the Velvet Underground, at Warhol's club, the Dom, he forgot about the "good society" and followed her obsessively all around New York.[9]

The songs that reflect the early influence of *The People's Songbook* are "The Partisan," "The Old Revolution," and "The Traitor" (*Recent Songs*, 1979).[10] "The Partisan," written by Anna Marley in 1944 and included in all of Cohen's tours between 1970 and 1988, was a response to the German occupation of France in World War II and Marley's role in the French Resistance. The song tells of the enemy pouring across the border and killing a woman who has given refuge to three soldiers. Only one of the three sheltered soldiers survives, and it is his voice that speaks the narrative. In contrast to the specific story of "The Partisan," "The Old Revolution" and "The Traitor" do not have a clear message. They may be inspired by actual events, but they are not ostensibly about those particular situations. Their imagery may reflect identifiable events, but the songs are woven into an imaginative web that conveys a mood rather than a message. They offer no solutions, merely invitations to share in the singer's suffering.[11] "Story of Isaac" (*Songs from a Room*), which one critic, Mikal Gilmore, described in 1985 as the best antiwar song written in the past thirty years, serves as an illustration. The song is ostensibly a retelling of the biblical story of Isaac, whose father, Abraham, was ordered by God to sacrifice. Throughout the song, however, the particular is universalized to deplore man's inhumanity to man and to extend the reprieve to our relations with each other in the contemporary world. Judy Collins's version was altered by her to fit in more specifically with the anti–Vietnam War sentiments of the late '60s. She ends the song with the lines "And may I never learn to scorn / The body out of chaos born / The woman and the man." Cohen himself denied that "Story of Isaac" could fit squarely into the antiwar camp. Indeed, his version concludes with the ambiguous lines "Man of peace, man of war—the peacock spreads his fan." He said in 1973 that he didn't need to have a song like John Lennon's "Give Peace a Chance." A song about conflict sung in a peaceful way would have the same message. In fact, he expressed his disdain for "slogan writers."[12] He nevertheless thought that all his songs were political in some sense. They were often strongly against one kind of authority or another.[13] In his song "A Singer Must Die" (*New Skin for the Old Ceremony,* 1974), he says:

> The courtroom is quiet, but who will confess? The answer is Yes. Then read me the list of the crimes that are mine. I will ask for the mercy that you love to decline. And all the ladies go moist, and the judge has no choice: *a singer must die for the lie in his voice.*[14]

The Future (1992), implicitly conveys a suspicion of all individuals or movements that promise perfection, such as communism, fascism, and certain types of religion. The extremes have become alluring and having left the middle ground exposed and vulnerable. It is a song that portends the future, but more disturbingly it is saying that the future is here and now. In the present the catastrophe is already evident. We are in the flood, the signposts are submerged, and the lights have gone out.[15] It is not something about which we can be indifferent: "The deluge is here and I care what happens."[16] There is a collective nervous breakdown taking place, testimony to which is the sale worldwide of fifty million Prozac pills a week.[17] The social contract between individuals has become frayed and is dissolving, and there is a return to tribalism where individuals are protecting their turf by reverting to homicide.

In such songs as "Democracy" (*The Future*) and "The Land of Plenty" (*Ten New Songs*) there is a sharp social criticism of the United States, in praise juxtaposed with irony and in satire portraying the light and the darkness, the delusions and the aspirations of the "land of the free." Each of these songs is an invitation to the country to transcend the blindness of greed and to redeem itself with a broader vision capable of a greater inclusivity, not only within society, but also between the society and races. Cohen implores the mighty ship of the American state to transcend corrosive hatred and the reefs of greed in order to land safely on the shores of need. Both songs are immensely optimistic; despite the squalor, degradation, violence, hatred, and sense of void, there is a huge potential to be realized and shared: "It's coming to America first / the cradle of the best and the worst. / It's here they got the range and the machinery for change / and it's here they got the spiritual thirst" ("Democracy"). "Democracy" is a spirited song, a call to maintain the rage against the dying of the flames of freedom, and to spread the flames of the white heat of resurrection. It has the same determination as "First We Take Manhattan" (*I'm Your Man*), without the sinister intent, but serves to remind us that the forces of good and evil have equally strong battalions in the struggle for survival. The song also is a caution to those who were exuberant over the fall of the Berlin wall in 1989 and believed, as Francis Fukuyama did in *The End of History and the Last Man* (1992), that liberalism had triumphed. Events in the former Soviet Union, Bosnia, Kosovo, Rwanda, and Afghanistan and the destruction of the Word Trade Center in New York, along with the rise of right-wing movements in France, Germany, and Eastern Europe, have sadly confirmed Cohen's skepticism as justified. Nevertheless, whatever may be unedifying about the United States, Cohen sees it as the great social experiment, the land where the races face each other, rich and poor are in confrontation, and the sexes battle for supremacy. It is the laboratory of democracy, with no guarantee that the experiment will work.[18]

In "The Land of Plenty" the crusader becomes the reluctant hero; after withdrawing to find a personal spiritual peace, he cannot renounce the social conscience that longs for the light of truth to illuminate the whole world. At the same time, not having the practical motivation, the fire to engage in the cause, or the will to fight, he is left, like Moses, wondering why he has been chosen to lead the exodus: "Don't really have the courage / to stand where I must stand. / Don't really have the temperament / To lend a helping hand." Both "Democracy" and "The Land of Plenty" continue themes that first emerged in *Flowers for Hitler*. Here Cohen is clearly repulsed by the greed, cruelty, and hypocrisy of modern society and politics and sees its transfiguration in religious revelation: "May the lights in The Land of Plenty / Shine on the truth some day" ("The Land of Plenty").

Political themes, without overt finger-pointing messages, permeate Cohen's poetry, and the power of his imagery, when it works, has a profound and disturbing effect. There is often overstatement, sometimes to the extent of voicing an extreme opinion more for effect than substance. The man known for his seriousness and intensity of mood finds it difficult to sustain this seriousness when asked to comment on serious issues. He may often self-mockingly call himself "laughing Lenny," but he is only half joking. Some poems are humorous and satirical, as, for example, his merciless mocking of the language issue in "The Only Tourist in Havana Turns His Thoughts Homeward" (*Flowers for Hitler*). In writing this poem, Cohen performed a political action by invoking the conventions of joking, overtly enough for everyone to get the joke, but subtle enough not to be too obvious and tiresome. He exhorts his compatriots to make the French speak English, to invent a completely new language, and to award a Canada Council fellowship for the most novel suggestion. The poem is a series of one- and two-line sketches that are juxtaposed but not thematic, united in their tone and overall point rather than in the details. Toward the end, alluding to fears that Canada may become the fifty-first state of America, Cohen says, "Let us threaten to join the USA / and pull out at the last moment."

Cohen has certainly not been reticent to voice political opinions in interviews. His experience of the darker side of New York life, the poverty and the despair, contrasted with immense wealth, puzzled him. Conspicuous consumption channeled into the living rooms of the poor through their television sets and the contrast between rich and poor on the streets generated for him a conundrum: Why did American society hold together? Why did the cohesiveness remain strong when everything to which the poor, both black and white, the oppressed, could not aspire to have or attain was constantly being rammed down their throats? Why didn't those who had little or no stake in society simple revolt? They were being infuriated by being exposed constantly to what they didn't have. Cohen further saw the cohesiveness of society being eroded by drugs and by the federal government's showing little interest in doing something concerted to stop the drug trade. For Cohen, the reformed drug abuser, the only way to arrest the almost deliberate targeting of white and black youth culture, destroying the life chances of the young, was to identify and attack those countries supplying drugs. The systematic supplying of drugs constituted an attack on the United States every bit as serious and perhaps more invidious than a conventional attack. Cohen responded to such an attack by using the conventional weaponry of war: "I think this is a real attack and I think that it should be met with real force . . . with the full force of the American armed community. So I would really go in and bomb the countries that are supplying drugs to America."[19]

The Man with the Golden Voice

We have seen that Leonard Cohen mixed with the usual suspects in the New York folk music scene, heard much the same music, and was subject to many of the same influences. So what made him stand out from the crowd as a performer, someone able to capture audiences in ways that most of his contemporaries in the genre were unable to do? What made the man of the sorrowful countenance touch the lives of so many? Kris Kristofferson was able to encapsulate the power of Cohen's understated persona when commenting on the way he projected his personality before crowds. At the Isle of Wight Festival in 1970, a weary audience, disgruntled with long delays in setting up equipment and sound level checks between acts, witnessed a disheveled, unshaven Cohen take the stage at 4:00 A.M. in battle fatigues and pajamas, semi-composed, tune-up for what seemed like an eternity, and begin to play. Kristofferson thought the audience would kill Cohen: "Then he did the damnest thing you ever saw: he charmed the beast. A lone sorrowful voice did what some of the best rockers in the world had tried to do for three days and failed."[20]

Besides the banal observation that Cohen's lyrical poetry had a depth and intensity that created a strange mood, that mood could not be set without the vehicle through which to do it. A hypnotic voice and good lyrics were not enough. Although Cohen himself did not rate his singing ability, and indeed mocks it in his song "Tower of Song" (*I'm Your Man*), it was recognized to have a mysterious and alluring quality. One reviewer remarked that Cohen's voice "has a magic incantatory quality which hypnotises his audiences, and especially teenage audiences, into a state of bliss if not grace."[21] The ingredient that crystallized the experience was the unusual musical forms and chord sequences. Although Cohen was in the American folk music scene, he was not of it. He did not rely on tried and tested melodies, nor did he play the guitar after any recognizable pattern. Yet there was a subtlety to the difference that did not make what he did jar with convention, but imperceptibly made listeners alert to a difference.

Buffy Sainte-Marie was immediately alert to this difference that set Cohen apart. She thought that it was probably his lack of musical training and ignorance of what he was doing that made his melodies exude originality. They are not conventional and certainly not predictable. Most songwriters, she suggested, use a very simple melodic line if the words are powerful and significant, and a very complex line if they are not. Cohen accompanies his forceful imagery with "outrageous modulations," often starting in one key and ending in another. Enchanted by the poetry, the listener is drawn into wanting to hear the song over and over again to grasp and appreciate what is happening in the music. Sainte-Marie argued that Cohen "has the delicious gall to ask us, who do not even know him, to follow him into a completely original and sometimes scary mind of words without the aid of any of the old folksy musical clichés we are used to holding on to as a guide-rail."[22]

In his mature life Cohen has become renowned for his immaculate and suave appearance. He always was meticulous about his appearance, but from time to time he has cultivated different styles. His famous blue raincoat ("Famous Blue Raincoat," *Songs of Love and Hate,* 1970) became part of his persona for a decade or more. It fit in with his fantasy of being discovered on Sunset Boulevard in Los Angeles and of playing the part of a detective in a Hollywood movie. He became so attached to his raincoat that it literally did become torn at the shoulder. In an interview he gave to *Duel* magazine in 1969, Cohen told the interviewer that he tended to wear clothes until they wore out. He found it difficult to find clothes that represented him. Clothes, he argued, have a magical quality in that they can really transform you in a day. In order to choose clothes that represent you, it is necessary to discover and know who you are. It is something that women have known for a long time and that men are only just beginning to acknowledge.

Songwriting for Cohen is not merely an expression of emotion; it is that, but it is also something much more disturbing, more akin to the exorcising of demons than to the calming of the spirit. It is certainly cathartic, serving to purge inner thoughts. The effect, however, is a severe withdrawal into himself, wounded with flesh torn and his personality under attack. The completion of each creative phase or projection is also the disintegration of the self, which each time has to be painfully and laboriously rebuilt. The process invoked, for Cohen, is whatever works: sex, drugs, antidepressants, religion, art, poetry.

Cohen's writings exude torment, the unending quest for redemption through troughs of deep depression, verging on insanity. With the release of *Ten New Songs* (2001), Cohen for the first time freely talked of his clinical illness, manic depression. It was for him a lifelong affliction with only brief and infrequent moments of respite. Interviews over the last three decades or so hint at his dark states of mind, periods of intense confusion, self-doubt, and self-hatred. Cohen spoke of being almost paralyzed by anxiety, unable to write, and filled with confusion. During the recording of *Songs of Leonard Cohen*, Richard Goldstein spoke to him in the Chelsea Hotel and was obviously irritated by what he took to be Cohen's affected fascination with "cracking up." Goldstein claimed that Cohen's favorite words were at that time *wiped out* and *bewildered*. Cohen told the interviewer that being wiped out was the "real" moment in life, and that around thirty or thirty-five was the traditional age for poets to commit suicide.[23] Goldstein remarked that Cohen appeared to judge episodes in his life by his inability to cope with them. In an interview published in the June 1972 issue of *Maclean's*, Cohen's response to the question "How are you feeling?" was, "I'm just reeling. . . . I'm staggering under the blows. No doubt I contrive these blows for myself." In other words, he took full responsibility for his state of mind, and with the exception of recent interviews, has never attributed the darker side of his thoughts to a clinical illness.

The songs Cohen wrote brought a degree, if only marginally, of coherence into his life, only to be almost immediately dissipated. He described his second album, *Songs from a Room*, as very bleak. The voice projected despair and pain and accurately reflected the state of mind of the singer. In *The Favourite Game* Cohen sensitively characterizes an extremely disturbed child, Martin, who dies at the summer camp where Breavman is working. Cohen felt an affinity with that boy, unable to communicate with the world, unable to make sense of it. As a youth, he himself was drawn to the people who the world called mad, as well as the socially aberrant, the drug addicts, tramps, and alcoholics who draped themselves all over Philips Square and Clark Street in Montreal. The completion of his second novel, *Beautiful Losers,* made him completely "flip out." His reason for writing it was that he considered himself a complete loser, both as a man and as a lover, morally and financially. He resented his own life and even vowed to fill the pages with black as an alternative to killing himself. When the book was finished, he fasted for ten days and had a nervous breakdown. He was taken to a hospital on the island of Hydra, where, he contended, the sky was black with storks who rested on the roofs of houses and took flight the next morning along with his depression.[24]

The 1971 tour included in its itinerary a series of unpublicized concerts at psychiatric institutions. Cohen did this tour not out of any sense of charity, but because he enjoyed playing to mentally ill patients and admired their honesty. If they did not like a song, they just got up and left.[25] Cohen maintained that "those people are in the same landscape as the songs come out of. I feel that they understand them."[26]

Daphne Richardson was a patient in a London psychiatric hospital whom Cohen visited on one of these trips. She had previously written to him, sending samples of her work, both prose and poetry. Some of her work juxtaposed lines from Cohen and Dylan, but she had failed to get permission for the use of the Dylan material. Cohen found on meeting Richardson that she was much more lucid and intelligent than he had expected. He was so impressed by her artwork that he asked her to illustrate his poetry collection *The Energy of Slaves* (1972). Richardson spoke to her caretakers of Cohen's invitation, but they did not believe that she had actually made contact with the famous poet. In responding to her subsequent anger and frustration, they were forced to restrain her. Richardson's letters and telegrams to Cohen asking for confirmation of his invitation to assure the hospital staff that she was not suffering from delusions did not reach him until after she had committed suicide in 1972. Ignorant of this, Cohen had actually instructed his agent to issue a contract and to confirm the truth of their professional relationship. The album *Leonard Cohen: Live Songs* (1973) includes an illustration that reproduces page 3 of Richardson's notebook. The first word of the first line of prose acts as the title: "Transfigurations." In the center of the page is a brightly colored eye, the corners of which are made up of red, blue, and green partial ellipses, with the remainder constituted by decreasing colored ellipses, the iris changing from orange, to green, to red, with the pupil colored blue and red. In capital letters following the line of the eye is the word *INTENSITY*. In this work, Richardson claims that, despite the fact that she could not substantiate her "outrageous claims," God had brought about a transfiguration by entering her body, in which, as a consequence, love bleeds and burns.

In the late 1970s, Cohen had a severe breakdown and found himself unable to write. He sought medical advice and was prescribed antidepressants. The drugs leveled out his mood, but they also put a ceiling on the heights of his emotions. He was semi-comatose, able to write a little but frustrated by the rate of progress. Cohen eventually threw away the drugs and regained his composure and determination. It was after this that he completed the songs for *I'm Your Man*, the album that resurrected his career.

In some moods Cohen thought of his songs within the genre of blues music. They were an expression of his low self-esteem and unhappiness. Leadbelly amusingly says in the prologue to "Good Morning Blues" that the white man does not have the blues because he's got nothing to worry about. Cohen's take on this is slightly different. He contends that "the blues as an art form didn't come from the black man being more miserable than the white man, but rather from his being more honest with himself about it."[27]

Since leaving the Buddhist monastery on Mount Baldy, near Los Angeles, where he had trained since 1993 and where he had become ordained as a monk, Cohen has talked more freely about his fight against depression. In talking about the song "Alexandra Leaving" (*Ten New Songs*) on the LeonardCohen.com Web site, he said that all his life he had been fighting against clinical depression and that all of his obsessions and indulgences, from sex and drugs to religious contemplation, were attempts to deal with it. That depression has now lifted, and he attributes the relief to nothing that he has done, but instead to a natural process. According to Cohen, he read once that as you grow older, the brain cells responsible for anxiety die more rapidly. He had expressed this same belief in 1993 while promoting *The Future*, but nevertheless he felt that he needed the disciplined guidance that the monastic life could give him.

After *The Future*, no new songs or poetry emerged until 1997, with the single entitled "Never Any Good." *Ten New Songs* was his first album since *The Future*. Cohen continues to write, but it is a painstaking process for him.

Endnotes

1. Quoted in Tom Chaffin, "Conversations from a Room," *Canadian Forum* (August/September 1983): 8; and Jim Devlin, *Leonard Cohen in His Own Words* (London: Omnibus Press, 1998), 82.
2. Cohen's introduction to folk music is also attributed to Alf Magerman.
3. Doug Beardsley, "On First Looking into Leonard Cohen," in *Intricate Preparations,* ed. Stephen Scobie (Toronto: ECW Press, 2000), 6–7.
4. See *Maclean's Review,* May 14, 1966; Robert Fulford, *Toronto Daily Star,* April 26, 1966; and Robert Arn, *Cambridge Review,* December 2, 1967.
5. Lawrence M. Bensky, "What Happened to Tekakwitha," reprinted in *Leonard Cohen: The Artist and His Critics,* ed. Michael Gnarowski (Toronto: McGraw-Hill, 1976), 28.
6. Dennis Duffy, "Beautiful Beginners," reprinted in *Leonard Cohen,* 29.
7. Quoted in Ira Mothner, "Songs Sacred and Profane," *Look,* June 10, 1969.
8. Judy Collins, *Singing Lessons* (New York: Pocket Books, 1998), 144.
9. Jim Devlin, ed., *In His Own Words* (London: Omnibus Press, 1998), 84.
10. Ira B. Nadel, *Various Positions* (London: Bloomsbury, 1996), 26.
11. Jim Devlin, *Leonard Cohen in Every Style of Passion* (London: Omnibus Press, 1996), 37.
12. Devlin, *In His Own Words,* 51.
13. Ibid., 59.
14. David Whiteis, in "It Seems So Long Ago: Random Memories and Vingettes of Leonard In Person" (wenheights.net/speakingcohen/whiteis.htm), has suggested that Leonard Cohen

passed on to him an anecdote: "[Cohen] said that 'A Singer Must Die' was written at least partially in response to his having learned that he was on President [Richard] Nixon's 'Enemies List'—the list Nixon and his henchmen drew up, consisting of dissidents and counterculture figures who were targeted for [Federal Bureau of Investigation] or [Internal Revenue Service] harassment. He asked me not to print this—'I don't want to inflame them even more'—but he definitely knew, or at least believed, that he'd been the subject of Nixonian surveillance."

15. Jim Slotek, "Cohen's Future Is Now," *Toronto Star*, November 19, 1993.
16. Michel Field, interviewing Leonard Cohen on the television program *Le Cercle de Minuit*, France2, December 1992.
17. Wayne Robbins, "The Loneliness of the Long-suffering Folkie," *Newsday*, November 22, 1992.
18. Ibid.
19. CBC documentary, "Leonard Cohen: A Portrait in the First Person," first broadcast 1988.
20. "How Was He for You? Famous Fans on Why Leonard Cohen Is Essential Listening," *The Observer*, October 14, 2001, 13.
21. Desmond Pacey, "The Phenomenon of Leonard Cohen," *Canadian Literature* 34 (1967): 5.
22. Buffy Sainte-Marie, "Leonard Cohen . . . His Songs," *Sing Out* (August/September 1967).
23. Richard Goldstein, "Beautiful Creep," *Village Voice*, December 28, 1967, 20. Reprinted in Gnarowksi, *Leonard Cohen*, 42.
24. Ibid., 27.
25. Paul Saltzman, "Famous Last Words from Leonard Cohen," *Maclean's* (June 1972).
26. Jack Hafferkamp, "Ladies and Gents, Leonard Cohen," *Rolling Stone*, April 2, 1971.
27. Paul Williams, "Leonard Cohen: The Romantic Ragpicker's Trade," *Crawdaddy* (March 1975).

$$\boxed{5}$$

HOW LONESOME DOES IT GET?

> Although Cohen may have a private affinity for the vitality, ease and emotive qualities of pop music at its best (as do most young people these days), this does not automatically provide him with the talent to sing. Cohen plainly cannot sing. His voice is dull and monotonous and has little range. Bob Dylan, on the other hand, does know how to sing and he makes his own rough and unsweet voice an attribute, not a liability. Unfortunately, Cohen has been able to do nothing with his voice and this fact turns up in his melodies, which are slow, deadeningly similar and wholly uninspiring.[1]

In this chapter I want to identify a variety of diverse and related factors that served to shape the experience of Dylan and Cohen in their formative years, ranging from country-and-western music to the place of New York's Chelsea Hotel in popular culture. This entails constructing a context of influences that passed through each singer in different ways. Dylan and Cohen were both deeply immersed in country-and-western music in their early teens, and both found inspiration in the more politically oriented folk tradition, which was not in itself as distinct from country-and-western music as it has now become. What is now called roots music encompassed a variety of styles and influences, as Harry Smith's compilation testifies. Dylan and Cohen, at different stages in the 1960s, found themselves closely associated with the Newport Folk Festival and all that that entailed, including the conventional distinctions between traditional and contemporary folk music, the former being regarded by the elder generation as more authentic than the latter. They were also both Jewish and, at the risk of being anachronistic, were caught up in what is now called the politics of identity and authenticity. Throughout their lives this search for identity manifested itself in different ways, and different aspects of their quests emerge and reemerge throughout this book. In this respect, I want to look at some features of the theory of multiculturalism in order to provide a context for understanding Dylan's and Cohen's location in the politics of the personal through self-exploration. Not only were Dylan and Cohen beneficiaries of the legacy of traditional American music, they were also the inheritors of political legacies: the aftermath of the McCarthy years and of the Holocaust, as the horrors of atrocities against humanity were graphically relived in the trial of Adolph Eichmann. I want to take the opportunity in this chapter to demonstrate the complexity of such phenomena, which are usually exhibited in a simplified monochrome instead of in technicolor in books on popular song, and the influences that shape the images.

Bob Dylan's and Leonard Cohen's interest in music began with the country-and-western songs of Hank Williams. Dylan claimed that Williams was the first and longest influence on him. He discovered Hank Williams in 1955, along with other country-and-western stars such as Hank Snow. Early bootleg recordings of Dylan show that, despite the many other sources of musical inspiration, he continued to sing Hank Williams songs. The early influence comes to the fore when he went through a country-and-western phase after *John Wesley Harding,* which was most pronounced on *Nashville Skyline* and *Self Portrait.* Dylan also had long admired Johnny Cash, and some evidence of their collaboration is to be found on *Nashville Skyline* with the duet "Girl from the North Country," taken from two days of recording with the Man in Black. The session resulted in a mixture of recordings of Dylan classics, such as "One Too Many Mornings" and traditional songs such as "Mountain Dew" and "Careless Love," as well as Cash standards such as "I Walk the Line" and "Ring of Fire."

Cohen had been playing guitar and singing since he was about fifteen, but he never regarded himself as a singer. He started his musical career at McGill University with a country-and-western group called the Buckskin Boys, playing square dance and barn dance music. It was while completing *Beautiful Losers* in Greece that Cohen listened to a lot of country-and-western music on the U.S. Armed Forces Radio station, and also a lot of Ray Charles on his Dansette record player. When he returned to Canada in 1966, he set out to reach Nashville, where he intended to become a country-and-western singer. But New York and the influence of Dylan distracted him, and Nashville would have to wait.

From 1964 onward Dylan tried to strike a balance between traditional, including country-and-western, and contemporary music. One avenue for this was the Newport Folk Festival, which also served as a political platform for much of the social concerns championed by the singers in the folk music revival of the late 1950s and early 1960s. They referred to themselves as a movement, and the sleeve notes of live recordings of the festivals boast of the involvement of folksingers and the messages in their songs in the process of protest and social change. For example, liner notes for the 1964 extended play album, (Fontana TFE 18010), featuring Bob Dylan and assembled friends singing "Blowin' in the Wind," states:

> A number of people from every background have joined hands with the Negroes in the movement against segregation and for equal rights. Those in the folk song movement are proud that so many of its leading figures have become identified, personally and musically, with this major social current of our time.

These singers deliberately and self-consciously set out to transform the political culture of the 1960s by reinforcing in people's minds what were already discernible signs of discontent with a failing political system. In an interview in *Vogue*, Phil Ochs contended that "young people are disillusioned: we want to reinforce that disillusionment so they'll get more involved and do something."[2] There was a certain smugness and self-assuredness to the movement that was often hard to take. Gene Lees complained, in an interview with TV host Steve Allen, that Bob Dylan "was distantly superior" and that Peter Yarrow was a pompous egomaniac in suggesting that the folk movement, and his trio in particular, was so powerful that it could campaign for the presidential elections with its own candidate and even sway the outcome. Lees disparagingly called Peter, Paul, and Mary "Peter, Paul and Jesus."[3]

The Newport Folk Festival, run by the nonprofit Newport Folk Foundation, was effectively an alternative political convention, bringing into public view the authenticity of an America that was lost. Performers who hadn't been seen or heard for thirty years or more were rediscovered and paraded across the stage along with the newly discovered talent. Those very voices that Harry Smith had revived and which inspired the folk revivalists were now also faces, literally living legends to the legions in search of the real America. Among those who played at Newport and who appeared on Smith's records were Mississippi John Hurt, Clarence Ashley, Eck Robertson, Buell Kazee, and Dock Boggs. The Newport Folk Festival was egalitarian in that it paid everyone who appeared the same daily rate, $50, plus transport and accommodation. The profits from the festival went toward assisting social causes and projects.

Politics of Identity and Authenticity

The folk revival of the 1960s brought together many strands in the "authentic" American voice. The human spirit when oppressed, deprived of security, and under threat of violence and starvation has traditionally expressed its anguish and pain in song. Slaves on galley ships, black plantation workers, criminals on chain gangs, those fighting for union rights, and political rebels of all sorts sang songs that were expressive of their plight and condemnatory of the society that oppressed them.[4]

The right to develop within one's own culture, on equal terms with those who enjoy similar rights, has been identified as the politics of authenticity. Recognition of one's cultural identity is deemed to be constitutive of the person. It is not only a demand for equal recognition of the right to pursue cultural values, but also a demand to acknowledge the equal worth of such pursuits. Blacks in the United States have a unique and peculiar place as a minority within a dominant culture. In modern theories of multiculturalism, Will Kymlicka, for example, has distinguished between national minorities and ethnic minorities. A national minority has a long-standing association with land or territory, which it may have occupied long before European settlement, and which therefore gives it a strong moral claim to some degree of autonomy and self-determination. Such groups would be the Maoris in New Zealand, the Aborigines in Australia, and the aboriginal Indians in the United States and Canada. Such groups require special rights, in addition to universal rights, in order to protect their traditions and way of life against the dominant culture. These are what Kymlicka would call "external protection rights." As a liberal who values freedom of choice and uncoerced consensus, he stops short of advocating rights of "internal restriction," in other words, rights that would restrict the freedom of members of a national minority to choose a different way of life. Alternatively, there are ethnic minorities who have chosen to be immigrants, and in doing so signal their willingness to integrate. These minorities, while not meriting special cultural rights of external protection, require special inclusion rights, for example, equal opportunities legislation.

American blacks in the early '60s were neither a national minority with a traditional claim on land nor an ethnic minority. Although by the late 1950s slavery had long been abolished, Jim Crow legislation was still prevalent and discrimination was rife. American society was segregated, with such public facilities as schools, churches, toilets, prisons, cemeteries, buses, and hospitals being provided on the basis of color. Blacks were excluded from political participation in some states, which required them in order to qualify for the vote to pass a literacy test, pay a poll tax, or be able to read and write any section of the state constitution, with the exception of those who could demonstrate that their relatives possessed the right to vote before January 1, 1866. In 1944 Gunnar Myrdal, in his famous study *An American Dilemma: The Negro Problem and Modern Democracy,* argued that, "any white man can strike or beat a Negro, steal or destroy his property, cheat him in a transaction and even take his life, without much fear of legal reprisal."[5]

The civil rights movement was demanding rights of inclusion, the demand to share in citizenship rights and enjoy the same social and political liberties as every other American citizen. It was not a terribly radical movement to begin with. The aspiration was for reform rather than revolution, and the perception was not that oppression is endemic in the system, but that there were anomalies that needed to be rectified. Blacks and students called upon the federal government to allow black people to sit next to white people and to be able to vote in free elections. In February 1960 a small group of black students staged a sit-in at the lunch counter in Woolworth, Greensboro, North Carolina. By March sit-ins had spontaneously spread to almost every Woolworth store in the nation, and Freedom Rides and Freedom Walks defying the policy of segregated buses became common. In April 1960 the Student Non-violent Co-ordinating Committee (SNCC) was established in Raleigh, North Carolina, which as its name suggests was designed to co-ordinate the non-violent protests. In August, 1961 the SNCC started a black voter registration campaign in Mississippi, and in 1963 along with the Congress on Racial Equality (CORE), the National Association for the Advancement of Colored People (NAACP), and the Southern Christian Leadership Conference (SCLC)— the organization which Martin Luther King helped found to spread non-violent means of protest to other groups—became allied in the Council of Federated Organizations (COFO) to co-ordinate voter registration. By 1963 over 5000 students had been jailed for taking part in the peaceful protest activities.

Martin Luther King was demanding rights of inclusion for black people, and he thought the objectives could be achieved through non-violent protest, despite the violent reactions of the authorities. King's major achievement came at the end of March 1965 with the voting rights march from Selma to Montgomery, Alabama, ending at the house of Governor George Wallace. The march provoked violent reactions culminating in the brutal battering to death of a white clergy-man which spurred Lyndon Johnson to throw his weight behind the Voting Rights Act which was passed by Congress in 1965. By this time Dylan had deserted the Civil Rights Movement, and King himself came under increasing attack from radical opponents such as the Black Muslims and Black Panthers (the Lowndes County, Alabama, Freedom Organization). Radicals demanded rights of autonomy and the freedom to national self-determination. Over the next two years violence flared-up in all the major cities, reaching a climax in the battle of Detroit in 1967. The assassination of King in 1968 bore witness to the demise of the non-violent campaign. Uprisings simultaneously broke out in 29 states and 125 cities, including particularly vicious violence in Washington D.C., leading to the arrest of 125,000 people.

Music played an important role in articulating the injustices perpetrated, but it also did much to revive the traditions of opposition to injustice by articulating in song, and injecting traditional songs with new meaning and purchase, the changing political climate of the 1960s. As Ron Everman and Andrew Jamison contend, "The 'folk revival' brought ideas into popular songs; it was in the songs that the critique of mass culture—with its dependence on war and weaponry—could be most effectively articulated."[6] The whole civil rights movement drew on the traditions of opposition to deep-rooted racism and spoke in a language that was a familiar form of expression. The vast resource of black music and white popularist protest provided the foundation on which the discontent of the new generation of youth could build.

Murray Edelman has argued that, contrary to popular opinion, which views art as separate from social issues, or at best reflective of them, art is integral to inspiring political behavior.[7] A society built on immigration and slavery, with low rates of literacy and a diversity of language, could find common forms of expression in music. Throughout its history, while the high-brow culture of the United States was imitative of Europe, the culture of the ordinary people has been much more innovative. The music of slavery, with its themes of solace and salvation, and the songs of the agrarian discontented are early examples of the power of song to forge common identities and to articulate cultural experiences. What the early-twentieth-century agrarian populist movement and the civil rights movement of the 1960s have in common is a shared sense of oppression and a clear sense of the oppressor. Capitalism, big business, and finance were seen by both to be exploitative of blacks and poor white farmers and farmworkers. Whereas blacks also had to contend with the racism of poor white agrarian populists, there was nevertheless a common cause and established focus.

To set the music of Dylan and Cohen in context, a quick review of the themes of critical movements in the twentieth century would be helpful. By the turn of the twentieth century, farmers and farmworkers in the United States didn't have sufficient numbers to constitute a significant political force, and labor unionism became the organized opposition to economic injustices. At the same time, there was a rise in evangelicalism, which opposed liberal liquor licensing laws and in this respect was at odds with the labor movement. The spiritual movement grew out of the Southern rural revivalist meetings and developed a form of music arising from the camp fire culture, of which country-and-western music became the direct heir. Country music arose as a distinct tradition in the 1920s and was fostered by the development of new technology. Radio and national recording companies sent talent scouts into the remote rural areas to discover new talents and new sounds. A. P. Carter of the Carter Family both collected and performed the rural country music, which, despite becoming commercialized, retained its domestic and homely themes. The labor movement, however, continued to provide a forum for and drew upon the experiences of cultural minorities. The likes of Woody Guthrie and Pete Seeger, while articulating and reiterating the plight of the common man, collaborated and shared the stage with leading articulators of the black experience, such as Sonny Terry and Brownie McGhee, Leadbelly and Big Bill Broonzy (real name William Lee Conley Broonzy). Members of the Industrial Workers of the World (IWW), known as the Wobblies, wrote and performed songs that articulated a utopian future, "One Big Union," free of workers' oppression. The labor movement was inclusive in orientation, demanding not minority cultural rights, but universal participation and emancipation, emphasizing workers' solidarity and a common cause, rather than distinctive ethnic identities. The most famous voice of the Wobblies was that of the Swedish immigrant Joseph Hillstrom, who emphasized his American identity by adopting the name Joe Hill. His own songs and those about his tragic life have burned themselves into the American imagination despite the fact that the social conditions and political struggles, of which he has become emblematic, have long become transformed. The songs of Joe Hill and the other Wobblies inspired the new generation of protest singers in the 1930s and '40s, among them Pete Seeger, Woody Guthrie, Earl Robinson, and Burl Ives, and were reincarnated once again in the topical song movement of the 1960s. Phil Ochs revived the memory of the famous unionist in one of his songs, and Bob Dylan parodied "I Dreamed I Saw Joe Hill Last Night" in his "I Dreamed I Saw St. Augustine." (In the 1980s the link was maintained in Billy Bragg's "I Dreamed I Saw Phil Ochs Last Night.")

Dylan was fully immersed in the civil rights and labor issues. He had soaked up the music that expressed the injustices and transformed his experiences into anthems that entered the collective consciousness of his contemporaries. Leonard Cohen's experience of multiculturalism was very different from that of Dylan. Dylan had come from a small country town in Minnesota and to a large extent learned of the injustices in society, the inequalities, land evictions, exploitations of refugees, and racial discrimination, through music. Cohen has maintained that the Canadian identity is defined in relation to its proximity to a great imperialist empire. Canadians, he has argued, understand that there is no alternative but to go along with the United States to a certain degree, yet to view the paranoia in the Canadian press about the extinction of Canadian identity as grossly exaggerated. Cohen's position has been more complicated by being part of a minority dominated by a majority French culture, which itself is a subculture of the dominant Anglophone community of Canada.

Within Quebec, both English speakers and English-speaking Jews like Cohen's family have felt somewhat alienated from the isolated pocket of French culture that surrounds them. Cohen himself has felt a foreigner in his own city, insufficiently conversant with French or Quebecois to feel comfortable in using French or its Canadian variant as the medium through which to express his art. In a letter to his sister Esther dated June 8, 1963, he thought that an independent Quebec was imminent, and somewhat tongue in cheek suggested that they transfer their documents and bonds out of Quebec banks for fear that they would be nationalized by a revolutionary government. His concern was genuine, and he reiterated it in a letter from March 29, 1964. Writing from Montreal, Cohen maintained that the separatist movement was very strong, and that the force of it had precipitated a fundamental reappraisal of the idea of Canada and the value of confederation. The formation of a secret army of liberation worried him, and he thought that the seriousness of the situation was not appreciated by the foreign press.[8] Cohen believed more in a Canadian nationalism that exhibited elements of jingoism and chauvinism as a counter to what Australians call the "cultural cringe," one culture genuflecting to another. Canadians, Cohen believed, had to have the courage to risk making fools of themselves, both politically and artistically.[9] To maintain his connection to Canada, Cohen has always kept a base in Montreal, even though his existence has been very much that of a cosmopolitan, living in Greece, New York, Tennessee, Mexico, and Los Angeles, among other places.[10] The political stance that is constant in Cohen's life is Canadian nationalism.

The Essential Tension

In the 1960s there was a tension between folk music conceived as the preservation of the past, a past that could not be interfered with or corrupted by commercialism, and folk music conceived as an ongoing changing tradition reflecting contemporary culture, in the same way that traditional folk music reflected its times. Alan and John Lomax, Francis Child, Bascom Lamar Lunsford, Paul Oliver, and Harry Smith in the United States, and Cecil Sharpe in Britain, set out to record and preserve cultural folklore in song. Folk music for them was a branch of ethnography, evidence of the beliefs and way of life of a passing culture whose spirit had to be preserved.

John Lomax was a pioneer in the collection of folk music and typically mirrored nineteenth-century anthropologists in his presuppositions and condescending tone. Like them, he worked on the assumption that he was studying and coming to understand a "primitive culture" whose ways were not altogether rational, being dominated as they were by emotions. The more isolated the community, the less likely it would contain the impurities of modern influences, but this did not preclude transforming the songs into modern packaging for greater appeal. Various versions of a song would be used by Lomax to compile a definitive composite version. This approach romanticized the primitive. Lomax was also ambivalent in the relationship of his work to black culture. He and his son, Alan, recorded hundreds of songs by black prisoners, most famously the convicted murderer Leadbelly, who was entrusted to Lomax's care. Lomax made a good deal of money out of Leadbelly, whom he presented on stage in convict's stripes. John Lomax recorded thousands of folk songs and helped to establish the Library of Congress's Archive of American Folk Music, which his son later came to direct, and initiated comprehensive oral histories of Leadbelly, Woody Guthrie, and Jelly Roll Morton, among others. It was an act of preserving for posterity a dying or dead past. Even Harry Smith's *Anthology of American Folk Music* exhibited a clear residue of this purist tendency. Moses Asch explained in his general notes to the collection that two principles of selection prevailed. First, the recording had to be of good enough quality for high-fidelity reproduction; second, the performance of the music had to be uninfluenced by the pervasive and insidious influence of radio and motion pictures. The period that fulfilled both criteria was 1926–1930, when electronic recording techniques developed and before the cinema infiltrated the remotest parts of rural life.

Dylan's attitude was very different. He saw it as a living heritage to be exploited, to be soaked up like a sponge, to be learned like a new language, which one acquires not to repeat what one has learned but to use in order to speak with one's own voice. He came into the company of Dave Van Ronk and Ramblin' Jack Elliott when he first arrived in New

York, and they provided the exemplar that Dylan followed. They had absorbed the tradition of folk and blues music, used black inflections in their "white" songs, and generally set out to extend, and not just to preserve, what they had inherited. This is exactly what Dylan did, and it initially disturbed the likes of the traditionalists because it did not display due reverence for the sacrosanct.

Dylan took songs from this heritage and invested his own distinctive style in them. Not only did he sing the songs in a way almost unrecognizable in intonation and rhythm, but he readily took traditional tunes and unashamedly injected contemporary themes into them, as he did, for example, with "Bob Dylan's Dream," set to the tune of "Lord Franklin," and "Masters of War," set to "Nottamun Town," both of which he had learned from Martin Carthy, and "Don't Think Twice, It's All Right," set to the tune of an Appalachian song called "Who's Gonna Buy Your Chickens When I'm Gone." Throughout his career Dylan returned to the traditional heritage that is so clearly evident on his first album, and he recorded versions of quite a few songs on *The Anthology of American Folk Music*. Selection 1 on the anthology, "Henry Lee," Bob Dylan recorded as "Love Henry" (*World Gone Wrong*, 1993); selection 3, "The House Carpenter," he recorded March 19, 1962 (*Bootleg Series*, vol. 1, 1991); selection 19, "Stackalee," appears on *World Gone Wrong*; selection 21, "Frankie," appears as "Frankie and Albert" on *Good As I Been to You* (1992); selection 25, "Down on Penny's Farm," is the inspiration for "Maggie's Farm" (*Bringing It All Back Home*, 1965); and selection 76, "See That My Grave Is Kept Clean," appears on *Bob Dylan* (1963). Others, such as Clarence Ashley's "The Coo Coo Bird," were included in Dylan's early repertoire, which is not surprising, given that Smith's anthology was the folk song Bible for the Greenwich Village folk revival. Harkening back to this revival and further back to the world of Clarence Ashley, Dylan includes a line from the song in his "High Water (For Charlie Patton)" on *Love and Theft*. The dedication is to "The Masked Marvel," Charlie Patton, who sings "Mississippi Boweavil Blues" on the anthology. Patton had a distinctive, gritty, gravelly voice that spits out the words with an earthy conviction, barely articulated. Dylan's voice has a distinct gravelly edge and lack of range on this album. Patton was one of the most influential of the early blues singers whose songs were mainly autobiographical, some of which betray a concern with social issues. Most famously, and to which Dylan's song alludes, is "High Water Everywhere." It tells of misery and havoc caused by the Mississippi River flooding its banks, having a heavy toll on lives and property. He sings it as one of those fleeing from the water and with a deep intensity and conviction, unnerving in the black mood he conjures.

It has been suggested that those who went in search of what Moses Asch called the "rich heritage of the American people" were a small number of restless youth of the 1950s and '60s in the wake of Eisenhower's new homogenized prepackaged plastic America sold to them through the media. They were looking for the authentic America in the vernacular regional musical cultures.[11] It is clear that the "authenticity" of the song is not what concerned Dylan. Take, for example, selection 1, "Henry Lee." Smith characterizes its content as "SCORNING OFFER OF COSTLY TRAPPINGS, BIRD REFUSES AID TO KNIGHT THROWN IN WELL BY LADY."[12] Dylan's characterization of the version he chose to sing has a much more contemporary resonance:

> LOVE HENRY is a "traditionalist" ballad. Tom Paley used to do it. A perverse tale. Henry-modern corporate man off some foreign boat, unable to handle his "psychosis" responsible for organizing the intelligentsia, disarming the people, and infantile sensualist-white teeth, wide smile, lotza money, kowtows to fairy queen exploiters and corrupt religious establishments, career minded, limousine double parked, imposing his will and dishonest garbage in popular magazines. He lays his head on pillow of down and falls asleep. He shoulda known better, he must have had a hearing problem.[13]

Indeed, Dylan's attitude to traditional folk music is worth quoting at length:

> All the authorities who write about what it is and what it should be when they say keep it simple, [that it] should be easily understood—folk music is the only music where it isn't simple. It's never been simple. It's weird. . . . I've never written anything hard to understand, not in my head anyway, and nothing as far out as some of the old songs. I have to think of all this as traditional music. Traditional music is based on hexagrams. It comes about from legends, Bibles, plagues, and it revolves around vegetables and death. There's nobody that's going to kill traditional music. All those songs about roses growing out of people's brains and lovers who are really geese and swans that turn into angels— they're not going to die. It's all those paranoid people who think that someone's going to come and take away their toilet paper—they're going to die. Songs like "Which Side Are You On?" and "I Love You Porgy"—they're not folk-music songs; they're political songs. They're already dead.
>
> Obviously, death is not very universally accepted. I mean, you'd think that the traditional-music people could gather from their songs that mystery is a fact, a traditional fact . . . traditional music is too

unreal to die. It doesn't need to be protected. Nobody's going to hurt it. In that music is the only true, valid death you can feel today off a record player.[14]

Dylan formed a rock-and-roll band in 1955, but by 1959, when he first heard Leadbelly, much of the vitality and rebelliousness of the genre had subsided, having been sanitized by the big companies for commercial reasons in the form of Pat Boone, Ricky Nelson, Paul Anka, Frankie Avalon, and Bobby Rydell, and the disappearance from the scene of some of rock and roll's great performers. Little Richard gave up to become a preacher; Carl Perkins was seriously injured in a car crash; Chuck Berry and Jerry Lee Lewis were personae non grata because of their involvement with girls barely in their teens; Buddy Holly, the Big Bopper, Ritchie Valens, Gene Vincent, and Eddie Cochran were killed in accidents; and Elvis Presley was drafted into the army.

At this time Dylan consciously latched himself to the long tradition of protest song. He has often been accused of opportunism and of unashamedly fulfilling his career aspirations by disingenuously adopting the protest mode. Such criticisms conveniently ignore the fact that it was Bob Dylan himself who gave the genre such mass appeal, and that when he expressed himself in the mode, it was hardly the most likely route to success. He was fortunate when he went to New York, not only in meeting and becoming friendly with performers deeply immersed in the folk and blues heritage, but also in having contacts close to the great folk collectors and preservers. Suze Rotolo's sister, Carla, worked for Alan Lomax, and through her and Bob and Sidsel Gleason, at whose house Dylan met regularly with Guthrie and his acolytes, he gained access to Harry Smith's classic six-album *Anthology of American Folk Music,* which was reissued in 1998, and Lomax's collection of *The Folk Songs of North America* (1935). Dylan was influenced by a whole array of protest song writers, such as Leadbelly, Bukka White, Cisco Houston, Sonny Terry and Brownie McGhee, Blind Lemon Jefferson, and Jesse Fuller.

In the 1930s, for example, J. K. Kinnard argued that the place to look for America's truly original poets was in the minstrel songs and spirituals of the black slaves stretching from the 1840s. The problem was, of course, as Ralph Ellison wrote in 1952, American blacks were invisible men—no one could see them.[15] The intense divide between black and white provided for well over a century the clearest focus for the folk song and produced some of the most interesting material, reflecting the social condition of black America. Big Bill Broonzy, for example, in his "Get Back," sang of the gradations of discrimination by whites against browns and blacks, different degrees of acceptability and different levels of pay, ending each verse with the chorus: "If you're white, you're all right. If you're brown stick around. But if you're black, get back, get back, get back."

The strongest influence on Bob Dylan was Woody Guthrie, whom he regularly visited in the hospital after arriving in New York in 1961. Dylan sang a tribute to Guthrie on his first album and recited a long poem written for him at a gathering in Guthrie's honor at New York's Town Hall on April 12, 1963, four years before Guthrie died. Guthrie, who came from Oklahoma, sang about the hard times of the '30s Dust Bowl farmers driven from their homes there to unwelcoming and inhospitable California, the "pastures of plenty," where, without the "do-re-mi," the refugees weren't welcome. He celebrated the dignity of working men in his songs, sympathizing with the hardships they endured and had perpetrated upon them. He highlighted the plight of itinerant works who traveled by rail to find work all over the United States. Such songs as "Vigilante Man," "Hard Travelin'," and "I Ain't Got No Home" express the brutality and injustice they suffered at the hands of self-appointed law enforcers, the official legal system, and the impersonal forces of the economic system:

I ain't got no home, I'm just a refugee
Just a wandering worker, I go from town to town
The police make it hard wherever I may go
and I ain't got no home in this world anymore

("I Ain't Got No Home," *Dust Bowl Ballads*)

Guthrie also sang about the exploitation of migrant workers who found their way to California from Mexico to pick fruit; some were on contract and paid much less than they were promised, while others were illegal immigrants whose contracts had expired. After the harvest, the farmers would routinely inform on them, and they were deported without pay. Guthrie wrote a famous song called "The Deportees" after a plane carrying Mexican workers caught fire over Los Gatos Canyon. Guthrie spent the last part of his career in New York City, where his appeal was as the outsider with the hick accent, seeing through the smoke screen of establishment lies.

The U.S. Supreme Court had declared unconstitutional the segregation of schools in its momentous *Brown* decision of 1954. Southern whites who organized to protest against its implications were also horrified by the growing popularity of black rhythm and blues among white youth. While they deplored the likes of Elvis Presley and Jerry Lee Lewis affecting black styles of music and sexually explicit movements, it was the black performers who were the major targets of protest. Nat King Cole, for example, was assaulted during a performance in Birmingham, Alabama, in 1956 by a faction of the local white citizens' council.[16] Woody Guthrie associated extensively and shared the stage with such black blues singers as Leadbelly, Sonny Terry, and Brownie McGhee, but Guthrie's illness rendered him less of a threat to authority by the mid-1950s. Pete Seeger and the Weavers, however, remained active, championing the cause against oppression, poverty, and segregation, even to the extent of singing Negro work songs.

Seeger attracted the attention of the McCarthyites. In 1956 he was investigated by the House Un-American Activities Committee and con- victed of contempt for refusing to answer questions about his political convictions. He also was blacklisted from national network television and was unable to appear at some college campuses. When Bob Dylan associated with him and his circle in 1961, Seeger's case, which was eventually to be dismissed by the courts, was still an issue. Robert Shelton, the *New York Times* music critic who championed Dylan, was himself hauled before the Senate Internal Security Subcommittee.

McCarthyism, though, was a one-issue phenomenon. While it was a force to be reckoned with in American politics, it did not seem to have the grass-roots basis that one has been led to believe. Furthermore, state and local anti-Communist legislation, though widespread at the time, is best understood as a reflection, not a cause, of national priorities.[17]

When Dylan moved to New York from Minnesota, he appealed to the radicalism that Woody Guthrie had exploited and effectively adopted the same stance as wise hick outsider with incisive and harsh observations.[18] The legacy of McCarthy and extreme right-wing politics was still very much in the air. As we saw, Seeger was blacklisted from appearing on the 1963 television series devoted to folk music, *Hootenanny*. McCarthyism was the most significant political phenomenon to arise in America in the post–World War II years. Joe McCarthy did little to enhance his reputation or political career during his first three years in Congress. He had some corrupt dealings with a soft drinks company that earned him the nick- name of 'the soft drinks kid'. He gave his support to a number of real- estate interests that enabled him to pay off his gambling debts. By 1949 the tax authorities and the bar commissioners were on his tail. An investigation showed that huge contributions to his campaign that purportedly came from family members could not have done so given the level of income declared in their tax returns.

A Republican speaking tour in the ensuing year saved his career. On February 9, 1950 he made his famous speech at Wheeling accusing the State Department of harboring 205 known communists. His information was gleaned from a letter written four years previously by the Secretary of State James F. Byrnes. He said that 284 cases had been investigated, of which 79 had been dismissed, and the remaining 205 after careful screening, proved dismissal unnecessary. McCarthyism was never a political movement. It had no candidates and formulated no platform. It was a one-issue phenomenon. There are numerous explanations for McCarthy's popularity, often linking it to historical factors in right wing politics, particularly American popularism, the sort for example, associated with Huey Long. We certainly need to distinguish between McCarthy and McCarthyism. McCarthy personally never translated into an electoral asset for the right, in that he did not unite elite and popular support. McCarthyism, however, for a short time did. Michael Paul Rogin has shown that there was little continuity between populism and McCarthyism, as some historians have contended. In fact almost the opposite was the case. Agrarian radicalism, when cohesive, contributed to the constituency of Democratic liberalism rather than to the Republican right. It seems from the evidence that I have analyzed that while McCarthyism was a force to be reckoned with in American politics it did not seem to have that grass roots basis that one has been led to believe and that state and local anti-communist legislation, though widespread, is best understood as a reflection, not a cause, of national priorities. The politics of the McCarthy era originated at national level and then spread to the states.[19]

At the time, Dylan sang mostly black folk blues and Guthrie's songs, but after encouragement from his friends, who recognized his talent, he started writing overtly political songs whose tales of injustices and social commentary no longer hark back to the 1930s and '40s, but were immediate.

Schools remained segregated in 1962 when Dylan wrote "Blowin' in the Wind," but blacks were becoming increasingly more militant, and their cause was gaining ground with a growing number of white socially conscious liberals. Dylan participated in many protests and sang the songs that were to be adopted as some of the anthems of social justice and civil rights. Dylan's girlfriend, Suze Rotolo, an aspiring artist, worked devotedly for the cause of civil rights as a secretary and activist with the Congress for Racial Equality (CORE). In February 1962 he did a benefit concert for CORE. As we saw earlier, in May 1963 Dylan was invited to appear on the *Ed Sullivan Show,* and he chose to sing one of his satirical political songs, "Talkin' John Birch Paranoid Blues," in which he ridicules the "Reds under the beds" paranoia still reverberating throughout American society. The song tells of a man, obsessed with investigating the Communist menace, "discovering" that Lincoln, Jefferson, Roosevelt, and Eisenhower were Russian spies and that the red stripes on the American flag were part of the socialist conspiracy. Columbia thought the song was too politically sensitive and wouldn't allow it to be broadcast. Amid a great deal of publicity, Dylan refused to sing a different song and was therefore not allowed to appear. Columbia also owned CBS, his recording company, and successfully sought to prevent the song from appearing on Dylan's second album. This was Dylan's first taste of being accused of selling out. He was not, however, really in a position to resist.

From Origins to Originality

It is not unusual in the life of a civilization, or a movement within that civilization, to revere the past. Looking back to a so-called golden age is a well-documented phenomenon. Being able to trace the origin of what currently exists to that golden age adds authenticity to what is happening in the present. This indeed was the attitude of many within the folk revival movement.

An example of the search for the origins of art in order to validate its worth can be seen in the efforts of artists during the Italian Renaissance, who tried to extract the worth of their art from its relation to its origins in classical times. It was in the process of trying to identify the authoritative origins of the present in the past that the people of the Renaissance were forced to confront their own historicity. The value of a work of art had become correlative with its source. Its ancient origin gave it its value. The artist and art historian Giorgio Vasari tried to break this link. He argued that even the ancients must have been preceded by works of art that are currently unknown to us. Historical priority itself could not be a source of the value of a work of art. Vasari forcefully contended that an artist's individual qualities signify an originality that transcends time. Originality and the quality of a work of art became almost synonymous.[20] The idea that the present has a value of its own and that its artistic productions have an intrinsic worth led, in the area of literature in particular, to an increasing resistance to traditional authorities. Innovation, or originality, as a criterion of value liberated the writer from a fixed canon of texts. On the basis of the criterion of originality, the canon was liberated and potentially open-ended. The predilection to be original came to inform all areas of activity in the post-Renaissance era.

In the field of the history of thought, the French philosopher Michel Foucault has endeavored to move the emphasis away from establishing continuities and stable discursive structure, to discerning the divisions within and limits of discourse. Instead of the search for permanent foundations, he identifies the transformations that act as new foundations.[21] He has tried to demonstrate that our established traditions and systems of analysis are arbitrary formations, the truth status of which depends on the rules of discourse that govern the various activities. Foucault exposed the often arbitrary changes in discursive practices that served to accentuate the realization that logic and rationality have little to contribute to discursive foundations.[22]

Foucault believed that it was the idea of a tradition that had encouraged the use of such terms as *origin* and *originality* in the history of ideas. The belief in tradition encouraged a fetish with continuity and gave a credence of legitimacy to the search for origins. Echoing the Renaissance opposition to the search for origins, Foucault claimed that origins are inaccessible because our attempts to discover an extended line of antecedents farther and farther in the past is never ending. Discourse, Foucault maintained, must not be referred back to some distant origin, but viewed in terms of when and where it occurs.[23]

Bob Dylan's first album was commercially unsuccessful, and although his popularity was growing, CBS executives were not convinced of his talent. He was kept on only because of the pressure that John Hammond and Johnny Cash brought to bear. Nevertheless, his second album, *The Freewheelin' Bob Dylan,* contained much more politically powerful songs, such as "Masters of War," "Oxford Town," and "Talking World War III Blues." It is generally the perception of these two albums that the first contains a derivative Dylan, absorbing and reexpressing the folk-blues tradition, with only a glimpse of his songwriting talents, whereas the second album brings the composer to the fore, with only a residue of his past. That is, we can identify a move from origins to originality.

Although this is substantially a sound judgment, it is only partially correct. It is well known that many of the songs on the second album had traditional tunes from English and American folk music. On his self-titled first album, Dylan used traditional and near-contemporary melodies, sometimes modified, but also substantially transformed the lyrics. The main difference is that the subject matter is substantially the same in the new lyrics as they had been in the originals to which they are related. So, for instance, Dylan's version of "Man of Constant Sorrow" is quite different from previously known recordings. The cover notes by Stacey Williams (Robert Shelton's pseudonym) suggest that the tune is a traditional Southern Mountain folk song, "but probably never sung in this fashion before." Of the various known versions, the basic theme is the same, a man of constant sorrow, invariably from Kentucky, saying farewell to his lover, with the promise of seeing her again on a beautiful, or God's, shore. The first verse of Dylan's version is substantially the same as that of the 1959 Newport Folk Festival version sung by the Stanley Brothers, but Colorado is substituted for Kentucky. Dylan's second verse resembles the fifth and last verse of the Stanley Brothers. Thereafter there are only occasional identities between the lines, such as "I'm abound to ramble," but thereafter the similarity between the verses ends. The album attributes the arrangement to Dylan.

On the *Freewheelin'* album, there is an even greater transformation in the version of "Honey, Just Allow Me One More Chance." The structure, tempo, and intonation are quite different from those of the original Henry Thomas version. Even the melody is significantly changed. What Dylan liked, and what he retained, was the plea in the title and little else. Henry Thomas starts with a verse and then sings the chorus: "Honey allow me one more chance / I always will treat you right / Honey won't you allow me a' one more chance / I won't stay out all night / Honey won't you allow me a' one more chance / I'll take you to the ball in France / One kind'a favor I ask of you / Just allow me just one more chance." On *Freewheelin'*, Dylan is credited with cowriting the song, but essentially he has authored it. He went a step further with "Nottamun Town," whose melody he appropriated for "Masters of War." Jean Ritchie had copyrighted it with her own publishing company, Geordie Music, which accused Bob Dylan of taking the melody. Dylan successfully claimed that both the variation of the melody and his new words constituted a new song.

By June 1963 Peter, Paul, and Mary had released "Blowin' in the Wind," and it quickly became Warner Brothers fastest selling single. Folk music was the common currency between Southern blacks and the Northern white civil rights supporters. Rhythm-and-blues stations played "Blowin' in the Wind," and it became the most widely sung "freedom" song in the movement. In early July 1963 Dylan sang at a benefit, with Pete Seeger and Theodore Bikel, supporting voter registration in Greenwood, Mississippi. He stayed a few days in Greenwood and Jackson, associating with black and student activists. His reputation as a protest singer and one of the spiritual leaders of the movement was gaining momentum. In August of the same year, after overwhelming success at the Newport Folk Festival, he sang to a crowd of over 200,000 people at the March on Washington rally, on same stage that the Reverend Dr. Martin Luther King Jr. delivered his famous "I Have a Dream" speech. Dylan sang "Only a Pawn in Their Game," and Peter, Paul, and Mary sang "Blowin' in the Wind."

Dylan's estrangement from the civil rights movement came when he himself felt that he was being used by its leaders, when he felt that he was a pawn in their game. A few weeks after the death of President Kennedy, Dylan was presented with the Tom Paine Award by the Emergency Civil Liberties Committee. He became distinctly uncomfortable at the ceremony because of his perceived alienation from the middle-aged, middle-class, well-educated, well-dressed liberals who were orchestrating the movement. He got drunk at the ceremony and gave a speech that both failed to express his meaning adequately and served to shock the assembled audience. After a rambling introduction, in which he told the audience that they were too old to lead the movement and that they should retire and spend their time on the beach, he declared that the categories of black and white and Left and Right meant nothing to him anymore, and that for him there was only up and down, and that the important thing was to move up from the ground without being hindered by trivia such as politics.[24] He then changed direction and said that he empathized with Lee Harvey Oswald, and saw something in him that he saw in himself. The assassination of Kennedy had profoundly affected Dylan, and he came to the troubled conclusion that Oswald was one of society's victims, and that everyone had something of Oswald in him. But it was not good enough to take collective responsibility for every crime perpetrated; it was time to say "I" rather than "we." Dylan's words and actions betrayed the fact that he felt his personality was being submerged in the collectivity, that what philosopher John Rawls calls the "separateness of persons" was being denied. The personality was being absorbed by the collective will of all. Dylan wanted to express what he was feeling, and not what everyone else was feeling. In justification of himself, which amounted to the expression of his own individuality, he explained to a friend what he had tried to convey and how the audience was incapable of understanding it:

> They couldn't understand that Oswald was like me, and like you. He was uptight about the times we're livin' in, about all the lies they feed ya, about the history books that tell ya facts not worth a damn, but never once tells you how somebody *feels*. That's what Oswald was about. That's what I'm about. . . . But those people can't understand. They don't know what's happening. All they can see is a cause, and using people for their cause. They're trying to use me for something, want me to carry a picket sign and have my picture taken and be a good little nigger and not mess up their little game.[25]

The assassination of John Kennedy brought it home to every American that being a public figure, taking a stand, was a risky business. Subsequently, of course, in addition to politicians and radicals such as Robert Kennedy and Malcolm X, who were murdered, and George Wallace, who was shot and permanently crippled, high-profile celebrities and religious leaders such as John Lennon and Martin Luther King were murdered, and others such as Pope John Paul II, Andy Warhol, and George Harrison had unsuccessful but serious attempts on their lives. The fear of death by assassination is now much more preeminent in the public psyche than it was in 1963. The strange paradox in Dylan's case is that it is often suggested that he moved away from finger-pointing songs and supporting high-profile collective causes because the assassination of Kennedy had so profoundly affected him. Although it now seems rather melodramatic, Dylan's betrayal of folk music and contamination of it with electric commercialism engendered fears for his own safety. After the Forest Hills show, the first after the infamous Newport electric set, Al Kooper confessed that he feared for the safety of the band in getting to their vehicles after the show, given that on stage he had been knocked off his stool and called a "fucking scumbag." Kooper pulled out of the band after the next show at the prospect of playing in Texas, exclaiming, "Look what they did to J.F.K. down there."[26] Phil Ochs voiced his opinion publicly, acknowledging the unspeakable trend in public life and despairing at what was happening to America. He said that he doubted Dylan could perform again, given the place that Dylan had in the American psyche and the pervasiveness of death in the public consciousness.[27]

I Remember You Well in the Chelsea Hotel

It was in 1966 that Leonard Cohen decided, in preference to pursuing the unattractive prospect of a university career, that he would become a singer, after reluctantly concluding that he couldn't make a reasonable living from writing. In January of that year he became interested in Bob Dylan, the Dylan of *Bringing It All Back Home* and *Highway 61 Revisited*. The songs on these albums were more influenced by poets such as T. S. Eliot and Ezra Pound than the American Beat poets Allen Ginsberg, Gregory Corso, and Jack Kerouac. Cohen actually said that he wanted to be the Canadian Dylan,[28] and that the future of poetry lay in pop music.[29]

It was immediately and perceptively noticed by the *New York Times* music critic John Rockwell that Cohen's "bitter sophistication" was indebted

more to the chanting of the Beat poets and the continental cabaret song
than to the folk and blues revivalists. Indeed, growing up in Montreal,
Cohen could not have escaped the moody, almost spoken, and barely sung
French *chanson*. He became tired of the fact that the critics were always
targeting his voice as weak rather than seeing his approach as that of a
musical stylist. He felt much more at ease with the tradition of the
chansonier, where the singer speaks the song and the aesthetic sound of
the voice determines the excellence of the work; for the *chansonier*, it is
style that matters and not perfect pitch or polished performance. A model
for Cohen was Jacques Brel, one of the foremost *chansoniers* in France
when Cohen first visited Europe. Brel was from Belgium and wrote songs
that were both passionate and disturbing. He was a romantic singer whose
cynicism expressed and articulated the confusion of life beautifully, without
offering any solutions. It is this capacity to characterize the disturbing, to
portray the uneasiness, and to convey the disorientation that unfamiliar
and grotesque situations can be all too familiar that became the hallmark
of many of Cohen's own more moving and powerful songs.

Cohen was already a successful poet and author and highly acclaimed
in literary circles in Canada. Thus, it was not that Dylan influenced Leonard
Cohen's songs, although Cohen recognized his genius. Instead, it was
Dylan's role that Cohen wanted to emulate, the voice and icon of an age.[30]

Cohen had intended to go to Nashville, but instead he stopped off in
New York in the autumn of 1966 and stayed more or less for two years,
starting at the Chelsea Hotel. This was when the Village was the center
of musical attention and the Chelsea was *the* place to stay.

The Chelsea, at 222 West Twenty-third Street, recently has been
restored, after a fashion, and capitalizes on its faded grandeur and fame
as the haunt of the bohemian set. Originally an apartment building, it was
converted to a hotel in 1905 and subsequently became famous for its cult
and underground status. The Chelsea has had a long tradition of literary
and artistic associations. It was where such luminaries as Mark Twain,
Sarah Bernhardt, Brendan Behan, and Arthur Miller stayed. (Miller actually
wrote *Death of a Salesman* there.)

The Chelsea was also where Dylan Thomas, who died in New York
in 1953, resided on his fourth visit to the States and where he recorded
a version of his now famous *Under Milk Wood* before being taken ill.
Thomas's wife, Caitlin, once lamented that poets were too highly regarded
in New York and not regarded highly enough in London. Indeed, Dylan
Thomas relied on New York's fascination with the poet to make money
when his talent was in decline and he was unable to raise money in Britain.
In New York, both he and Brendan Behan were as famous for their

notorious drinking and bad behavior as they were for their writing talents. In fact, the central character in Cohen's *The Favourite Game*, Lawrence Breavman, who exhibits many of the character traits and lived many of the experiences of the young Cohen, wanted partially to emulate Dylan Thomas. Cohen writes of Breavman, alluding to aspects of himself, "He was a kind of mild Dylan Thomas, talent and behaviour modified for Canadian tastes."[31]

From the 1950s the Chelsea was intermittently home to various Beat writers and poets, including Kerouac, Ginsberg, Corso, and Herbert Huncke. The publisher Raymond Foye was attracted to stay there when he saw Corso smash a pay phone in the lobby. The corridors over the decades were graced by the likes of famous eccentrics such as Quentin Crisp, the "naked civil servant," and Virgil Thompson, the composer and music critic for the *International Herald Tribune*. It was also where Phil Ochs adopted the identity of John Train and Sid Vicious of the Sex Pistols later murdered his girlfriend, Nancy Spungen. Actors such as Dennis Hopper, Bette Davis, Kris Kristofferson, and Woody Allen used the hotel, and it is the setting for numerous music videos and films, including Warhol's *The Chelsea Girls* (1966) and Allen's *Manhattan Murder Mystery* (1993).

In the 1960s Stanley Bard became the manager of the hotel and Jerry Weinstein the concierge. Bard was then tolerant of the bohemian artists who could only pay their bills with canvases and whose works of art adorn the hallways and rooms. The former ladies' reception room, with frescos around the frieze, is now the office for Bard and his son David, the managing director. The entrance lobby has been restructured and is home to many of the same sculptures and paintings given in lieu of rent. The artist Taylor Mead has commented that "[f]or years Stanley put up with a lot, which made the Chelsea a natural place for original people. I guess he had enough of the 'crazies.' "[32] Poets, however, were never as favorably treated as artists. Corso complained that "I lived in rooms where junkies go and die, where painters never paid rent, but the poet always had to pay."[33]

Cohen spent a large part of his time at the Chelsea. The bohemian atmosphere of the hotel and its vibrant drug culture suited him fine. As Linda Hutcheon suggests, Cohen deliberately cultivated his counterculture image from as early as 1967.[34] He was part of the New York "scene" that Bob Dylan joined after turning away from the movement. Among the residents at the Chelsea at one time or another during his stay were Bob Dylan, whose future wife, Sara Lownds, had an apartment there with her daughter; Robbie Robertson of The Band; and Nico of the Velvet Underground who Dylan met in Paris in 1964, stayed with for about a week, and for whom he wrote "I'll Keep It With Mine" (*Biograph* and *Bootleg Series*). Nico had worked in New York since 1959 and was influenced by Dylan, who introduced her to Andy Warhol. Warhol persuaded the Velvet Underground to include her as a singer. She was tall, blonde and beautiful, and made an enormous impression on the men associated with the New York scene, including Dylan. Cohen had met Nico at Warhol's club, the Dom, and he became infatuated with her. He introduced her to macrobiotic food and wrote "Joan of Arc" (*Songs from a Room*), "Take This Longing" (*New Skin for the Old Ceremony*), and "Memories" (*Death of a Ladies' Man*) for her.[35] Nico in turn introduced Cohen to Lou Reed, who admired Cohen's books *Flowers for Hitler* and *Beautiful Losers*. At the Chelsea Cohen also met Edie Sedgwick, the star of many of Warhol's films. At the time, she was permanently on various cocktails of drugs. Sedgwick had dated Dylan for a while in 1966, at a time, Jonathan Taplin suggests, when "[Dylan's] transition from folk purity to the rock insanity was overwhelming him."[36] Her flamboyant and confident exterior disguised a deep inner fragility that inspired Dylan's "Just Like a Woman."[37]

Danny Fields, who had introduced Cohen to Sedgwick, describes Cohen at the time as heavily into incense, candles, and reading material that he got from a magic/witchcraft shop. He was always burning incense, and the management kept threatening to throw him out because the smoke would set off the fire alarms. Cohen, in fact, warned Sedgwick that the candles she burned on her mantelpiece were arranged in such a way as to cast a dark spell.[38] This was prophetic, given that shortly afterwards her suite caught fire and nearly burned down the hotel.

Drugs were so endemic to the Chelsea Hotel culture, where there was a danger of having LSD and other noxious substances served with everything, that Cohen eventually vacated and went to live in the less fashionable hotel with the name evocative of pioneer Canada, the Henry Hudson.

Politics of the Personal

Cohen was much more concerned with the politics of the personal, before that phrase was coined, than with the assorted movements that were popular then. For him, that meant an obsession with women and his relations with them.

His musical idols at the time were many: traditional folk and blues singers, particularly Pete Seeger, whose music and life he greatly admired;

country singers, especially Hank Williams; and jazz-blues singers such as Billie Holiday, whose haunting voice and sometimes biting, bitter lyrics are echoed in Cohen's own work. One of her most powerful and disturbing songs that always totally captured audiences was "Strange Fruit," which is a chilling condemnation of Southern white racist lynching:

Southern trees bear a strange fruit
Blood on the leaves and blood at the roots.
Black bodies swinging in the Southern breeze.
Strange fruit hanging from the poplar trees.

Cohen had gained considerable exposure during his stay in London in 1959–1960 to jazz and blues through his encounters with the West Indian "blues" parties, which had become fashionable as the alternative night life of the city.

A performer of note, of course, never ceases to draw upon the resources he finds around him, and because Cohen had eclectic interests in Eastern philosophy and religion, as well as in the Christian tradition, his musical range is broad. On *Recent Songs,* for example, Cohen draws upon Persian and Chinese poetry. "Ballad of the Absent Mare" is based on the ancient Chinese text *Ten Ox-herding Pictures* by Ka-Kuan, and the imagery of the Persian poets Attar and Rumi inform both "The Guests" and "The Window." The sounds draw upon Middle Eastern and Eastern European instruments and melodies, reflecting his own Russian Jewish background.

In 1968, Cohen finally made it to Nashville to record his second album, *Songs from a Room.* Bob Dylan had recorded part of *Blonde on Blonde* in Nashville as well as *John Wesley Harding* and *Nashville Skyline,* the latter two albums betraying a heavy country influence. Cohen's album, however, bears no traces of the home of country music. There are certainly country traces on subsequent albums, as, for example, in "The Captain" on *Various Positions.* Indeed, Cohen famously described himself as a "country and eastern" singer.

Also of note was Cohen's collaboration with Phil Spector on the album *Death of a Ladies' Man.* The almost unimaginable combination of Spector and Cohen has been well documented. Spector's obsession with guns, his heavy drinking, his tendency to surround himself with menacing henchmen, and his penchant to threaten musicians. The now infamous stories of Spector holding a gun to Cohen's neck as a sign of his unswerving affection and his obsessive possessiveness of the master tapes, to the extent that Cohen was prevented from hearing the mixes before the album was released, are now legendary. The sound and style of *Ladies' Man* were in such contrast to Cohen's previous work that it came as a great disappointment to him. However, with the intervention of time, Cohen has mellowed and warmed toward the album and has now developed a great affection for it, even to the extent that he has entertained the possibility of working with Spector again. Spector, for his part, expressed great admiration for Cohen, and warmly cherished the honor of working with Cohen and of sharing in the writing and production of *Death of a Ladies' Man*.[39]

Endnotes

1. Juan Rodriguez, "Poet's Progress—To Sainthood and Back." Reprinted in *Leonard Cohen: The Artist and His Critics,* ed. Michael Gnarowski (Toronto: McGraw-Hill, 1976), 67.
2. Cited in Ron Everman and Andrew Jamison, *Music and Social Movements* (Cambridge: Cambridge University Press, 1998), 106.
3. In Gene Lees, *HiFi/Stereo Review* (November 1964): 57.
4. See Robert Cantwell, *When We Were Good: The Folk Revival* (Cambridge, Mass.: Harvard University Press, 1996).
5. Cited in Marvin J. Folkerstrom, Jr., *Ideology and Leadership* (Englewood Cliffs, New Jersey: Prentice Hall, 1988), 86.
6. Everman and Jamison, *Music and Social Movements,* 122.
7. Murray Edelman, *From Art to Politics* (Chicago: University of Chicago Press, 1995), 2.
8. Cohen to Marion McNamara, March 29, 1964 (Leonard Cohen Papers, box 11, file 12, Thomas Fisher Library, University of Toronto).
9. "Let's Be Ourselves Is Poets Advice," *The Toronto Gazette,* November 17, 1964.
10. Paul Williams, "Leonard Cohen: The Romantic in a Ragpicker's Trade," *Crawdaddy* (March 1975).
11. Jon Pankake, "The Brotherhood of the Anthology," in *A Booklet of Essays: Appreciation, and Annotations Pertaining to the Anthology of American Folk Music* (Washington, DC: Smithsonian Folkways Recording, 1997), 26.
12. Harry Smith, booklet accompanying *The Anthology of American Folk Music.*
13. Bob Dylan, notes to *World Gone Wrong.*
14. Quoted by Greil Marcus, *Invisible Republic: Bob Dylan's Basement Tapes* (London: Picador, 1998), 113–114, and Greil Marcus, "The Old Weird America," in *A Booklet of Essays, Appreciations, and Annotations Pertaining to the Anthology of American Folk Music,* 5–25.
15. Ralph Ellison, *Invisible Man* (New York: New American Library, 1952).
16. See Brian Ward, *Just My Soul Responding: Rhythm and Blues, Black Consciousness and Race Relations* (London: UCL Press, 1998).
17. For a variety of reviews on McCarthyism, see Robert Griffith and Athan Theoharis, *The Specter: Original Essays on the Cold War and the Origin of McCarthyism* (New York: New Viewpoints, 1974).
18. See Tom Smucker, "Arlo Guthrie and the Communist Mystical Tradition (A Tall Tale)," *Village Voice,* August 29, 1977, 38.
19. See Robert Griffith and Athan Theoharis, *The Specter: Original Essays on the Cold War and the Origins of McCarthyism.*
20. David Quint, *Origins and Originality in Renaissance Literature: Versions of the Source* (London and New Haven, CT: Yale University Press, 1983), 5.
21. Michel Foucault, *The Archaeology of Knowledge* (London: Pantheon, 1974), 5.

22. Mark Philp, "Michel Foucault," in *The Return of Grand Theory in the Human Sciences,* ed. Quentin Skinner (Cambridge: Cambridge University Press, 1985), 70.
23. Foucault, *Archaeology of Knowledge,* 8, 12, 25.
24. Dylan's "As I Went Out One Morning" (*John Wesley Harding*) makes mention of Tom Paine and is believed to be a response to this incident.
25. Anthony Scaduto, *Bob Dylan* (London: Tavistock, 1972), 163.
26. Marcus, *Invisible Republic,* 17–18.
27. Ibid., 18–19.
28. Ira B. Nadel, *Various Positions* (London: Bloomsbury, 1996), 142.
29. Cited in Nadel, *Various Positions,* 150.
30. Jim Devlin, ed., *In His Own Words: Leonard Cohen* (London: Omnibus, 1998), 82.
31. Leonard Cohen, *The Favourite Game* (Toronto: McClelland & Stewart, 1994), 108.
32. Cited in Rita Barros, *Chelsea Hotel: Fifteen Years* (Lisbon: Lisboa Camera Municipal, 2000), 77.
33. Cited in Barros, *Chelsea Hotel,* 39.
34. Linda Hutcheon, *Leonard Cohen and His Works* (Toronto: ECW Press, nd), 2.
35. Dave Thompson, *Beyond the Velvet Underground* (London: Omnibus, 1989), 28–29.
36. George Stein, *Edie: An American Biography* (New York: Dell, 1983), 228.
37. Marianne Faithfull says, however, that Ginsberg thought most of Dylan's songs were about him. Faithfull maintains that the one that is really about Ginsberg was "Just Like a Woman." Marianne Faithfull and David Dalton, *Faithfull: An Autobiography* (New York: Cooper Square Press, 1994/2000), 49.
38. See Stein, *Edie,* 264–265.
39. Susan Nunziata, "The *Billboard* Interview," *Billboard,* November 28, 1998.

6

INTERPRETING DYLAN AND COHEN:
MAGIC, IMAGINING, AND INSPIRATION

One might apply that contrast of [William] Blake and [P. B.] Shelley to one of the essential differences between Dylan and another poet-singer, Leonard Cohen. Cohen in any case often paddles in the maudlin, but an associated weakness in his work is exactly that Shelleyan quality of saying, as it were, "Look at me: God, I'm sensitive!" A fundamental strength of Dylan's sensitivity is to avoid calling attention to itself.[1]

How are we to compare the work of Dylan and Cohen as poet-songwriters? Initially, they differ in their responses to society and the ways in which people are alienated. Dylan wrote and sang explicit protest songs, whereas Cohen expressed the angst of alienation. The differences in the poetry, or song, of Dylan and Cohen can be understood as a result of the different directions from which they invested their lyrics with integrity. Dylan didn't consciously set out to be a poet. His aim was to become an accomplished folksinger; he even described his early self as a Guthrie jukebox, playing, talking, and singing in the style of his hero. Bonnie Beecher recalls how when the young Dylan was drunk, he would only answer to the name Woody. It was through her that he gained his first exposure to many of the folk and blues artists from which he drew his early repertoire.[2] His poetry very much draws upon the American heritage and fascinating imagery found in the folk and blues tradition. Allen Ginsberg recognized that using these resources, Dylan "built a great twentieth century art out of roots, out of ground minstrelsy, which was a mighty achievement."[3] There is a spontaneity in the imagery and language derived from this tradition, whereas Cohen's language and imagery are characterized by precision and clinical execution, emerging out of his studies of poetry in college. He wrote and recited formalistic poetry, then decided that lyric poetry of integrity could also make good songs.[4]

Cohen's transition from poetry and prose to lyric poetry in song was for him a natural progression. He did not feel that he was rejecting what he had previously embraced, but merely changing the mode of communication. He had collected and sung folk songs for a long time, and while on the island of Hydra he had decided to write some of his own. In conversation with Adrienne Clarkson of *Take Thirty,* a CBC arts television show, Cohen commented with a note of irony, after singing on television for the first time: "The time is over, Adrienne, when poets sit on marble steps wearing long black capes."[5] Like Dylan, but not as severely, Cohen incurred the wrath of those who thought he had sold out to popularism. Art simply could not be commercial, and became debased if it tried. Louis Dudek was representative of this view when he stated: "It's a critical delusion that folk-poetry is the mother tongue of the human race, or that the immediately popularist is the touchstone of art."[6]

When faced with two different views, implicit and explicit, about the appropriate way to "read" Dylan's and Cohen's lyric poetry, how do we differentiate between the validity of the claims? In other words, how should we read Dylan and Cohen? What I will try to develop here is some basic distinctions that will enable us to determine what are and what are not appropriate questions to ask of a particular song/poem. I want to suggest that it is not a uniform set of questions that we ask of the work of an author, and that the key to gaining a better understanding is to be able to identify what questions to ask of what songs/poems. To ask the wrong questions gives rise to misleading or distorted answers.

In order to do this, I am going to distinguish between two approaches to appreciating the lyric poetry of Dylan and Cohen, and for that matter a whole range of other poets and poet-singers. I then want to go on to articulate the aesthetic theories of the philosophers Michael Oakeshott and R. G. Collingwood, and of the Spanish poet and playwright Federico García Lorca, to show how they are useful in helping us to distinguish the right kinds of questions to ask of which poems/songs. The purpose of invoking such theories is to suggest a pathway beyond the current dominant approaches, not to suggest that this is the only way out. It is a path that allows us to proceed in an interesting and intellectually stimulating direction, but this is not to deny that there may not be others that also lead to equally valid destinations.

The first claim is widespread and dominates the literature and Internet discussion on Dylan; in fact, a whole Web site is devoted to it—Dylan Lyric Commentaries.[7] We can call this the search for referents, and it can be divided into two subcategories: (1) the search for referents in people, places, and objects, or the satisfaction of curiosity; and (2) the search for referents in influences, or the concordance approach. James Abbott McNeill Whistler was less than kind in describing such activities as "collecting—comparing—compiling—classifying—contradicting,"[8] but they do help to compare and interpret, in this case, the approaches of Dylan and Cohen as poets.

The Search for Referents

Referents in People, Places, and Objects

The first predilection for referents in people, places, and objects assumes that the more you know about to what a song refers, the better appreciation you have of it. This is exemplified by Aidan Day in *Jokerman: Reading the Lyrics of Bob Dylan*.[9] It is an approach that has bedeviled poetry appreciation for decades and has emerged in relation to contemporary music wherever there was an interesting lyric. In 1967, for example, Richard Poirier complained that much of the commentary on the Beatles was marred by research that was largely irrelevant. Knowing the details of Tara Brown's death, a friend of the Beatles who died in a motor crash and who is alluded to in "A Day in the Life" (*Sgt. Pepper's Lonely Hearts Club Band*), serves to obstruct rather than illuminate the song's reference to a man in a car and the circumstances of his death at a traffic light.[10] In Dylan's case, take, for example, "Positively 4th Street," the single that immediately followed "Like a Rolling Stone" and was recorded four days after the 1965 Newport Folk Festival. The song has been widely interpreted as a bitter attack on Dylan's former friends in the folk world and suggested that the title refers to where he was living on West Fourth Street in Greenwich Village at the time. Alternatively, it has been suggested that the song refers to Fourth Street in Minneapolis, where Dylan went to college and dropped out. For this same approach, it is a matter of importance to determine that "Just Like a Woman" is about Edie Sedgwick, or indeed that the "tallest and the blondest girl" in Leonard Cohen's "Memories" is Sedgwick's rival,

Nico, or that Janis Joplin is the subject of "Chelsea Hotel No. 2." For example, something like the following story illuminates or gives meaning to "Just like a Woman." During the period 1963–1965, Sedgwick was featured in several high-profile magazines, including *Time, Life,* and *Vogue.* She was a fashion icon, as well as the star of many of Andy Warhol's films. She also dated Dylan at a time, Jonathan Taplin suggests, when "his transition from folk purity to the rock insanity was overwhelming him."[11] Sedgwick lived life on the edge, subject to extreme highs and lows induced by a vicious circle of uppers and downers to keep pace with her frenetic lifestyle. Her flamboyant and confident exterior disguised a deep inner fragility, however. The lines in Dylan's "Just Like a Woman" are taken to be propositions about an identifiable woman, but the Sedgwick referent makes sense of such lines as "with her fog, her amphetamines and her pearls" and "But lately I see her ribbons and her bows / Have fallen from her curls," and the famous last line of the refrain, "But she breaks just like a little girl."

Maurice Ratcliff takes the same approach to all of Cohen's songs. While fully acknowledging that the poet trades in ambiguity, he implicitly conveys the view that we ought to be able to unravel what is ambiguous, and indeed thinks that there are limits to ambiguity beyond which meaning is unintelligible or lost. In discussing "The Old Revolution" (*Songs from a Room*), Ratcliff asks: "What is the protagonist talking about and why? Ambiguity is all very well, but it seems that here Cohen strayed over the boundary into impression."[12] The assumption is that the song must have an authorial meaning, and that it is a failure on the part of the poet if he or she does not convey it. The author is much more at home in discussing "Hey, That's No Way to Say Goodbye" (*Songs of Leonard Cohen*), because he is able to disentangle the referents and discern the subject matter of the song. "Goodbye," which was written in 1966 at the Penn Terminal Hotel in New York, although similar in theme to "So Long, Marianne," which is on the same album, is actually about a different but parallel relationship that had run its course. Ratcliff does raise a note of caution when searching for referents to give a song meaning. He argues, but does not heed the warning himself, that "the story of the song's genesis underlines the perils of reading too much autobiography into a work of art."[13] He even concedes that sometimes with poets who thrive on ambiguity the audience has to find the meaning for itself, and in certain songs, such as "The Butcher" (*Songs from a Room*), the meaning is not easily yielded.

We can find ourselves in terrible tangles if we try to tie meaning too literally to outside referents. Ratcliff contends that "First We Take Manhattan" (*I'm Your Man*) is not a political song because "it neither identifies the causes of problems nor proposes solutions to them."[14] He is quite right that this is not a finger-pointing song, but wrong to think it is not political because he cannot find the events or injustices to which it refers. Instead, he attaches it to an entirely inappropriate referent by suggesting that it is an allegory for "girding the loins for the rigours of [Cohen's] forthcoming tour, a call to arms directed at his hand."[15] The itinerary of touring may well have suggested the imagery, but it does nothing to explain it or to help us appreciate it more. As we have already seen, a poem or a song can be deeply political, representative of a counterculture, and unnervingly unsettling because of what it brings into question, or because the mood is dark and threatening. The disturbing imagery may have no referent that we can identify, the language and meaning may be inseparable, yet they may be profound in their impact on the reader or hearer, as, for example, the menacing tone and allusions in the following lines:

> *Ah you loved me as a loser, but now you're worried that I just might win.*
> *You know the way to stop me, but you don't have the discipline*
> *How many nights I prayed for this, to let my work begin.*
> *First we take Manhattan, then we take Berlin.*

("First We Take Manhattan")

Or the equally disturbing and apocryphal "The Future," from the album of the same name:

> *Your servant here, he has been told*
> *to say it clear, to say it cold:*
> *It's over, it ain't going*
> *any further*
> *And now the wheels of heaven stop*
> *you feel the devil's riding crop*
> *Get ready for the future*
> *it is murder*

Another danger in such an approach, the amassing of more and more detail, to use a cliché, is that we won't see the forest for the trees. It is a fallacy to believe that gathering new facts about a subject leads to cumulative understanding. Mark Twain puts this much more eloquently when in his *Life on the Mississippi* he tells of how he came to know every feature of the great river as well as he knew the letters of the alphabet. This in itself was an achievement: "But I had lost something, too. I had lost something which could never be restored to me while I lived. All the grace, the beauty, the poetry had gone out of the majestic river."[16]

Even where the author appears to invite the link with outside referents, they may serve to obscure rather than illuminate, complicate rather than elucidate, and perhaps intentionally. Take the following lines from Dylan's "You're Gonna Make Me Lonesome When You Go" (*Blood on the Tracks*): "Situations have ended sad / Relationships have all been bad / Mine've been like Verlaine's and Rimbaud." At the level of generality the lines are self-explanatory and self-referential. Without knowing anything about Verlaine and Rimbaud, the previous lines indicate that the relationship was certainly less than happy. If we descend into the particulars, however, and anchor the poem to the specifics of the relation between Verlaine and Rimbaud, we raise more questions than we can answer: for example, who in this relation does Dylan identify with? The older Verlaine or the younger, dominant Rimbaud? Although neither admitted that his relationship was homosexual, and in fact denied it in print, it was widely believed to have been so throughout their stormy intermittent periods together, character-ized by drunkenness, violent quarrels, and Rimbaud's quest for power and its exercise by experiencing every type of sin. Their relationship in Paris, London, and Brussels was intermittent between 1871 and 1873, when Verlaine was imprisoned for attempted manslaughter after shooting Rimbaud in the wrist and trying to prevent him from leaving Brussels.[17]

The meaning of statements in this first approach is similar to Friedrich Gottlob Frege's correlation of the sense and reference of a sentence in the use of language. Frege added a distinction that he deemed irrelevant to the meaning of an expression, what he called its color.[18] Thus, the use of *guy, chap*, or *man* as synonyms in a sentence is a matter of coloration rather than propositions. The sense of a sentence has to do with the dictionary definition of the words in the context of the sentence, or at least those that are relevant to the truth value of an expression, and those things to which they refer, the referents of the words. Basically, by identifying Edie Sedgwick as the subject of "Just Like a Woman," we are able to determine the truth value of the statements. In this respect, we understand poetry just as we would understand any other sentence, as a statement about the world. In this approach meaning is equated with the psychology of the author, that is, with authorial intention, and building up the context assists us in retrieving the intention. In philosophical hermeneutics it has a long and distinguished heritage in Wilhelm Dilthey, and more recently with E. D. Hirsch Jr. As Hirsch suggests, "A text cannot be interpreted from a perspective different from the original author's. Meaning is understood from the perspective that lends existence to meaning. Any other procedure is not interpretation but authorship."[19] Stephen Scobie strongly criticizes this approach in his comments on Cohen's "Suzanne," when he argues that knowing the subject is Suzanne Vaillancourt adds nothing to our appreciation of the song. What is important is the song itself.[20] Anal retentive textual interpretation is often dismissed as too intellectualist, as, for example, by Robert Sandall, who accuses Aidan Day of subjecting Dylan's lyrics to tortuous scrutiny.[21] However, it is not that the approach is too intellectualist, but that it is instead noncriteriological, by which I mean that there are very little by way of criteria in terms of which to pronounce one interpretation more convincing than another, and relies more on imaginative creation than reasoned interpretation.

The problem may best be illustrated with reference to the interpretation of political philosophy. One of the most influential historians of political thought in the United States in the latter part of the twentieth century was Leo Strauss. He argued that political philosophy by its very nature is subversive and constituted a threat to authority by questioning the very assumptions upon which political life was organized in any particular community. During periods of persecution it was particularly important that the real meaning of philosophical texts be disguised, for fear of being convicted of heresy and condemned to death. Although the practice of concealing hidden meaning was most imperative during times of persecution, it was in fact a widespread method by which initiates conveyed their secret meanings to each other. In other words, the great texts include an exoteric doctrine designed for general public consumption and an esoteric one addressed to fellow initiates that only they could understand. There is a great difference, however, in claiming that there are hidden meanings in a text and the conceptually different activity of providing the key, or the principles, by which to unlock the meaning. It is at this point that the most tortuous and convoluted interpretative gymnastics are performed. Among Strauss's assumptions, for example, is that philosophers are so intelligent that they could not possibly make mistakes, so that when we discover an apparent contradiction or mistake, it must be intentional and point to a hidden meaning.[22] Such an assumption is often made of Dylan. For example, Dylan's misspelling of Hardin, the real-life outlaw in "John Wesley Harding," the song and the album, has been taken to be meaningful and significant. In Hebrew there are no separate letters for vowels, and the Jewish names for God, Jehovah, or Jaweh may be transliterated as

149

JWH, the initials of John Wesley Hardin.[23] The addition of the *g* to Hardin is further evidence for some interpreters that the actual referent of the song is God.

Referents in Poetic and Musical Sources

The second subspecies of the search for referents is the identification of influences in poetic and musical sources. This approach is exemplified by Michael Gray, Greil Marcus, Christopher Ricks, George Woodcock, Stephen Scobie, Michael Ondaatje, and Desmond Pacey, to different degrees. The assumption is that if we can discover that someone wrote or sang something similar elsewhere, this adds to our understanding of what Dylan or Cohen have wrote and sung. Both Marcus and Gray are dismissive of what the latter calls "superficial message hunting."[24] In direct criticism of A. J. Weberman, the inventor of garbology, who maintains that the contents of a subject's garbage can help draw conclusions about that person's life, Marcus argues that it is impossible to understand "Just Like a Woman" by making logical connections between it and transvestites because of the reference to Queen Mary, or Britain because of the use of the word *fog*, even if they are the correct referents.[25] Scobie goes in for extensive interpretation of this kind, as, for example, in *Alias Bob Dylan*.[26] Although Scobie explicitly disavows the search for factual referents, for example, by pointing out the futility of linking Edie Sedgwick and Bob Neuwirth with "She's Your Lover Now" (*The Bootleg Series*), he nevertheless thinks that the critic has to engage with the complexity of the text. He deals with the text almost like a crossword puzzle, in which the clues point us toward the answers.

So the question remains, is the alternative nothing more than superficial influence hunting? Certainly the method is one that could be affected by the use of a poetry, or blues, concordance. We put in a search for certain words or phrases and match them with similar words and phrases in Dylan's songs. When we find such resemblances, they are linked together not by evidence, but by subjective intuitions. The connections are extremely tenuous, made by the use of deliberately imprecise language. Hence, for example, when linking Dylan's work with other poets, Michael Gray uses such connecting lines as "It seems to me to contain many recollections of major English poets," it "sometimes calls John Donne to mind," "The techniques resemble each other," it "seems to remind one vaguely," "There is a keen correspondence," a "minor correspondence," and even "an exact echo." We are also told that "Dylan inherits ideas from [Kenneth] Patchen too, I think—or again, perhaps just from the milieu that Patchen was a creative part of."[27]

Patrick Crotty is similarly imprecise in linking influences to Dylan by using tentative and evasive language. For example, he says, "There *may* [my emphasis] be a number of scriptural citations in 'When the Ship Comes In': The opening phrase of the [Syrian Apocalypse of] Baruch quotation raises the intriguing possibility that the title track of *The Times They Are A-Changin'* should be counted among Dylan's Apocalyptic songs." In reference to "When the Ship Comes In," Crotty says it "appears to allude to what is perhaps the most famous phrase in Revelation, 'And there was no more sea' (21:1)."[28] Greil Marcus's approach is much more sophisticated and evocative. In exploring the breadth and depth of the *The Basement Tapes* (1975), he tries to capture what Dylan and The Band "took out of the air" and what they put back into it. They captured, not abstractions, but the ghosts of the real sons and daughters of American history, manifest for a moment on Harry Smith's *Anthology of American Folk Music*, "the founding document of the American folk revival."[29] *The Basement Tapes* were in fact a "shambling" version of this anthology.

Cohen's work has been approached in the same way by, for example, Michael Ondaatje, George Woodcock, Desmond Pacey, and Stephen Scobie. Ondaatje suggests the poem "Lovers," from *Let Us Compare Mythologies*, exhibits a bitter irony reminiscent of A. M. Klein. Both writers, he claims, employ similar poetic and rhetorical tricks: "Apart from the obvious similarities—such as the exotic words and worlds, and a biblical style— there is the same gentle irony about oneself and about one's childhood heroism."[30] In *Collected Poems* we find Dylan Thomas's "tousled ghost," as well as some deft parodying of T. S. Eliot. We also find borrowings from and echoes of W. H. Auden and Edith Sitwell.[31] In *Recent Songs*, "The Gypsy's Wife," for example, "echoes, if it does not rely on, the *Blood Wedding* of [Federico García] Lorca, no less."[32] The fact that Lorca wrote *Gypsy Ballads* is hardly sufficient grounds to link Lorca's relentlessly bleak play, with Cohen's lyrics, which he says himself relate to the stained relationship he was in with Suzanne Elrod at the time it was breaking down. The emotion expressed is that of the conflicting feelings of wanting to break free, while at the same time jealousy that someone else may be in her arms. Desmond Pacey juxtaposes Cohen with William Wordsworth, because the former resembles the latter in achieving magical clarity, not by looking at the world in generalities or through scientific concepts, but by close examination of detail, such as the streaks on a designated tulip. This juxtaposition is justified because at least once there is "an obvious echo" of Wordsworth's "Tintern Abbey" in *Beautiful Losers.*[33] Both poets exemplify a search for sensual exactitude. This is not to suggest, of course, that what is borrowed may occasionally be transformed into an original statement, as, for example, in "Travel" from *The Spice-Box of Earth,* in which the lines "Horizons keep the soft line of your cheeks / The windy sky's a locket for your hair" follows lines that are no more than serviceable Yeats, but with the word *horizons,* "a new spirit enters—that of a poet capable of utterly individual statement within the convention, and from this point the resemblance to Yeats becomes ambivalent. These lines are no longer good imitation Yeats; they are lines which only Yeats could have imitated."[34] Scobie, in reading *Let Us Compare Mythologies,* sees "reminiscences of Eliot" in "Rededication," and of John Donne in "The Fly." He contends that Cohen's poem is a pale imitation of Donne's "The Flea."[35]

The problem with the search for influence and origins, as we have seen, is that of infinite regress. For example, to say something like "Dylan shares with Eliot the use of urban imagery and the expression of urban disillusionment"[36] is to invite the process of infinite regress. It is very obvious that Dylan shares this with a whole range of other poets, including his contemporary Leonard Cohen and his predecessors Baudelaire, Rimbaud, and Lorca. It should come as no surprise that poets, artists, and philosophers share things with others of their kind. Indeed, Pablo Picasso made no apology for his pillaging of past art, which he nevertheless transformed and made his own. He famously said, "When there is something to steal, I steal." The hermeneutic theorist Wilhelm Dilthey pronounced one of the most telling indictments. Rudolph Makkreel nicely encapsulates Dilthey's view: "Origins as such cannot provide meaning: they, in effect, take away the meaning that the phenomenon possesses by deriving it as a mere effect of something else."[37]

Let us look at the case of Robert Browning to illustrate more concretely the point that I am trying to make. Gray spends a great deal of time detailing what he sees as the resemblances between Dylan and Browning. In this concordance approach, what Gray misses entirely is the scientific and philosophical worldviews that converge in Browning, and which are completely absent from Dylan, and without which any resemblances are superficial. What is called the metaphysical element, the underlying philosophy that gives unity to all his works is an important factor in understanding him and the work that he produced. Browning tries to explain all things, even good and evil, as manifestations of the principle of love. Browning relies in his poetry on the underlying assumptions of the day. He assumes, for example, the principle of evolution at work in human experience, and also subscribes to philosophical idealism, the view that the mind constitutes reality, the idea that nature and spirit are inseparable, not that nature is intelligent, but that it is intelligible to mind and is therefore mind dependent. Ultimately, however, and at considerable variance from Dylan, Browning's whole outlook of life expressed in his poems rests upon agnosticism and the idea that truth is unattainable.[38]

The same philosophical influence pervades T. S. Eliot. Eliot made a thorough study of F. H. Bradley while at Oxford University in 1914, had studied under the American idealist Josiah Royce at Harvard University, and while at Oxford came under the sway of the likes of J. A. Smith, who introduced Italian idealism into Britain. Eliot wrote a Ph.D. thesis on Bradley, which he never formally defended, thus failing to fulfill a condition of receiving the degree. Gray cites an appreciation by F. R. Leavis of Eliot's poetry, remarking that it is every bit as applicable to Dylan's *Highway 61 Revisited* and *Blonde on Blonde* as it is of Eliot. The line quoted from Leavis relates to "poetry that freely expresses a modern sensibility, the . . . modes of experience of one fully alive in his own age."[39] This was written in 1932 while Leavis was at Cambridge University and shortly after he established the literary criticism journal *Scrutiny*. Leavis's reference to the "modes of experience" is in fact an allusion to the philosophical idealism of Michael Oakeshott, who was also working at Cambridge and a contributor to *Scrutiny* in 1931, as well as editor of *The Cambridge Review*.[40]

The Emotional Response

The second approach to appreciating the lyrical poetry of a song is what we may call, for want of a better term, the emotional response, and it implicitly rejects this narrow conception of language. In this respect, the words are not taken as statements. The words are indeed colors on the poet's palette that are used to conjure powerful images that have the capacity to move us emotionally without having a determinate meaning or propositional value. This is what Neil Tennant of the Pet Shop Boys meant when he said that the lyrics of REM's "Losing My Religion" were brilliant, despite the fact that he didn't have a clue what they meant.[41] Kenneth Allsop was quick to pick up the significance of Dylan's shift to art as the expression of emotion, or what Lorca described as inspirational poetry. Certain types of questions were not applicable. After quoting a few lines of "She Belongs to Me" (*Bringing It All Back Home,* 1965), Allsop exclaims: "What does it mean? What does it matter? It arrows, as poetry should, beyond the compartments of literal meaning . . . "[42] This is also what Paul Williams means when he writes that asking who the real Bob Dylan is and what he is really trying to say is not, strictly speaking, answerable. Williams argues that he can listen to "Sad-Eyed Lady of the Lowlands" (*Blonde on Blonde*) and empathize with the song, feel what it is about, because the words successfully communicate an emotion despite the fact that the line "My warehouse eyes and my Arabian drum" have no clear meaning to him, but nevertheless have a clear relevance in his own understanding of the song. In his view, art is not interpreted, but experienced.[43] For Williams, *The Basement Tapes* signifies the point at which Dylan purposely goes beyond the conscious statement. More recently, after quoting the first four lines of "I Want You," John Harris asks: "What is all that about? It probably doesn't matter. It sounds beautiful . . . "[44] Though not wanting to banish analysis from art, Henry Jones warns that it destroys the very thing that it analyzes: "The beauty of form and the music of speech which criticism destroys, and to which philosophy is, at best, indifferent, are elements essential to poetry."[45] At the less adventurous end of the scale, it is the determination to take texts out of their contexts, and read them as self-contained works.[46]

Here the text distances itself from the author in a process that Paul Ricoeur calls distanciation.[47] The text is gradually severed from the intention of the author, its contextual referents, and joins the company of a quasi-world of texts. It represents the move away from epistemological hermeneutics, which links the meaning of a text to the author's intentions. Dylan himself was well aware of this process. He maintained that anyone who has a message learns from experience that it cannot be represented in song without becoming something different: "A song leaves your mouth just as soon as it leaves your hands."[48]

Instead of linking the meaning of a text to the intention of the author, Hans-Georg Gadamer puts forward an ontological hermeneutics, which is suggested to him by Martin Heidegger's notion of "being there in the world." The question for Gadamer becomes not how should we interpret texts, which is an epistemological question relating to the acquisition of knowledge, but instead, what happens to us every time we interpret a text, which is an ontological question about the nature of our being. The answer is that a text is articulated within a tradition, even if it is reacting to that tradition, and projects in front of itself a horizon. The person trying to understand such a text also stands at a point in this tradition, and has a forestructure of meanings with which to encounter the text, what Gadamer calls prejudice in a nonpejorative sense. Any understanding or experiencing of texts constitutes a "fusion of horizons."[49]

Some Aesthetic Theories

At this point, I want to enlist the service of R. G. Collingwood's widely read and influential theory of art, which covers not only fine art, but all forms of artistic expression. I want to contrast this with the less well known theory of Michael Oakeshott, who denies that art is the expression of emotion. I will then extend the typology by looking briefly at Lorca's theory. The reason for doing this is to have some point of reference by which to explore the changes within Bob Dylan's work, and between his poetry and that of Leonard Cohen. The purpose is not to deny or confirm any of the three theories.

R. G. Collingwood's *The Principles of Art* (1937) is a book that tries to distinguish art from craft, and pseudo-art from art proper. Craft is essentially utilitarian, having a value not in itself, but for the use to which it is put. By acquiring and developing certain technical skills, the craftsperson can conceive of an object and produce it according to that plan. Take, for example, the various statues and paintings found inside the tombs of Egyptian pharaohs. Craftsmen produced the artifacts according to the religious conventions of the time, designed to assist the body of the pharaoh into the afterlife. Although they may be beautifully executed, they are not meant to be viewed or displayed. They are objects conceived of as a means–end relation. The objects are the means to an end, in this case to ward off evil spirits and to assist the pharaoh on his journey. Here the objects do not express the emotion of the craftsman. It is undoubtedly the case that they may incidentally do this, and border upon something like art. Art proper, Collingwood argues, is often confused with art as magic and art as amusement. Art as magic shares with craft a utilitarian function, but in addition it is designed to arouse emotions in the community to which it is addressed. It has a practical purpose in that the emotions that are aroused are channeled into an activity for some perceived social benefit. A fertility dance, for example, is designed to arouse emotions of love and desire, to be channeled into socially beneficial and institutionally sanctioned relationships between men and women. In so far as art as emotion also suppresses some emotions that are not socially beneficial, art as magic is a denial and perversion of art. A war dance, for example, is meant to arouse emotions of fearfulness and suppress those of fear, channeling the positive emotions into the activity of war. Art proper, in Collingwood's view, is the expression of emotion. The emotion that is expressed is not preconceived. It is not first formulated and then expressed. It is expressed in the artistic act itself and inseparable from it. Nor does the production of the work of art have an ulterior purpose, but its success depends on evoking that same emotion in the audience and thus contributes to the viewer's own self-understanding of his or her emotional life.[50]

Although many of the details of Collingwood's theory may be challenged by aestheticians, the idea that art is the expression of emotion has widespread support. Paul Williams in his book on Dylan talks of artistic performance as the expression of emotion, or of what the performer is feeling at that particular time.[51] In contrast to this view, Michael Oakeshott takes poetry to be a certain way of imagining, distinct from practical, scientific, or historical images. What distinguishes the voice of poetry in the conversation of humanity from the other voices is its manner of being active. This activity is contemplating or delighting in the making of images. They are, as opposed to the images in other idioms of discourse, "mere" images. They are not facts about the world, because they are not propositions, and here truth and falsity are inappropriate terms in which to appreciate them. You do not ask of the images, could this have happened, is it possible or probable or just an illusion or make-believe, because to ask these questions assumes the distinction between fact and not fact, which is out of place in poetic contemplative imagining.

Furthermore, they are present images; they have no past or future. They are delighted in for what they are, rather than for what they are related to, that is, the occasions that may have inspired them. A photograph may lie if it purports to be a true likeness of its subject, but a poetic image cannot lie because it affirms nothing. It is irrelevant to the work of art that it does not faithfully represent the subject. Paul Cézanne's *Rocky Scenery of Provence* is a composition of irregular shapes of color comprising an image whose aesthetic quality has nothing to do with whether it looks like Provence or not, and the appeal of Vincent van Gogh's cornfields does not require that the corn and the clouds really swirl in harmony in the south of France.

Van Gogh's *Starry Night* is of no practical use to the traveler wanting to get from one place to another without the aid of a map, and scientifically it is a travesty, but to judge its practical or scientific value is to misunderstand it. Van Gogh's *Starry Night* exists only in the poetic image that he has created. The arrangement and diction of the contemplative images are what distinguishes one poet from another; the symbols are not interchangeable. To substitute one as a synonym for another destroys the image. Take, for example, the following lines: "In this room the heat pipes just cough" ("Visions of Johanna"). To substitute "The central heating in this room is inadequate" is practically to say the same thing, but the poetic image is destroyed.

Why, then, are poetic images mere images? It is because the relation between symbol (language) and meaning (thought) is different in poetry from the relation in other modes of experience. This is a view Oakeshott shares with Collingwood who, in *Speculum Mentis*,[52] distinguishes, art, religion, science, history, and philosophy with reference to their different relations between symbol and meaning. In our everyday practical lives, for example, each symbol, or word has a determinate referent or signification. The more determinate, the better the communication. If I ask for a loaf of bread, I am using a symbol to evoke an image, not to create one. I am not trying to give a novel nuance to the symbol, merely to be understood in a settled language. In other words, meaning and symbol are distinct, but not radically separable, because in this mode "every word has its proper reference or signification."[53] The symbol is separable from and the means by which we convey meaning. The reason why art or poetry is different is because there is no separation of symbol and meaning: a poetic image is its meaning; it symbolizes nothing outside of itself.[54] This view is confirmed by fellow idealist Henry Jones in his study of Browning. He contends that the worth of a work of art "must be recognised as lying wholly within itself," and that in it "thought and expression are inseparable."[55]

Oakeshott explicitly denies that poetry is the expression of emotion designed to evoke the same emotion in the audience. If he intended his target to be Collingwood, then he misses it. Collingwood is unequivocal in ruling out a means to an end relationship in art, which the idea of design and execution posits. The emotion is only discovered in its expression. The ability to evoke that same emotion in others is the criterion of good art. Oakeshott argues that although the idea that art is the expression of emotion is commonly held, it rests on the mistaken view that poetry must be in some way informative and instructive. The poet must have undergone the emotion from which the poetic image derives. This, Oakeshott argues, "makes a necessity of what is no more than an unlikely possibility."[56] It is important to emphasize that Oakeshott is trying to establish what makes the poetic utterance unique; he is not suggesting that poets only contemplate or delight in images, only that when they do anything else, it is not poetry.

Let us now look at how the distinction between art as magic, art as delighting in and contemplating imaginings, may further be extended. Lorca's New York poems mark a significant development in his style, from what he calls the poetry of imagination to the poetry of inspiration. This distinction is elaborated in a number of lectures variously reported in the press and collected under the title "Imagination, Inspiration, Evasion." Imagination is synonymous with the aptitude we have for discovery. It enables us to illuminate what is hidden and to breathe life into fragments of reality to which humanity is blind. Imaginative poetry, however, has horizons and is constrained by reality. Imaginative poetry is constrained by the laws of logic and reason; it makes connections with the world, discovering unexpected relations between objects and ideas, and in doing so abates mystery. It is the poetry that explores and describes the universe. As Lorca suggests: "One's imagination needs objects, landscapes, numbers and planets and the relationship between them within the purest form of logic is vital."[57] It is the poetry that explores and describes the universe.

Lorca argues that imagination is located within human logic and controlled by reason. It is a special way of creating that requires order and boundaries. Imagination is the starting point in poetry, and the poet constructs a tower against the elements and against mystery. His voice is listened to because he creates order, but he finds it difficult to inspire intense emotions free from constraints. Imagination is ultimately impoverished, and poetic imagination even more so. Visible reality is far more nuanced than we imagine, and far more poetic than imagination can comprehend, as is often evidenced in the conflict between scientific reality and imaginary myths. For example, imagination has attributed to giants the construction of huge grottoes and cities of enchantment. We have subsequently realized that they were created by continuous patient and eternal drops of water, the triumph of reality over imagination. Or more correctly, imagination becomes conscious of its shortcomings. Lorca argues that

> imagination seemed to be operating in a logical manner when it attributed to giants that which did, indeed, seem to be the work of giants. However, scientific reality, poetic to the extreme and beyond the logical field, showed us that the truth was to be found in eternal, crystal-clear water droplets. It is a great deal more beautiful to think that a grotto is the

158

result of the mysterious caprice of water bound and governed by eternal laws, than the caprices of some giants which have no more meaning than that of an explanation.[58]

The poetry of inspiration, on the other hand, acknowledges mystery and moves in a world of poetic harmony and order that avoids imaginative reality with its currently perceived norms of beauty and ugliness, and enters instead into a poetic reality far more astonishing, sometimes characterized by tenderness and sometimes by immensely deep cruelty. It is elusive and evades reality by tracing the pathway of dreams that leads in the subconscious to an unsuspected fact. The traditional metaphor in poetry gives way to the poetic fact, which is tied to poetic logic. The order and balance of imagination often give way to the incongruity of inspiration. In this respect, the poem is a "self-sufficient entity without reference to any reality outside itself."[59] Poetry of inspiration breaks free from logical control and passionately rejects the temptation to be understood. In Lorca's view, poetry cannot be understood; it is received, not analyzed. It is counter to intelligence and the received order of things. The poet of inspiration has to look at the world with the eyes of a child, and when asking for the moon truly believe that someone will reach out and place it in his hands.[60] In sum, then, the poet of imagination is constrained by human logic, abating mystery by explaining the inexplicable, whereas the poet of inspiration is set free by poetic logic, acknowledging that not everything has a cause and effect, and that pure reality evades explanation. The implication seems to be that imaginative poetry craves to be understood and makes propositions about reality that can be explored and refuted. Inspirational poetry delights in mystery, rejects the temptation to be understood, and presents images to which truth and falsity are inapplicable.

The poetry of inspiration, on the other hand, acknowledges mystery; it is elusive and evades reality. The traditional metaphor in poetry gives way to the poetic fact that is tied to poetic logic. Michael Oakeshott has something similar in mind when he characterizes poetic imagining as contemplative. You do not ask of the images whether they are fact or not fact. They are not propositions about the world to which truth and falsity are applicable; they are images to be delighted in.[61]

Bringing It All Back Home

Taken together, these theorists enable us to construct a view of poetry that is capable of characterizing the overlapping and concurrent forms of poetic expression found in Dylan's work. The first phase is pseudo art, or art as magic, having a preconceived purpose and desired practical effect, represented by the "topical" or "finger-pointing" songs. Second, we have art as the expression of emotion, or imaginative art, which has no preconceived purpose or desired practical effect, but which nevertheless expresses what the artist is feeling. Here the logic of reality is explored, the unexpected connections exposed, and the imagery embedded in occasions or situations. In this category we can place such songs as "My Back Pages," "Ballad in Plain D" and "Chimes of Freedom" (all from *Another Side of Bob Dylan*), and "Subterranean Homesick Blues" (*Bringing It All Back Home*). Third, we have what Oakeshott refers to as a delighting in images, and what Lorca calls inspirational poetry, with no necessary external referents and with an internal logic of its own. This form of poetry is typically represented by such songs as "Hard Rain's A-Gonna Fall" (*Freewheelin' Bob Dylan*), "Tombstone Blues" and "Desolation Row" (*Highway 61 Revisited*), and "Sad-Eyed Lady of the Lowlands" and "Visions of Johanna" (*Blonde on Blonde*). Dylan appears to be acknowledging this distinction in an interview he gave in the summer of 1965. When asked whether he was trying to bring order from the chaos of the world, Dylan answered "No." He simply accepted the world, saying "I don't know what the songs I write are. That's all I do is write songs, right?"[62] Furthermore, I want to suggest that Leonard Cohen predominantly inhabits the world of the second and third under-standings of art.

To misunderstand the poetic phase may lead to absurd conclusions. Let me illustrate with an example from C. P. Lee's *Like the Night*. In interpreting Bob Dylan's "Just Like a Woman," Lee cites the opening line: "Nobody feels any pain." In taking this statement to be a proposition, Lee offers a contorted and absurdly literal analysis of the song: "Is this one of the greatest ironic statements in the history of the universe? Everybody feels pain of some sort at some time or another."[63] When taken as an expression of emotion, or as imaginative poetry, the question of whether the statement is right or wrong does not arise: "Nobody feels any pain / Tonight as I stand inside the rain." Taken as an expression of emotion, it conveys self-absorption, despondency, resignation—an obliviousness to the world and the feelings of other individuals, because rain serves to isolate the self and its thoughts. As imaginative poetry, the lyrics are a series of images:

> Nobody feels any pain
> Tonight as I stand inside the rain.
> Everybody knows that baby's got new clothes,

But lately I see her ribbons and her bows
Have fallen from her curls.

Each line is an image, and it makes no difference to the appreciation of that imagery whether Edie Sedgwick is or is not the subject of the song. This is the point that Bob Dylan is making when, in talking of the film *Renaldo and Clara*, he says, "When you go to a movie, do you ask what does that person do in real life?"[64]

What I want to suggest, then, is that there is a point at which Dylan ceases to be only a craftsman, ceases to have only a preconceived idea with a determinate purpose, ceases to express his emotion, which was largely anger, only *by* writing songs, and came to express it instead *in* writing songs. This, I think, is what he was trying to say in October 1965 when he commented that "I don't write now unless it just happens."[65] In the 1966 *Playboy* interview he asserted: "I've stopped composing and singing anything that has either a reason to be written or a motive to be sung."[66] The process by which "Like a Rolling Stone" became a song confirms this. Dylan's diversions into free-form prose and poetry, and even playwriting, were an expression of his frustration at the restrictiveness of the medium of the song in which to express himself. "Like a Rolling Stone" was a spontaneous expression of the anger and frustration he felt at the sterility of his art. He was bored with what he was doing and dissatisfied with what he had produced. On the airplane home from London after his short 1965 acoustic tour and his disastrous and abortive attempt to create a new sound with John Mayall's Blues Breakers, he vented his anger in a flow of consciousness with no preconceived subject and at an abstract focal point. At this stage, "it was ten pages long, it wasn't called anything, just a rhythm thing on paper all about my steady hatred directed at some point that was honest."[67]

M. L. Rosenthal, the New York teacher and well-known critic, disparaged Cohen's lyric poetry for having little or no meaning. Paul Barrera at first glance seems to imply that the search for the author's meaning is futile, but then relents by suggesting that Cohen's ambiguities are something like cryptic crossword clues, and the reader must try to break the poetic code. There is a note of disappointment when he declares that *Book of Mercy* (1984) is so personal that "it is impossible to break through to the inner meanings."[68] Doug Beardsley, a contemporary of Cohen in Montreal, perceptively appreciated that such comments, though literally true, miss the whole point of what some poets, at least, are doing. It was the aura and sense of the mysterious that the lyrics conjured, not their meaning that mattered.[69] Douglas Barbour emphasizes the nonpropositional character of poetry in reviewing Cohen's *Selected Poems* (1968). Barbour talks of "a poetry of enigma, where often it is impossible to know what is happening in the poem even while it exercises its charm upon you."[70] Lorca's understanding of the poetry of inspiration shows a sensitivity to the medium far more sophisticated than that of Rosenthal, and is consistent with Cohen's description of what is appropriate and inappropriate to ask of a poem. The poet is not absolved from clarity by immersing himself in ambiguity:

> There is a clarity that is perceived by the heart and clarity that is perceived by the mind. You know, clarity is not a fixed idea. Sometimes something that is clear to the heart needs quite complex expression. You just let the words or tune speak to you and it's very clear. You give yourself to the kiss or the embrace and while it is going on there's not any need to know what is going on. You just dissolve into it. . . . But if there is an obscurity in my work, it's something that no one can penetrate, not even me. . . . You just try to be faithful to that interior landscape that has its own rules, its own mechanisms, and it's important to be faithful to them. If someone says "I love the song, what the fuck does it mean?" the question is not as important as the declaration.[71]

The work itself, Cohen argued elsewhere, is beyond significance and meaning. Metaphorically the work is a diamond that the poet cuts and polishes, reflecting, refracting, and amplifying light. Poetry is nevertheless an activity that is not merely summoned or invoked; it is not self-consciously premeditated, and the images present themselves as a consequence of the desperate and dismal lost battles of life.[72]

I think that we can detect in Cohen a self-conscious move from the poetry of imagination to the poetry of inspiration. I am not suggesting a discontinuity here, because many of the themes are enduring; it is the imagery with which the themes are portrayed that become more surrealistic, sinister, and even starkly frightening. *Flowers for Hitler* is the collection that manifests this completion of the transition that had already been taking place in individual poems previously. It is a book that is far less discerning than his previous books of poetry, and which includes poems that are awkward and underworked, many of which exhibit the philosophy of Irving Layton that the poet should just publish everything and that time will filter out the bad. Cohen deliberately sets out to shock, by casting off an image that he misleadingly calls "the golden boy," implying that his previous poetry did not contain similarly disturbing images. He wanted to move, he said, in the less socially acceptable dung pile of the writer at the front line. The subjects he used for the poems were not addressed directly, but tackled by employing symbolist and surrealist imagery. The book is, in a sense, a self-conscious revolt against style, a deliberate attempt to deny that the poems have any style. As Scobie points out, the pose of denying that the poems have style is itself a style. He recognizes that what Cohen is doing in much of the imagery is not to convey a literal or propositional meaning but instead to project the general atmosphere and tone of the book.[73] The content is political, not in any finger-pointing way, but in that it accentuates for view the most ugly, decadent, disjointed, sinister and threatening underlying realities, not as aspects of life, but present in all of life—the extraordinary in the ordinary, and, what is worst, the ordinariness of the extraordinary.

Endnotes

1. Michael Gray, *Song and Dance Man III* (London: Cassel, 2000), 59.
2. "The Girl from the North Country," in *Wanted Man: In Search of Bob Dylan,* ed. John Bauldie (New York: Citadel Press, 1991), 20.
3. Allen Ginsberg, "On the New Dylan," *Georgia Straight,* May 25, 1971.
4. Frank Davey, "Leonard Cohen and Bob Dylan: Poetry and the Popular Song," available at http://www.terabit.net/icho/cohint-davey69.htm.
5. Adrienne Clarkson, "Counterpoint Leonard Cohen," in *Intricate Preparations,* ed. Stephen Scobie (Toronto: ECW Press, 2000), 2.
6. Cited in L. S. Dorman and C. L. Rawlins, *Leonard Cohen: Prophet of the Heart* (London: Omnibus Press, 1990), 178.
7. www.geocities.com/Athens/Forum/2667.
8. James Abbott McNeill Whistler, "The Ten O'Clock Lecture," in *The New Oxford Book of English Prose* (Oxford: Oxford University Press, 1998), 532.
9. Aidan Day, *Jokerman: Reading the Lyrics of Bob Dylan* (Oxford: Basil Blackwell, 1988).
10. Richard Poirier, "Learning from the Beatles," in *The Performing Self* (London: Chatto & Windus, 1971), 134–135.
11. Quoted in George Stein, *Edie: An American Biography* (New York: Dell, 1983), 228.
12. Maurice Ratcliff, *The Complete Guide to the Music of Leonard Cohen* (London: Omnibus, 1999), 29.
13. Ibid., 19.
14. Ibid., 80.
15. Ibid.
16. From *The New Oxford Book of English Prose,* ed. John Gross (Oxford: Oxford University Press, 1998), 533–534.
17. Wallace Fowlie, *Rimbaud and Jim Morrison* (Durham, NC, and London: Duke University Press, 1994), 43–44.
18. Michael Beaney, ed., *The Frege Reader* (Oxford: Blackwell Publishers, 1997).
19. E. D. Hirsch Jr., *The Aims of Interpretation* (Chicago: University of Chicago Press, 1976), 49.
20. Stephen Scobie, *Leonard Cohen* (Vancouver: Douglas & McIntyre, 1978), xi.
21. *London Sunday Times,* July 17, 1988.
22. Leo Strauss, *Persecution and the Art of Writing* (Glencoe, IL: The Free Press, 1952). One of his most famous interpretations is that of Niccolò Machiavelli as the most evil man in history. See Leo Strauss, *Thoughts on Machiavelli* (Seattle and London: University of Washington Press, 1969).

23. Geoffrey Stokes, *The Rolling Stone History of Rock and Roll* (New York: Summit Books, 1986), 390.

24. Gray, *Song and Dance Man III*, 1.

25. Greil Marcus, "Let the Record Play Itself," *San Francisco Express-Times*, February 11, 1969.

26. Stephen Scobie, *Alias Bob Dylan* (Alberta, Canada: Red Deer Press, 1991).

27. Gray, *Song and Dance Man III*, 54, 65, 70, 76, 77.

28. Patrick Crotty, "Bob Dylan's Last Words," in *Do You Mr Jones?: Bob Dylan with the Poets and Professors*, ed. Neil Corcoran (London: Chatto & Windus, 2002), 322–323.

29. Greil Marcus, *Invisible Republic: Bob Dylan's Basement Tapes* (London: Picador, 1998), 87.

30. Michael Ondaatje, *Leonard Cohen* (Toronto: McClelland & Stewart, 1970), 6.

31. George Woodcock, "The Song of the Sirens: Reflections on Leonard Cohen," in *Leonard Cohen: The Artist and His Critics,* ed. Michael Gnarowski (Toronto: McGraw-Hill, 1976), 155–156.

32. Rowman and Rawlins, *Prophet of the Heart*, 306.

33. Desmond Pacey, "The Phenomenon of Leonard Cohen," *Canadian Literature* 34 (1967). In fairness, it must be added that Pacey's intention is to show how the book *Beautiful Losers* is the culmination of Cohen's own work and artistic development and not the intimation of that of others.

34. Woodcock, "The Song of the Sirens," 156–157.

35. Scobie, *Leonard Cohen,* 24.

36. Gray, *Song and Dance Man III*, 72.

37. Rudolf Makkreel, *Dilthey: Philosopher of the Human Studies* (Princeton, NJ: Princeton University Press, 1975), 328.

38. Henry Jones, *Browning as a Philosophical and Religious Teacher* (Glasgow: Maclehose, 1896), 321–322.

39. Gray, *Song and Dance Man III,* 71, citing F. R. Leavis, *New Bearings in English Poetry* (1932).

40. Michael Oakeshott, *The Modes of Experience* (Cambridge: Cambridge University Press, 1933).

41. Cited in Roddy Lumsden, "While the King Was Looking Down," in *The Message: Crossing the Tracks between Poetry and Pop,* ed. Roddy Lumsden and Stephen Troussé (London: The Poetry Society, 1999), 95.

42. Kenneth Allsop, "Beat and Ballad," in *The Dylan Companion,* ed. Elizabeth Thompson and David Gutman (New York: Da Capo, 2001), 98.

43. Paul Williams, *Bob Dylan, Watching the River Flow: Observations in Progress, 1966–1995* (London: Omnibus, 1996), 19.

44. John Harris, "In Praise of Bob Dylan," *Q Dylan* (2000): 12.

45. Jones, *Browning as a Philosophical and Religious Teacher*, 2nd ed., 3.

46. Scobie, *Leonard Cohen,* xi.

47. Paul Ricoeur, "The Hermeneutical Function of Distanciation," in *Hermeneutics and the Human Sciences*, ed. and trans. John B. Thompson (Cambridge: Cambridge University Press, 1981).

48. Bob Dylan, in the 1966 *Playboy* interview, reprinted in *Bob Dylan: The Early Years—a Retrospective,* ed. Craig McGregor (New York: Da Capo Press, 1990; first published 1972), 132.

49. See Hans-Georg Gadamer, *Truth and Method* (London: Sheed & Ward, 1985).

50. R. G. Collingwood, *The Principles of Art* (Oxford: Oxford University Press, 1937).

51. Paul Williams, *Bob Dylan, Performing Artist 1960–73* (London: Omnibus, 1994), 3.

52. R. G. Collingwood, *Speculum Mentis or the Map of Knowledge* (Oxford: Oxford University Press, 1924).

53. Michael Oakeshott, "The Voice of Poetry in the Conversation of Mankind," in *Rationalism in Politics and Other Essays,* ed. Timothy Fuller (Indianapolis: Liberty Press, 1991), 503.

54. Ibid., 527.

55. Jones, *Browning as a Religious and Philosophical Teacher,* 3.

56. Oakeshott, "Voice of Poetry," 524.

57. Federico García Lorca, "Imaginación, inspiración, evasión," in *Obras completas III: prosa,* ed. Miguel García-Posada (Barcelona: Galaxia Gutenberg, 1997). The quotation comes from "El

Defensor de Grenada," *Granada,* October 11, 1928. I am indebted to Lisa Davies for translating the text.

58. Ibid.

59. Derek Harris, cited in Federico García Lorca, *Poet in New York,* ed. Christopher Maurer, trans. Greg Simon and Steven F. White (London: Penguin, 1990), xiv.

60. The text comes from "El Sol," *Madrid,* February 16, 1929.

61. Oakeshott, "Voice of Poetry," 488–541.

62. Nora Epron and Susan Edmiston, "Bob Dylan Interview," in *Bob Dylan: The Early Years, a Retrospective,* ed. Craig McGregor (New York: Da Capo Press, 1990), 86.

63. C. P. Lee, *Like the Night: Bob Dylan and the Road to the Manchester Free Trade Hall* (London: Helter Skelter, 1998), 124.

64. Cited by Allen Ginsberg, "Bob Dylan and Renaldo and Clara," in *Wanted Man: In Search of Bob Dylan,* ed. John Bauldie (New York: Citadel Press, 1991), 122.

65. Cited in Clinton Heylin, *Dylan the Biography: Behind the Shades* (Harmondsworth: Penguin, 1998: first published 1991), 125.

66. Dylan, "The *Playboy* Interview," in McGregor, *Bob Dylan,* 132.

67. Cited in Heylin, *Behind the Shades,* 129.

68. Paul Barrera, *Leonard Cohen: Came So Far for Love* (Andover, NH: Agenda, 1997), 17, 57.

69. Doug Beardsley, "On First Looking into Leonard Cohen," in *Intricate Preparations,* ed. Stephen Scobie (Toronto: ECW Press, 2000), 8.

70. Douglas Barbour, "Canadian Books," *Dalhousie Review* 58 (1968): 568. Reprinted in *Leonard Cohen: The Artist and His Critics,* ed. Michael Gnarowski (Toronto: McGraw-Hill: 1976), 39.

71. Biba Kopf, "Jenny Sings Lenny," *The New Musical Express,* March 14, 1987.

72. Cohen interviewed by Stephen Williams, "The Confessions of Leonard Cohen," *Toronto Life* (February 1978): 48.

73. Scobie, *Leonard Cohen,* 46.

7

DYLAN FROM MAGIC TO POETRY

"What do you think of Bob Dylan?" The premier songwriter of our generation. Still and always. He happens to be resting. He deserves a rest but have no fear, he will be back with much information and data about repose in the '90s.[1]

At this point, I want to apply the theories we have discussed in Chapter 6 to Bob Dylan's writings, but first I would like to deal with a possible objection. Given that Dylan is so unequivocally associated with the political activism of the civil rights movement, wouldn't it be more appropriate to explore his work through a theory directly applicable to social movements? Serge Denisoff, for example, has attempted to classify protest songs and their function in American left-wing social movements.[2] The first type of songs he calls magnetic, in that they serve the function of attracting new adherents to the cause or strengthen the resolve of those already committed. They are songs that encourage mobilization by relying on relatively simple and often well-known melodies, use repetitive verse for audience participation, and have uncomplicated and direct messages. Their music itself is secondary, merely vehicles for delivering simple messages.

The second category of songs is what he calls rhetorical. Their focus is on expressing indignation and dissent, a counter to the dominant images of the age, but bereft of solutions to the problems they highlight. They are, in general, much more of a vehicle for musical innovation and sophistication than the "magnet" songs allow, but nevertheless they allow scope for lyrical expression. Denisoff argues that these are the types of protest songs that became prevalent in the 1960s, but they had very little measurable political impact.

This functionalist approach has many limitations. First, it is utilitarian, equating means and ends, demanding justification in terms of utility, the measure of the usefulness of the songs being political activism. However, political activism is not the only measure of the purpose of a song and, indeed, may be almost impossible to measure in any meaningful way. The expression of discomfort, dissatisfaction, disillusionment, and despair may have a corrosive effect on the fundamental and unquestioned principles of society without having to incite direct action. Second, the songs may keep alive the continuity of the struggle against perceived injustice and provide the necessary social cohesiveness in holding common-minded people together, by linking them with the past and with their fellow sufferers or protesters. In other words, they serve to forge and perpetuate identities, which are alternatives to the identities that the authorities seek to impose on them. The songs demand that their identities be recognized and implicitly realize that misrecognition, an imposed alien identity, is just as much a form of oppression as any other, and perhaps more insidious in that it deprives one of one's self-respect and the cultural and ideological roots to which one belongs. Third, this approach is not sensitive to the poetic element in song, and indeed dismisses anything that is not overtly political or "magnetic" as of questionable value. It is not a theory that allows us to explore the diversity of Dylan's songs and doesn't really enable us to distinguish the early Dylan from the later, or from the whole host of his contemporaries, such as Phil Ochs, Tom Paxton, and P. F. Sloan. In that the theory's criterion of worth is the song's utility, it is questionable whether the usefulness of the poetic is a legitimate avenue to explore, and even if it is, it cannot be taken to be exhaustive.

Dylan wrote many overtly political songs that reflected the growing unrest in the country with racism, war, social injustice, and bigotry. For a two-year period from January 1962 Dylan wrote an almost endless flow of topical or protest songs. This coincides with the time he and Suze Rotolo lived together. Rotolo came from a family whose sympathies were with the Left, and at the age of seventeen she was working as a volunteer, filling envelopes for the Congress of Racial Equality (CORE). As we've mentioned, Dylan's first serious protest song, "The Death of Emmett Till" (does not appear on any Dylan LP), which condemns racial violence and segregation, was written for a benefit concert on February 23, 1963. It was entirely congruent with the work of CORE but not, strictly speaking, a topical song, in that its subject was a racial murder that had been committed in 1955. "The Death of Emmett Till" relates the story of the murder of a young black man by a white gang and the subsequent acquittal of two of the accused by a jury that included some of their accomplices. The song says that there was a reason for the killing, but it doesn't say what it was. (In fact, Emmett Till had whistled at a white woman.) The song lacks the subtlety that Dylan was gradually to develop and was indistinguishable from the type of expression common among fellow finger pointers, who spelled out the problem in great detail and gave the prescriptions for solving it. More explicit than most of his protest songs, in "The Death of Emmett Till" Dylan is forceful in his injunction to resist and to condemn the Ku Klux Klan and all racial hatred. He followed this song with "Talkin' John Birch Paranoid Blues" (*The Bootleg Series*), a powerful attack on the extreme right-wing John Birch Society, ridiculing its paranoia about Communists.

Dylan was nevertheless uncomfortable about being called a writer of protest songs. Most of these songs have not appeared on his officially released albums and exist only in bootleg versions or in radio archives. In 1991 Sony released a set of three bootleg albums, the first of which included such songs as "Let Me Die In My Footsteps," "Talkin' John Birch Paranoid Blues," "Walls of Red Wing," and "Who Killed Davey Moore?" Dylan himself viewed the composition of his earlier songs in the same way that Collingwood viewed art as magic. Dylan maintained that "the songs before the fourth record, I used to know what I wanted to say before I wrote the song."[3]

Dylan's early protest songs are clearly injunctive in their intent. Most even draw the moral for the listener. These songs are meant to charge the audience emotionally, channeling this emotion into active support for political causes. Some are direct exhortations to act, calling upon the audience to do something about a particular situation or injustice. In an interview in 1963, Dylan was explicit about his intent: "What comes out in my music is a call to action."[4] Indeed, in 1963 what was important for him were not the melodies, many of which he borrowed anyway, but the words.[5] In other songs, Dylan sought the same effect more subtly through graphic images, like the powerful "Only a Pawn in Their Game," about the murder of Medgar Evers, the leader of the Mississippi branch of the National Association for the Advancement of Colored People, in June 1963, or "The Lonesome Death of Hattie Carroll," or sometimes in songs with a poignant tale of hardship, like "North Country Blues," which are meant to evoke the appropriate emotion—dread, disgust, despair, anger, sympathy—but rarely resignation. Their purpose is to generate a collective revulsion, a growing tide of outrage against the "system."

A number of songs sum up Dylan's whole attitude to the conventional and accepted inheritance from the previous generation. His topical songs of this period are typical yet distinctive in the civil rights movement. They are songs that engender collective identity, not through the originality of their lyrics or innovative musical style, but because they lent themselves to be communally sung. The folk revival was very much based on a collective identity and common form of expression, and the success of performers such as Paxton, Ochs, Pete Seeger, Joan Baez, Judy Collins, and Buffy Sainte-Marie was the participatory nature of their songs and the emotive content of their lyrics. The singers demanded participation and often led by example in gathering an ensemble of performers on stage. Songs of this type include Dylan's "Ye Playboys and Playgirls," "Blowin' in the Wind," and "The Times They Are A-Changin'." In "Ye Playboys and Playgirls," Dylan defiantly announces that he won't be beaten into submission by fashionable society, war profiteers, racist lynch mobs, and Jim Crow (segregationist) laws. He will not, he says, allow any of these to dictate his own way of behaving, "not now or no other time." When he says "They ain't gonna run my world," it is a rallying cry to the collective, not a personal statement, but the expression of the stance of a generation of people determined to bring about political change, emotion-ally charged and willing to give their practical support to political causes. In fact, the version of this song was sung by Dylan with Pete Seeger at the 1963 Newport Folk Festival (*Newport Broadside*, Vanguard); here, the audience was encouraged to sing along, emphasizing the collective rather than the individual defiance of the song. Another song sung at this same festival and to the same purpose and effect was "Blowin' in the Wind," which Dylan sang with Peter, Paul, and Mary, Joan Baez, the Freedom Singers, Pete Seeger, and Theodore Bikel (*Evening Concerts at Newport*, vol. 1, Vanguard). This is one of the classic protest songs of the 1960s and appeared first on *The Freewheelin' Bob Dylan*.

The album *The Times They Are A-Changin'* has been criticized by Clinton Heylin for its almost unrelenting pessimism and its monotone, even monot-onous, intensity and high moralism, adding up to a "gruelling listening experience."[6] This seems to me to be an unduly harsh criticism of a collection of material that is far from homogeneous and continues the transformation of finger-pointing songs. Both "The Times They Are A-Changin' " and "When the Ship Comes In" are not pessimistic. It is true that they are songs about destruction, but they exude a confidence in renewal—a renewal that transcends the injustices and corruption of the present. Both songs have similar messages and are defiantly optimistic in the face of adversity because of the belief in the inevitability of the tide of change. The metaphor of water is used to drive home the same message in both songs: accept the inevitability of change or drown, like Pharaoh's army, in the growing tide of resistance and demands for social justice.

"The Times They Are A-Changin' " became the anthem of a generation. Such songs unite people and allow them to feel that they belong to a like-minded community, that they believe in the same cause. "The Times They Are A-Changin' " exudes confidence, effectively articulating for the first time a social change that began to occur in the 1950s and what later became known as the generation gap. It is conciliatory in that it offers the opportunity for the older generation, particularly politicians, not merely to accept, but to go with the flow. It is uncompromising in that they are told to participate on the terms of the new generation, or get out of the way:

Come mothers and fathers throughout the land
And don't criticize what you can't understand
Your sons and your daughters are beyond your command
The old road is rapidly agin'
Please get out of the new one if you can't lend your hand
For the times they are a-changin'.

It is definitely a song with a preconceived purpose and a clear sense of who Dylan's audience is, as Dylan himself explained in the notes to his retrospective album *Biograph*.

Like many of the singers he admired, Dylan continued to mine the rich seam of topical song material, the division between blacks and whites. "Ballad of Donald White," "The Death of Emmett Till," and "The Lonesome Death of Hattie Carroll" deal with the injustices and prejudices of the American legal system from the point of view of the victim. In the first, the victim is the convicted murderer who sought help but whose voice was not heard. He was a man who had no parents and no friends, and who could not adjust to society. He realized that society needed protecting from him and asked to be returned to an institution. He was sentenced to death for his crime, and the song ends with White wondering how many had taken heed of his words, how many unfortunate boys deprived of opportunities in life would walk the same road as him, and asks if they are really enemies or victims of society. The second, preserved as a recording of the show *Broadsider* in May 1962, tells of the murder of a black man from Chicago by a group of white men out for "some fun" in a Mississippi town. After stirring the emotions of the listener, the song ends with an exhortation to all like-minded people who want to make America a greater place in which to live, to act in order to bring about justice and make human rights a reality. It is very much in the populist, rousing style of Woody Guthrie, patriotic with a cutting-edge, antiestablishment bent.

This populist tendency in Dylan surfaces throughout his career. "Union Sundown" on the album *Infidels*, for example, bemoans the cosmopolitanism of capitalism manifest in the array of countries from which everyday consumables emanate. His point is that capitalism is unscrupulous and immoral, always ready to exploit cheap labor in foreign countries at the expense of American jobs. Unions, the traditional protectors of working people, have themselves become big business, and they have ceased to serve their purpose and are becoming obsolete. Democracy, Dylan asserts, is an illusion, and it is force and violence that rule the world. It is a championing of the working man and the principles of enterprise and adventure that permeated the New World, and a condemnation of the greed that has undermined and subverted those principles.

To further illustrate Dylan's use of art to arouse emotion and motivate a politically conscious public to act, let us look at his antiwar songs. Among them we find reflected the growing fear among the population in general of nuclear war. On *The Freewheelin' Bob Dylan* there are two explicitly antiwar songs, "Masters of War" and "Talking World War III Blues." There was to have been a third, "Let Me Die in My Footsteps," which is a defiant protest against civil defense advocates, or "fall-out shelter sellers," as he calls them in "Ye Playboys and Playgirls." Dylan sings that he would rather die in his footsteps than go underground and suffer a living death. In the final verse he exhorts everyone to delight in the natural beauty of the American landscape, and like him to refuse to cooperate with the peddlers of nuclear war.

"Masters of War" is a venomous attack on those in authority who use war as an extension of policy, orchestrating destruction and hiding behind their desks in mansions while young men are sent to their deaths. It is an expression of utter contempt for the evil inflicted on the world by these men. Dylan likens them to the filth that runs down drains, and he expresses his wish that they all die, leaving the world a much better place. Their sins are so horrendous that "even Jesus would never forgive" what they do. (After Dylan became a born-again Christian, he dropped the reference to Jesus.) Dylan himself never saw the song as antiwar. Instead, it was directed at the vast military-industrial complex in the United States, of which President Eisenhower had warned and which had a vested interest in initiating and conducting wars. Dylan's song and concern reflect that of the Beat Generation's opposition to the civilizational values that the military-industrial complex generated. The writings of Burroughs, Hunke,

Ginsberg, and Kerouac warned of the dangers of those people in whose hands such vast power was entrusted.

I want to emphasize again that Dylan's finger-pointing phase may have been eclipsed for a time, but it continued to reemerge periodically throughout his recording career. For example, his born-again Christianity is not the only surprising thing about the album *Slow Train Coming* (1979). It also heralds a return to social criticism that so clearly distinguished the material of the early 1960s. In it there are no extended narratives, as we find on the earlier albums, such as "Oxford Town," "Only a Pawn in Their Game," and "The Lonesome Death of Hattie Carroll," but there is the reemergence of the community ethic. Here, Dylan condemns the hedonism, materialism, and individualism that partially characterized the albums of 1965–1967, as well as adultery, hypocrisy, corruption, pornography, and failing to live by one's conscience. He despairs at the oppression perpetrated by the old upon the young, by the young upon the old, and by the rich upon the poor. Dylan warns of the spiritual wars between religions, making it clear that Buddhism and Islam are threats to the "true" religion. He condemns false ideologies, including Marxism and capitalism, for polluting people's thoughts, multinational corporations and foreign interests for controlling and manipulating the American economy through oil ownership, and the conspicuous consumption of the Arab oil producers: "Sheikhs walkin' around like kings, wearing fancy jewels and nose rings" ("Slow Train").

These themes continued to preoccupy Dylan throughout the succeeding years, as, for example, in the moral stand he takes in "Political World" on the 1989 album *Oh Mercy*. Again, from a deep religious conviction, Dylan paints a picture of decaying values, a degenerate world "where mercy walks the plank," of directionless masses, the devaluation and denigration of wisdom, and the rejection of peace as the ultimate aim among nations. This presaged a period when Dylan's songwriting ability eluded him, and he reverted to recording some of the blues and country-blues songs he had encountered in his youth. It also marked a return to solo acoustic guitar and harmonica accompaniment. The most interesting feature of the reversion, however, is the heavily political terms in which he describes what each song is about on *World Gone Wrong* (1993). This is best illustrated by juxtaposing what Harry Smith says about the song "Stackalee" (sometimes seen as "Stack A Lee," as on Dylan's album, and as "Stagger Lee") on *The Anthology of American Folk Music*. Smith, in his usual cryptic manner, says: "THEFT OF STETSON HAT CAUSES DEADLY DISPUTE. VICTIM IDENTIFIES SELF AS FAMILY MAN." He goes on to say that the murder happened in Memphis in about 1900, and that

CBS publicity to coincide with Dylan's 1965 tour of Britain.

"Stackalee" was probably related to the Lee family, who owned a fleet of steamliners on the Mississippi.[7] (The real "Stag" Lee Shelton, the apparent subject of this song, is legendary for his ferocity. On Christmas Day, 1895, he killed Billy Lyons in a saloon in St. Louis and thereafter embarked upon an unrelenting wave of violence.)

Contrast Smith's explanation with Dylan's attempt to make the theme more relevant to contemporary times. Dylan maintains in the liner notes to *World Gone Wrong* that the song says

> no man gains immortality thru public acclaim. truth is shadowy. . . . the song says that a man's hat is his crown. . . . No rights without duties is the name of the game and fame is a trick. He is not some egotistical degraded existentialist dionysian idiot, neither does he represent any alternative lifestyle scam (give me a thousand acres of tractable land and all the gang members that exist and you'll see the Authentic lifestyle, the Agrarian one).

In fact, all of the songs on the album are chosen not because they represent a traditional musical genre, but because they have continuing relevance. They may have been composed at a certain time, but their relevance is timeless.

Dylan constantly reworked his old protest songs and included them in his sets. In 1975, for example, in the Rolling Thunder Revue (released as volume 5 in *The Bootleg Series*) and the autumn 2002 Stateswide Tour, he included a powerful version of "The Lonesome Death of Hattie Carroll." On the *Bootleg* recording, Dylan called upon those in the audience who might have some political pull to help get Rubin Carter released from prison. He then launched into one of his most powerful finger-pointing songs, "Hurricane" (cowritten with Jacques Levy).

Even now, when he is inclined to say very little other than to introduce his band, political points are often made forcefully. Take, for example, the two concerts at New York's Madison Square Garden on November 11 and 13, 2002. On the first night, Dylan entered the stage wearing a military-style jacket with red trim and red piping down the outside leg of the trousers. The suit was black and served to highlight the scarlet red. The paramilitary uniform introduced a note of irony into the event, held on Veterans Day, which in 2002 was dedicated to those U.S. soldiers currently in service in the war against terrorism. Veterans had marched down Fifth Avenue that same morning, and President George W. Bush had warned of the threat that Iraq posed to the United States and of the determination of his administration to invade if Saddam Hussein failed to comply with the United Nations resolution to readmit weapons inspectors. Dylan stood at an electric piano for the opening numbers of the set, the first of which was "Tweedle Dee and Tweedle Dum" off *Love and Theft*. He and his band then reverted to acoustic guitars for the most pointed song of the night—"Masters of War." Its significance was not lost on the audience, who spontaneously cheered as Dylan rasped, "And I hope that you die, and that your death will come soon." (The song was dropped from the set on the next night, however.) The next song, for which Dylan returned to the piano, was a different, but effective, rendition of "It's Alright Ma," and in recognition of the continuation of the theme, the audience cheered on hearing the words "But even the president of the United States sometimes must have to stand naked."[8] In the second show at Madison Square Garden Dylan substituted "Blowin' in the Wind" and "The Times They Are A-Changin" for "Masters of War" and "The Lonesome Death of Hattie Carroll," demonstrating unequivocally that he had lost none of the political edge in forty years of performing.

These are only two of many occasions when Dylan's political consciousness has surfaced at significant and poignant moments. Before television cameras in 1991, while receiving a National Association of Recording Arts and Sciences Lifetime Achievement Award, Dylan sang "Masters of War" in response to the ongoing Gulf War. The words were enunciated in a rushed and mumbled manner, and the song was almost indecipherable. The political point was lost, as actor Jack Nicholson, obviously and unashamedly amused, then handed Dylan the award. Dylan's faltering speech of acceptance silenced the audience, however, when he related some wisdom his father had passed on to him: "Son, it's possible to become so defiled in this world that your own mother and father will abandon you. And if that happens, God will always believe in your ability to mend your ways."[9] This explains why, when Dylan sings "Masters of War," he has ceased to use the line "Even Jesus would never forgive what you do."

What Makes Dylan Special?

Dylan, of course, is only one in a long line of protest singers and balladeers who chronicled the injustices of their societies. What makes his protest songs so special? Dylan's own explanation is overly modest. He maintains that what differentiates him is "attitude." He plays folk music with a rock-and-roll attitude that has enabled him to cut through the mundane and be heard.[10] Like Woody Guthrie, he has a talent for using humor and irony, even sarcasm, in conveying a political message. But in addition, his songs are on the whole subtle rather than sloganeering, powerful without being crass, emotional without being sentimental. Joan Baez thought the beauty of Dylan's protest songs in comparison with others was their understatement: "He wrote songs that hadn't been written yet."[11]

Michael Gray criticizes Dylan's protest songs for having hardly anything in them but clichéd messages. He argues that it is not so much the clichés but the fact that Dylan thinks clichés are necessary for emphasis that mar the songs.[12] Here, I think that Gray has missed the subtlety of the songs and fails to appreciate their uniqueness in relation to the tradition to which Dylan belongs. This is because he is too concerned with identifying the similarities between Dylan and his so-called influences rather than detecting the very real differences. Dylan elevates the protest song into an altogether more sophisticated medium.

The music and the delivery of the words are congruent with the subtlety of the message. There are songs, such as "Ballad of Donald White" and "The Death of Emmett Till," in which Dylan plays the traditional role of the folksinger, reporting and highlighting the social condition of his times, but he is never merely doing this. There is a strong sense of social conditioning in his songs: the perpetrators of crime are just as much victims as the victims themselves. Personal responsibility is often absorbed into societal responsibility. In both "Who Killed Davey Moore?" and "Only a Pawn in Their Game," the guitar is biting and the voice of the interrogator raspingly accusatory. In the former, the accused are assertively defensive. "Who Killed Davey Moore / Why an' what's the reason for?" elicits denials from the referee, the angry crowd, Moore's manager, the gambler, the boxing writer, and finally the opponent. The song doesn't actually attribute blame to any of them individually, but to society collectively for encouraging and condoning boxing as a sport. Dylan uses the same technique in his account of the murder of Medgar Evers in "Only a Pawn in Their Game." His death shocked more liberal-minded Americans and impelled President Kennedy to abandon his attempts at appeasement and take a more aggressive stance toward desegregation in the South. Both he and his brother Robert Kennedy, the attorney general, attended the funeral, and the Evers family were invited to the White House as a gesture of solidarity. The incident was one that immediately aroused the condemnation of protest singers. Phil Ochs, for example, labored the moral of the story in a dull and dreary narrative form in "The Ballad of Medgar Evers," doing little to arouse passion or indignation because of its sanctimonious tone.

In "Only a Pawn in Their Game," the killer of Medgar Evers is himself portrayed as the victim of institutionalized racism, taught to believe that the laws justifiably protect his white skin. He is filled with irrational hatred and used by the officers of law and order to perpetuate racially motivated criminal acts that promote and protect their vested interests. It is an indictment of the whole of society, portraying both the murdered and the murderer as victims. Dylan performed this song for the first time at a voters' registration rally in Greenwood, Mississippi, on July 6, 1963, footage of which provides the retrospective in D. A. Pennebaker's film *Don't Look Back* as an answer to the question asked for the listeners of the BBC World Service, "where did it all begin?"

Again, in "The Lonesome Death of Hattie Carroll," Dylan does not employ a simple hectoring style. Instead, the song builds to an intensity of feeling by taking the listener through different degrees of indignation and pity, postponing their expression at the end of each verse with the words "Now ain't the time for your tears." The particular incident itself, a true story of murder by a young socialite of a black waitress in Maryland who was slow to bring the drink he had ordered, is used to build the emotional intensity, but the expression of grief and sadness is reserved for institutional failure and hypocrisy. The charade of courtroom dignity, honor, justice, and equality before the law is exposed by the murderer's six-month sentence. What Dylan is saying is that while we have a deep sympathy with the victim, what we really need to weep for is a society that feigns justice and equality with a false dignity and grace in establishment institutions that exude an appearance of equality divorced from the reality of racism.

The whole force of these songs is not merely in the words, but in the performance. These songs are particularistic in that they identify a specific incident or subject from which generalizations are drawn or which can be inferred by the listener. But Dylan was also capable of writing protest songs without a specific point of reference, but which were nevertheless capable of summing up the human predicament in a way that resonated with every sympathetic and disaffected individual. "Blowin' in the Wind," for example, celebrates the dynamic progressive feature of humankind, inquisitiveness. It does not pretend to give answers, but instead emphasizes the importance of the questioning activity: there never will be any answers if the questions are not first asked. The song has a surface appearance of fatality and resignation, with an undercurrent of self-assertion. It raises the question, how many—How many deaths? How many times?—and implies that collectively we will determine when all such injustices cease. The inspiration for the song came from the idea that those who didn't speak out were betraying themselves by their silence.[13] To be silent was to be complicit in the crime; to speak out, to ask questions, was at the very least to begin the process of collective self-reflection, a demand of the authorities to justify and defend what they take for granted.

It would be a mistake to think that because Dylan often puts an emphasis on social responsibility that he wishes to absolve the individual of personal responsibility and guilt. We saw earlier that, in his acceptance speech for the Tom Paine Award, Dylan had implied that there was something of Lee Harvey Oswald in all of us, and that society was so confused and mixed up that this was bound to be reflected in the individuals who comprise it. After the furor, Dylan took the opportunity to clarify his position on collective and individual responsibility in a letter he sent to the Emergency Civil Liberties Committee. In it, Dylan expressed his unease at having to give an acceptance speech. The uncertainty he felt was exactly that which Mister Jones was later to be characterized as feeling in "Ballad of a Thin Man" (*Highway 61 Revisited*): "Because something is happening here / But you don't know what it is." He explained that perhaps he should have sung, but that the award was not for singing, but for what he had sung. Something else was expected of him, but he didn't know what it was, and it made him feel uncomfortable. He explained that when he spoke of Oswald, he was speaking of the times and not the deed of the assassination itself. He did not want to say that we all share in the blame for every church bombing, gun killing, person in poverty, or presidential assassination. Each person must take responsibility for his or her actions. The times affect each person, and if there is violence in the times, some of that violence is in each of us. We each receive what is there to be received, we are not deaf or mute, yet we can go on from there to do something about it.[14]

Using his art as magic, the arousal of emotions for their practical effects, is only one side of Bob Dylan in the early albums. We also get intimations of a sense of art as the expression of emotion. "Don't Think Twice, It's All Right" (*Freewheelin' Bob Dylan*) and "Boots of Spanish Leather" (*The Times They Are A-Changin'*) are love songs about the personal relationship he had with Suze Rotolo.

These songs portray art as representation. The subject matter in each is unambiguous, although its point of reference may not be explicit. They are emotionally expressive songs depicting a state or condition in which the singer finds himself. These are essentially a foretaste of the personal exploration of relationships that we find on *Another Side of Bob Dylan*, the album that generated a great deal of criticism from Dylan's Greenwich

Village friends. Regarding these songs, you could ask questions about outside referents. But on that album we also get a foretaste of what Dylan called a "hallucination . . . atery song." Here art is no longer representation, but fragmentation, abstract images, emotionally demanding yet having no direct intent. One such song on the album is "Chimes of Freedom," which he began to write in February 1964 while traveling with three companions around America almost permanently stoned, and which he performed in May of that year on Granada Television's *Hallelujah*, introduced by Sidney Carter, who told the audience that Dylan was hailed as the new Guthrie and was one of the foremost voices of social protest. Dylan sang both an up-tempo version of "Don't Think Twice, It's All Right" and "Chimes of Freedom," neither of which conformed to the picture painted by Carter in the introduction. What, then, did Dylan mean by "hallucination . . . atery song"? Essentially he is talking about an abstract song, not necessarily induced by hallucinogenics, whose lyrics conjure up images with scattered referents, with no particular story, but which may have a point or many points, without needing to be stated. "Chimes of Freedom" was in fact influenced by Rimbaud. Rimbaud, as we saw, recommended a disorienting of the senses in order to induce the gift of visionary imagery.

Unlike many other protest singers of the 1960s, Dylan had an ability to conjure up the image, without having to spell out the message in literal terms. That is, he had an ability to stimulate the imagination of the listener, rather than foreclose it with too literal a representation of his message.

How can someone say something without saying it? There are all sorts of things that we do with words without having to use the words themselves. A joke relies on the audience picking up on the fact that, in saying what you are saying, you intend to be humorous. This is what John Austin called the illocutionary force of a sentence and what Quentin Skinner elaborated into the idea of what someone intends to mean *in* saying something as opposed to *by* saying it.[15] By singing "Chimes of Freedom," Dylan intended to fulfill his commitment to Granada Television and pick up his pay check. *In* singing "Chimes of Freedom," he may have intended to convey a glimmer of hope to all those oppressed by psychological, sociological, or physiological afflictions, without explicitly articulating the idea that fate or destiny is on their side in the tolling of the bells of liberty. In Phil Ochs' "There But for Fortune" and Ralph McTell's "Streets of London," whose melodies and intonations are incongruous with the lyrics, we are introduced to the victims of society and told not to be judgmental of them, but of the system. There but for the grace of God, they say, we could all be the drunk, the down and out, the prisoner.

Take the subtlety of Dylan's treatment of the subject of the nuclear threat in comparison with that of his contemporaries. P. F. Sloan's "Eve of Destruction," the 1965 hit for Barry McGuire, for example, leaves you in no doubt after hearing a graphic catalog of war, hatred, and violence, that those who don't "believe we are on the eve of destruction" are somehow deficient in their powers of comprehension. It is a stark, literal, berating account, designed to cajole and intimidate those in power with rather a crass and an obvious narrative. (The song at the time was banned on many radio stations out on the West Coast because critics maintained it gave "aid and comfort" to the Vietcong and could possibly incite violence in the "hot" urban ghettos.[16])

Even in relation to some of the other protest songs, Dylan talks of them as expressions of what "he" is feeling, portraying them in an intensely personal way, and almost severing them from the audience in his mind. One of his most intense songs is "A Hard Rain's A-Gonna Fall." In it, Dylan expresses his emotions not in any literal, narrative, or descriptive way, but abstractly, often through disconnected images, not through a story or a portrayal of a situation. It is doubtful that he had any intention to arouse any particular emotions in his audience to any practical effect. In "Rain," the singer responds to a series of questions posed by an interested, nonjudgmental, caring parent figure. The questions are simple: Where have you been? What have you seen? What have you heard? Who have you met? What will you do now? The answers are a series of evocative images, mostly disconnected, but in the first three verses the number 10,000 is repeated. The singer has been "ten thousand miles in the mouth of a graveyard," has seen "ten thousand talkers whose tongues were all broken," has heard "ten thousand whisperin' and nobody listenin'." The notes to *The Freewheelin' Bob Dylan* suggest that this song was written during the Cuban missile crisis of 1962 (although there is some doubt about this) and represents an expression of what feelings the crisis generated in Dylan. Anthony Scaduto is sensitive to what Dylan is doing when he writes: " 'Hard Rain' is filled with spare, sparkling images that evoke the terrors of national injustice and of international-insanity-diplomacy[,] [n]ever mentioning nuclear war or fallout, the evils of segregation or man's inhumanity to his own kind, but forcing the listener to conjure with such terror out of his own emotions."[17] It is not a polemical protest song, but as Nat Hentoff says in the liner notes, it is a transmutation of Dylan's "fierce convictions into what can only be called art." Tom Paxton, one of the first to hear the song, said that it very quickly became acclaimed by Dylan's fans as his greatest work to date, and Dave Van Ronk maintained

181

that everyone became intensely aware that it heralded an artistic revolution.[18] Paul Williams talks about the song in terms similar to those that inform R. G. Collingwood's characterization of art proper. He suggests that Dylan wrote it with no preconceived idea of what it should mean, nor with a calculated intent on what it should evoke in his audience, but nevertheless with a sensitivity to the effect upon the listener.[19]

As we saw earlier, by the end of 1964 Dylan had already distanced himself considerably from those who hailed him as a great writer of topical songs, as Dylan's disturbed comment to Joan Baez about not wanting to be responsible for the political aspirations of his audience and Irwin Silber's complaint about Dylan's entourage serving to distance him from reality testify. By mid-1965 he was consciously rejecting the significance that those songs had for the civil rights movement. Asked about those songs in an interview in September of that year, Dylan reacted by saying: "I'm not a preacher. Songs can't save the world, I know that. Whatever you have to give, you give. That's the way it is."[20] And on December 3 of the same year, in a press conference for San Francisco's KQED-TV, he remarked: "The protest thing is old. And how valid is it anyway? Is it going to stop anything? Is anybody going to listen? People think this helps. . . . But songs aren't going to change the world."[21]

The fact that Dylan moved away from what he called finger-pointing songs does not mean that his songs became apolitical. By the time he recorded *Bringing It All Back Home* in 1965, Dylan was fed up with everyone wanting him to be just like them ("Maggie's Farm"), and declared that he was going to be just like he wanted to be. Dylan was actually describing himself in "She Belongs to Me" when he sang "She's got everything she needs / She's an artist, she don't look back. / She can take the dark out of the nighttime / And paint the daytime black." Others have seen the song as an ironic putdown of Saint Joan (Baez).

Art, of course, is not precluded from having multiple meanings, and reflecting different images from different angles, nor for that matter, as Hans-Georg Gadamer's and Paul Ricoeur's hermeneutic theories demonstrate, need its meaning be restricted to the intentions of the author or artist. Furthermore, the appreciation of a piece of art, a poem, or even a philosophy is not a passive encounter. The situatedness, or being there in the world, of the appreciater, as Heidegger has shown us, has a marked effect on what we can achieve in an encounter with art. We take with us a forestructure of meanings that constitute our horizons, which, as Gadamer argues, "fuse" with the horizon projected by the text or work of art.[22] The "fusion of horizons" that occurs between the artist and the appreciater of art is a reciprocal process expanding the horizon of both.

In Ricoeur's view, this process of "appropriation" is itself a creative pro-cess.[23] As Dylan himself commented, he wanted to write songs that worked on many different levels. The same words with an interchanging subject may be both sincere and ironic through the gestalt switches. Because appreciation is a matter of fusion between horizons, a work of art may mean nothing to a person whose horizon is not open to the experience. Benedetto Croce tried to explain this experience in distinguishing between history and chronicle.[24] Chronicle is the retelling of a dead past whose life does not connect with the present. The historian must be driven by a contemporary problem in his or her fascination with the past. The issue must resonate in the soul. But in order for a history book to be history for a reader, the reader too must have that same passion, the same resonance of the issue in his or her soul. Without it, the book is simply chronicle. The fascinating proposition with which Croce presents us is the suggestion that the very same book may be a work of history or of chronicle depending on whether the issues with which it deals resonate in the soul of the reader.

What characterizes much of Dylan's work in the albums of 1965–1967 is what was intimated in "A Hard Rain's A-Gonna Fall." Although "Chimes of Freedom" appears on *Another Side of Bob Dylan*, many of the songs lack its abstract, impressionistic, and symbolic character. Most of the songs were written over the course of a week in Greece and reflect the intense personal turmoil that his breakup with Suze Rotolo inflicted on him. This is most clearly understood in Collingwood's terms as art as the expression of emotion, or what Lorca called imaginative poetry, where the logic of the expression is not self-referential but explores connections and pursues meanings in the world. They attempt to understand and abate the mystery of emotional experiences. "Ballad in Plain D," for example, is vitriolic and describes the night of the three-way venomous battle at Suze's sister's apartment that marked the breakdown of their relationship. Even though Dylan was serially unfaithful, his expectations of Suze were unreasonable and colored by uncompromising possessiveness and jealousy, to the point that he refused to allow her a life that was not totally wrapped up in his, which in turn was wrapped up in his own career and image formation. The album expresses emotion, but without subtlety, and "Ballad in Plain D" was a song he later very much regretted writing. In 1965 he described the songs of the previous year as one dimensional in contrast with the three-dimensional songs that he was now aiming for. The new songs, which were to appear on *Bringing It All Back Home* and *Highway 61 Revisited*, contained more symbolism and moved on different levels within and between verses. In contrast with the earlier albums, in which he knew what he wanted to say in his songs and then wrote them, he characterized his new phase quite differently. Now, he said, "I just write a song like I *know* that it's just going to be all right and I don't know exactly what it's all about, but I do the layers of what it's all about."[25]

It is the world around Dylan that provided the inspiration, often a specific incident or event, which stimulated his creative talent, resulting in a series of images, mostly abstract, evocative of a mood or feeling. However, you could not say that these later songs were about the particular situations that proved inspirational. It would be difficult on hearing "A Hard Rain's A-Gonna Fall," for instance, to identify the Cuban missile crisis as the subject matter, and even though the Vietnam War weighed heavily on Dylan's mind when he wrote "Tombstone Blues" (*Highway 61 Revisited*), and the poetic images are inspired by it, the song is not a narrative but instead a series of metaphors about the war:

> The king of the Philistines his soldiers to save
> Put jawbones on their tombstones and flatters their graves
> Puts the pied pipers in prison and fattens the slaves
> Then sends them out to the jungle.

President Lyndon Johnson is the Philistine leader who threw the draft dodgers into prison and had a program of inner city rejuvenation meant to improve the condition of blacks, who were disproportionately represented in the battalions in Vietnam. These may or may not be the referents to the images, but the images are meant to stand alone. Nevertheless, the referents in both "A Hard Rain's A-Gonna Fall" and "Tombstone Blues" are important to a subtle appreciation of the songs. They are examples of poetry that abate mystery.

A song can evoke the mood of an era, without having specific referents within it. Jon Landau realized this in his review of *John Wesley Harding*. He contended that Dylan exhibited a profound awareness of the war and the effect that it was having on everyone, just as the country was about to split apart over the assassinations of Martin Luther King Jr. and Robert Kennedy, over race, political and police riots, the presidential election, and the carnage in Vietnam. Landau did not claim that any of the songs were about Vietnam, or a protest against it: "All I mean to say is that Dylan has felt the war, and there is an awareness of it contained within the mood of the album as a whole."[26]

The song that most epitomizes this phase of Dylan's career is "Desolation Row." Many names evoked in it are familiar, such as Casanova, Einstein, T. S. Eliot, and Ezra Pound, but they are contemplative images, not persons:

Einstein, disguised as Robin Hood
With his memories in a trunk
Passed this way an hour ago
With his friend, a jealous monk
He looked so immaculately frightful
As he bummed a cigarette
Then he went off sniffing drainpipes
And reciting the alphabet
Now you would not think to look at him
But he was famous long ago
For playing the electric violin on Desolation Row

By this time Dylan had come to see his songs as experiences, and comprehending the meaning of the words was not necessary to understanding the experience; too much intellectualizing could destroy it. Indeed, he said that he was writing for those who shared his feelings: "The point is not understanding what I write but feeling it."[27] Irwin Silber, who wrote the open letter to Bob Dylan following the release of *Another Side of Bob Dylan*, understood very well where Dylan was coming from when he reviewed *Highway 61 Revisited* in *Sing Out!* in March 1966.[28] He linked Dylan's new visionary poetry to existentialism, and by implication to aspects of the philosophy that underpinned the Beat Generation. The songs on the album, he argued, represent life as an absurd amalgam of meaningless events and episodes encapsulated in the arbitrary reference points of birth and death. To search for meaning or purpose in life is a pointless and futile exercise. As social critique, it is powerful, but in offering a remedy, it is mute, a philosophy bereft of a positive vision. Silber was not, then, an unthinking traditionalist reactionary. He understood well what Dylan was doing: he thought it destructive of the community that the folk music he represented had striven to create and sustain.[29]

Even though *John Wesley Harding* signaled another musical transformation, it did not herald a transformation in Dylan's poetry, but instead a steadier control of the imagery. The songs are still characterized by the presentation of images unfolding as narratives in dramatic form; at the same time, the songs elude those who seek to discern a meaning by appearing to have a direction and point, but suddenly veering off in a different direction or unexpected turn. One reviewer, commenting on "The Ballad of Frankie Lee and Judas Priest," asserted that "[t]here is a frightening delight in meaninglessness: drawled words . . . irrelevant details and nonsequiturs."[30]

I have argued that the protest song phase in Dylan's early career may best be understood as pseudo art, or what Collingwood called art as magic.

The songs are faithful in many respects to the form of the genre, but also unique in the subtlety of the message, portraying the murderers and murdered as victims of a sick society. Dylan in these early songs is not offering a structural analysis of society in which the forces at work are impersonal. Instead, he attributes agency to the officers of the institutions who have a vested interest in perpetuating racism, the arms race, or the running down of traditional industries. These songs, I have suggested, are quite different from those that are expressive of personal rather than collective emotion and whose referents are still anchored in the logic of everyday reality, what Lorca called imaginative poetry. Finally, both the finger-pointing injunctive and the expression of personal emotion are to be distinguished from the abstract expressionism of Dylan's later "inspirational" phase. Here we are presented with a parallel universe made up of the accentuated absurdities of our own, a series of images, but not propositions, about which it makes no sense to ask whether they are right or wrong, and whose images, to use Oakeshott's words, are to be delighted in. I don't want to suggest that these are exclusive or discrete phases in Dylan's career. They are notionally distinct, but in reality they overlap and run concurrently.

Endnotes

1. Leonard Cohen, "Q Questionnaire—Leonard Cohen," Q, (September 1994).
2. R. Serge Denisoff, Sing a Song of Significance (Bowling Green, OH: Bowling Green University Press, 1972).
3. Cited in Ralph J. Gleason, "The Children's Parade," Ramparts (March 1966): 33.
4. Cited in Clinton Heylin, Dylan the Biography: Behind the Shades (Harmondsworth: Penguin, 1998; first published 1991), 77.
5. Christian Williams, Bob Dylan in His Own Words (London: Ominbus Press, 1993), 29.
6. Heylin, Behind the Shades, 78, 79.
7. Smith describes each song included in The Anthology of American Folk Music in the handbook that accompanies the set. The collection was reissued in 1997 (Smithsonian Folkways Recordings) on three CDs and included an additional booklet of essays.
8. This type of audience reaction has persisted over the decades. Reports of Dylan's 1974 U.S. tour highlight that line as having the greatest single impact on audiences.
9. Cited in Neil Corcoran, "Death's Honest," in Do You Mr. Jones: Bob Dylan with the Poets and Professors, ed. Neil Corcoran (London: Chatto & Windus, 2002), 147.
10. Bob Dylan in His Own Words, ed. Christian Williams (London: Omnibus Press, 1993), 29.
11. Cited in Anthony Scaduto, Bob Dylan (London: Helter Skelter, 1996), 111.
12. Michael Gray, Song and Dance Man III (London: Cassell, 2000), 22.
13. Andy Gill, My Back Pages: Classic Bob Dylan 1962–69 (London: Carlton, 1998), 23.
14. See "A Message from Bob Dylan," sent to the Emergency Civil Liberties Committee after he received the Tom Paine Award at the Bill of Rights dinner on December 13, 1963 (Robert Shelton Archives, Institute for Popular Music, Liverpool University).

15. J. L. Austin, *How to Do Things with Words*, ed. J. O. Urmson (Oxford: Oxford University Press, 1962); Q. Skinner, *Meaning and Context: Quentin Skinner and His Critics*, ed. James Tully (Cambridge: Cambridge University Press, 1988).
16. Robbie Woliver, *Hoot: A Twenty-five-Year History of the Greenwich Village Music Scene* (New York: St. Martin's Press, 1994), 131.
17. Scaduto, *Bob Dylan*, 127.
18. Andy Gill, *My Back Pages: Classic Bob Dylan 1962–69* (London: Carlton, 1998), 30.
19. Williams says that the poet, in whose company he includes Dylan at this point, "does not premeditate, and in a real sense is inspired, and yet at the same time must work very hard and have a talent that is uniquely his own, in order to seize the moment and be the voice of his times, his generation." Paul Williams, *Bob Dylan, Performing Artist 1960–73* (London: Omnibus, 1994), 60.
20. Beverly Hills, California, press conference, September 4, 1965. Reprinted in *The Bob Dylan Companion*, ed. Carl Benson (New York: Schirmer Books, 1998), 59.
21. Cited in Robert Shelton, *No Direction Home* (New York: Da Capo Press, 1997; first published 1986), 286.
22. Hans-Georg Gadamer, *Truth and Method* (New York: Crossroad, 1982).
23. Paul Ricouer, *Interpretation Theory: Discourse and the Surplus of Meaning* (Fort Worth: Texas Christian University Press, 1976).
24. Benedetto Croce, *Theory and History of Historiography*, trans. Douglas Ainslie (London: Harrap, 1921), esp. 12, 19, 134.
25. Cited in Gleason, "The Children's Crusade," 33.
26. Cited in Greil Marcus, *Invisible Republic: Bob Dylan's Basement Tapes* (London: Picador, 1998), 55.
27. Frances Taylor, "Dylan Disowns His Protest Songs." Reprinted in *Bob Dylan: The Early Years, a Retrospective*, ed. Craig McGregor (New York: Da Capo Press, 1990), 97.
28. Reprinted in ibid., 66–68.
29. Reprinted in ibid., 102–103.
30. Jean Strouse, "Bob Dylan's Gentle Anarchy," *Commonweal*, 1968. Reprinted in Benson, *The Bob Dylan Companion*, 87.

$$\boxed{8}$$

FIELD COMMANDER COHEN

> As you get older, you get less willing to buy the latest version
> of reality.
>
> —Leonard Cohen, 1988[1]

Leonard Cohen's own political stance has always been ambivalent; it is anarchic in an intensely personal way. Early in his career, he was somewhat overawed with the idea that he, like Bob Dylan, was considered a spokesman for a whole generation. Shortly after the release of Cohen's first album, William Kloman, writing in the *New York Times*, prophesied that "Cohen seems on the verge of becoming a major spokesman for the ageing pilgrims of his generation, the so-called 'Silent Generation' who came of age under Eisenhower."[2]

It was Cohen's ability to engage with the audience at a deeply personal and intimate level that made him so alluring. He was said to have seduced his young audience through their identification with his anguish and experience of the narrow range of emotions with which he dealt. A German translation of his work described him as "the incarnation of unfulfilled wishes and unanswered questions of the young generation."[3] He was appointed "spokesman for its emotions and actor of its own unachievable scramble out of squareness and aloneness."[4]

Cohen himself maintained that the only way he could be regarded in this way was because deep down he was the same as everyone else and that his songs reflected this universal affinity. He has always been the reluctant political commentator and has rarely become directly involved in any cause. Like Dylan, he felt distinctively uncomfortable with the idea of defining a generation and of being the spokesman for someone else.

He was, he said, used to illustrate how love had become a cultural phenomenon; on the contrary, he thought society, far from manifesting love, was on the precipice of violence, if not physical, then psychic. He had no special gift or insight to share with the world. In "Stranger Song," he makes this clear: "Please understand, I never had a secret chart / to get me to the heart of this / or any other matter."

Faithful to the idea that the individual poet does not have a mission, although Cohen is religious, he does not regard himself as a priest whose role is to propagate his beliefs. The great strength of Cohen's lyric poetry, in Barbara Arniel's view, is his ability to transform his own experience "into something approaching universal pain and ecstasy."[5] Cohen claimed that he had no political program and no political identity, and that in fact he hardly had any personal identity at all.[6] Any impressive piece of work, however, has a subversive element, and it only becomes uncomfortable or disturbing when political and social activity results from it. According to Cohen, subversiveness is one of the most desirable characteristics of a piece of art, because of that feeling of groundlessness you experience in hearing, seeing, or reading it.[7]

There are many references in Cohen's work that allude to the idea that the intention *to* write a poem is something quite different from the intention expressed *in* writing. For example, Cohen has explained what his intentions are when he writes a song or poem. They say nothing about the meaning of what is authored as such, but relate to the quality that he aims to achieve. The musical intention is to achieve excellence, whereas the textual intention is to achieve accuracy and honesty. The mood or emotion that a song expresses is not first premeditated, then executed, but just happens in the course of writing. Cohen says: "When I have my guitar in my hand, I can like hit the chord of A major and the mood just falls right out, all over the place." Again, he denies this preconceived intention when he maintains that "[a]nybody who writes songs knows that it's nothing they command. You are the instrument of something else."[8]

We find very little in Cohen's poetry of what R. G. Collingwood called art as magic. There is little of the finger pointing, but a great deal of art as the expression of emotion. Cohen also alludes to the fact that some of his poems, at least, move toward Oakeshott's idea that, in poetry, symbol and meaning are inseparable; they do not stand outside of each other as they do in ordinary language and science. Without explicitly formulating a theory, we see in Cohen's different responses to questions about his work that, in relation to some of his lyric poems, he is willing to talk at length about the emotion expressed and the referents that give it meaning, whereas in relation to questions about other poems, he is either unwilling or unable to explain, justify, or articulate any meaning beyond what the work itself encapsulates, where sense and reference, language and meaning are internal to the poem.

Cohen, for instance, readily explains the referents that give meaning to such songs as "Suzanne" and "Chelsea Hotel No. 2." "Suzanne" is a reworked version of a poem from Cohen's book *Parasites of Heaven*. Its references are real people, places, and encounters. Cohen even describes the first verse as reportage, in which he gives us a characterization of the subject and the relation in which he stands to her. The impression given is that the relationship was platonic, but recent interviews with Suzanne Vaillancourt, who now lives in Los Angeles, indicate that their empathy went much deeper. Suzanne and her husband were a stylish Montreal couple, and Cohen was deeply attracted to her. She had grace, charm, and wit, and, as Cohen says, she was "half crazy" in an endearing way. She had a home near the St. Lawrence River, where she would serve Constant Comment tea flavored with orange peel. The second verse conveys the religious feel of old Montreal and the religiosity that exudes over the harbor front. The harbor in the song is on the St. Lawrence River, and "our lady of the harbour" is the mariners' chapel of Notre Dame de Bon Secours, on top of which a statue of the Virgin Mary stands with her arms outstretched toward the river. The reference in the song to Jesus betrays the religious aura that surrounds old Montreal on the waterfront. Even here the beauty of the song is unimpaired by ignorance of these facts. Indeed, the image that each person has of "our lady of the harbour" is conjured by the poetry and has a character unique in each person's vision. The building is in fact much more imposing than the song conveys, and far less beautiful, simple, and quaint than the imagery portrays.

The third verse is both particular and universal, in that, through the encounter with a particular person, Cohen is trying to express the kind of tender and compassionate care and attention that a man looks for in a woman. The specificity of the song is transcended by the universal. "The song," Cohen says, "could have been called by any name because I had the guitar pattern before I had the name of a woman."[9]

It is now well known that the subject of "Chelsea Hotel No. 2" is Janis Joplin. Cohen tells the story that he met Joplin in the elevator in the Chelsea Hotel. She asked him if he had seen Kris Kristofferson, and he answered, "I'm him." The lines "Ah but you got away, didn't you, babe, / you just threw it all to the ground" become more intelligible as a result of knowing the referent. Without knowing the woman is Janis Joplin, we would not know that the escape was in fact suicide. Cohen himself saw it as an act of indiscretion to reveal the name of the woman, and he very much regretted that he had identified Joplin as the subject of the song. But the regret may partly be because the song is not wholly based on Janis Joplin but expresses an amalgam of emotions that he felt toward a number of women at that time. The self-deprecating line "You told me again you preferred handsome men" was in fact something that Nico had said to him. Maurice Ratcliff suggests that the song is also about Suzanne Elrod, the mother of Cohen's son, Adam, and daughter, Lorca. Their relationship was strained at the time, and Cohen felt that he was being "jived around."[10]

In relation to other songs, Cohen has been unable to account for what they mean. Instead, he sees them as experiences, as something that happen to you as a listener or reader, and you feel moved in some way without being able to articulate what a particular song is saying. When asked, for example, to justify and explain the powerful, venomous language used in the poem "French and English" (*Stranger Music*), which denounces the narrowness of the French and English mentality in Montreal, Cohen simply replied: "I just can't . . . go beyond the poem itself. Everything that I have thought about the matter is there and I think the language is appropriate. I wouldn't want to . . . make a commentary."[11] He has been more explicit about the free-standing quality of a poem or song when he says: "I am interested in the song standing without footnotes or commentaries. And that's the mark of a completed song—that it doesn't need anything else said about it."[12] Again, he confirms the nature of poetry when he says: "It's hard to look back at a song and try to really discover the aesthetic or the argument of a song. A real song has no argument."[13] "Story of Isaac," for example, clearly has a biblical reference, but it is not that which gives it its force or power. It is the imagery, the conflicting senses of trust and betrayal, the universal in the particular, and our ability to empathize without fully understanding what the song is saying that give it true meaning. Cohen himself is at a loss as to its meaning: "As to its meaning . . . I don't know except that it exists as psychic reality."[14]

Images of War

Themes and images of war surface in all sorts of contexts in the writings of Leonard Cohen. He frequently sees his own life being played out on the front line, with "missiles and shrapnel flying through the air."[15] His most recent CD of live recordings, compiled from his 1979 tour, is called

Field Commander Cohen (2001). Cohen commented that "field commander" is an ironic description, but that he always did have a love of the army. For one, his father had intended to send him to the military academy in Kingston, Ontario, about three hours by train from Montreal. Also, the rank of officer somewhat describes the qualities of leadership needed on a tour, when a diverse group of men and women have to be kept together over months of grueling traveling and performing. The military imagery often betrays a worldview that is indicative of struggle. Cohen's own inner life is lived on the front line, and his albums are his artillery not only against an industry that has not always treated him with dignity and respect, but also against those injustices that are never clearly defined, but which he feels are subterranean and undermining the very fabric of social cohesiveness. He describes his album *The Future*, for example, as "a tank of a record—it can go over anything, it can meet all resistance."[16] Shortly after he retreated to the monastery on Mount Baldy, which was itself as much about military discipline as spiritual quest, he described Zen Buddhism as an excessively rigorous, severe, and disciplined religion: "You may just as well join the Marines if you're interested in that kind of life."[17]

The images of war are sometimes invoked in a literal, but not representational, sense, as in "The Partisan" and "Story of Isaac," or metaphorically to characterize human relationships, as in "There Is a War," or as an allegory for liberation, as in "First We Take Manhattan." "Story of Isaac," for example, was introduced by Cohen as about the sacrifice of one generation by another. Although it is not immediately apparent, it is also an anti–Vietnam War protest.

Cohen was six years old when World War II began. Both Cohen's father and uncle had served in World War I, the former with the Canadian Expeditionary Force. Cohen's father had wanted him to become an officer in the army, and his uncle Boris had expected him to enlist during the Korean War. Cohen himself did have a brief flirtation with combat during the 1973 Arab-Israeli conflict (referred to as the Yom Kippur War), but the nearest he got to becoming an officer was to imagine himself as "Field Commander Cohen" in the song of the same name. He called his 1970s backing band The Army, and dispositionally he was obsessed with discipline. For one whose life often fell into chaos, and where the absence of discipline manifested itself in self-indulgence, he introduced discipline and order into his life from without. In interviews he always speaks fondly of how Marianne Ihlen (with whom Cohen had lived on Hydra and who is the subject of the song "So Long, Marianne") had introduced a sense of order and discipline into his life, and one of the attractions of Zen Buddhism for him was its disciplinarian regime—what could not be self-imposed had to be imposed from without. Pico Iyer commented, after interviewing Cohen at the Zen Center on Mount Baldy in 1998, that he "has managed to turn it into mountain training more rigorous than the army."[18] Strangely enough, Cohen describes his monastic existence in military imagery: "We feel we're like the Marines of the spiritual world: tougher, more reckless, more daring, more brave."[19] In "First We Take Manhattan," the singer's conquering spirit is guided by the beauty of weapons, and the only person able to stop him is unable to do so because of impotence through the lack of discipline. Cohen's psychological attachment to discipline is not frivolous. Indeed, his solution to the problem of social dysfunctionalism and violence in Los Angeles, where he now lives, was the rather reactionary and unimaginative view that the authorities "should put boys and girls into uniform. There should be universal North American conscription again. It's us against drugs. If you don't understand that you're gonna lose."[20]

In 1961 Cohen was curious to see Fidel Castro's Cuba firsthand. His motives, however, were not entirely clear. The Spanish poet Federico García Lorca, who was a considerable influence on Cohen, had visited there thirty years earlier. Cohen saw his Cuban trip as an adventure, an opportunity to experience danger and excitement. It was *his* civil war, without the political commitment. He was not a Communist sympathizer when he went down to Havana, but by the time he left, he was vehemently anti-Communist.[21]

In 1961 Castro's government was only two years old, and the United States was almost paranoid about the Communist threat off the coast of Florida. In 1964 Cohen claimed that "I was very interested in what it really meant for men to carry arms and kill other men. . . . The real truth is that I wanted to kill or be killed."[22] Havana was decaying, but many of the decadent bars and entertainments had been re-introduced to slow down the economic decay. Cohen continued his bourgeois bohemian seminocturnal existence in Cuba by associating with petty criminals, gamblers, pimps, and prostitutes. He also met Cuban artists and writers with whom he discussed political oppression and artistic freedom. He disliked the American Communists he met there, and they disliked him, denouncing him as a "bourgeois individualist." This reaction was not new to him. In Montreal, although the Communists fascinated him with their paranoia and absolute conviction, they in turn were less than kind to him. For them, Cohen claimed, he was a symbol of the decline of the enemy. He could never quite affect the style, and his family, after all, did own a clothing factory.[23]

Cohen's position in Havana became precarious as tension mounted over the prospect of an impending invasion, which culminated in the Bay of Pigs invasion on April 17, 1961.[24] It was an operation that went disastrously wrong. Naturally, Cuban troops became vigilant and suspicious of anyone with an American-sounding accent. Cohen "escaped" from Cuba on April 26 after being detained at the airport. It is not surprising that he was detained: He had grown a Che Guevara–style beard and wore paramilitary clothing, which, given the circumstances, immediately drew attention to himself.

Although Cohen's motives may have been ambivalent, his conclusions were not. In defending himself during the Cuban missile crisis against the accusation that he was pro-Castro and anti-American, he claimed that he had gone to Cuba to see a socialist revolution firsthand, and not blindly to support it. For him, Castro's regime was oppressive and repugnant because of its obsession with control through censorship and collectivism. In the censorship of "bourgeois intellectuals," Cohen found himself aptly categorized. He lived the excitement and energy of the Cuban revolution, but hated the loud, obtrusive anthems and overbearing posters. In 1976 he acknowledged that much of what he saw in Cuba was great, but for him personally, "everything was too public and up-front. You had to participate all the time and I'm just a bourgeois individualist."[25] Capitalism, he observed in 1993, with all its faults, has a more benign grip on people than any other system yet invented.[26]

Democracy, for Cohen, is part and parcel of this system. It is the faith of the West, which affirms all other faiths, a thing that most religions cannot do. Cohen claims that in its affirmation of the idea of a fraternity of men and women, it is the highest expression of the Western experience. What he has to say about it, however, is heavy in irony. The land of the free, where personal liberty and self-determination are valued above all else, where democratic principles fill the rhetoric of politicians, is, in Cohen's song "Democracy" (*The Future*), the place to which democracy is coming but has not yet arrived:

> From the wars against disorder,
> from the sirens night and day;
> from the fires of the homeless,
> from the ashes of the gay:
> Democracy is coming to the USA.

The song was inspired by the fall of the Berlin Wall and by the popular belief that democracy was coming to the East. The sentiment in the song is that if it is coming anywhere, it is to the United States. Cohen claims that there is a dissolution of the irony in the song through its sense of conviction and passion working on a higher, mysterious, and urgent dimension.[27]

Cohen repeated his experiment in danger again in late September 1973, when he flew to Tel Aviv to join the Israeli Army a few days before the Yom Kippur War. Again, his motives were ambivalent. His immediate reason seems to have been to escape from the situation he was in with Suzanne Elrod on the island of Hydra. In the past, he had supported the Arab demands that Israel return the territory captured in the 1967 Six-Day War, but he was now on the side of the Israelis. Cohen was assigned to an Israeli Air Force entertainment troupe, and he traveled around Israel and sang to the soldiers, giving various ad hoc performances. He seemed to be excited by the danger of war, and romanticized it, but the sight of wounded Egyptians disturbed him and caused him to become less enthusiastic. He returned to Jerusalem and flew back to Hydra to join Suzanne and his son, Adam.

War is in fact a continuing theme in Cohen's work. It is the only activity, along with earning a living, he suggests, that justifies a man leaving a woman. In fact, he characterizes the whole of life as a war. His songs resound with images and imaginations of war, even fantasies of world domination. They are evocative of situations and themes rather than commentaries or injunctions to act. They are instead invitations to delight in the images and feel something of the same emotions: despair, exhilaration, demonic passion. Cohen himself has said that he writes what he feels as honestly as he can, and is delighted if others can empathize or feel part of themselves in the songs.[28] In other words, they are what Collingwood would call art proper. Cohen's songs are rarely representative; the situations that inspire them are rarely immediately apparent. Songs that appear to have a story are allegorical. They are not a means to an end; they are not designed to arouse a certain emotion and channel it to some practical effect, but instead are expressions of emotion. Take, for example, "Dance Me to the End of Love" (*Various Positions*). Ostensibly, it is a love song with some religious imagery: the olive branch and Babylon. It is, however, a song with "a chilling scenario" inspired by Nazi concentration camps. It is optimistic in its assertion of the joy of the will to survive in the struggle against evil.[29] "The Old Revolution" (*Songs from a Room*) includes images of soldiers, war, and killing, recurrent themes in Cohen's songs. Often they are not literal but instead are metaphors for the daily struggle of life.

The male-female relationship is often portrayed as a battlefield, where comrades fight a common enemy and become war weary, or in which they are enemies locked in immortal combat. "Winter Lady" (*Songs of Leonard Cohen*) talks of Marianne Ihlen as the "child of snow" he defends in his military guise against all men. In "There Is a War" (*New Skin for the Old Ceremony*) he characterizes the human condition in the following terms:

> *There is a war between the rich and poor,*
> *a war between the man and the woman.*
> *There is a war between the left and right,*
> *a war between the black and white,*
> *a war between the odd and the even.*

This war between men and women to which he refers is one that is a battle of wills, a ruthless and vicious struggle to the psychic death, and in which women have the upper hand. Everyone knows, Cohen says, that women are the mind and force that hold everything in place.[30] His album *I'm Your Man* represents for him a truce in this war, perhaps even a peace.

The songs inspired by the Yom Kippur War are not about the war itself, but express something more universal. "The Night Comes On" (*Various Positions*), for example, was written because of what Cohen felt when the Egyptians crossed the Suez Canal, but what it means is that everyone is in a place that is not free, living under a certain tyranny that it is our duty to throw off by leaving Egypt and entering the Promised Land. The song is a metaphor for escaping from slavery for the Promised Land.[31] There is a brief reference to Egypt in the song, but the continuing metaphor is that of coming back to the world, the place of freedom and safety:

> *Yes, and here's to the few*
> *Who forgive what you do*
> *And the fewer who don't even care*
> *And the night comes on*
> *It's very calm*
> *I want to cross over, I want to go home,*
> *But she says, Go back, go back to the World*

"Field Commander Cohen" is inspired by the war, but it evokes Cohen's earlier experience in Cuba. It is a surrealistic fantasy in which Cohen characterizes himself as a spy, "parachuting acid into drinks at diplomatic cocktail parties" and trying to persuade Fidel Castro to give up his military and political power to return to the mundane, "such as waiting rooms and ticket lines, / silver bullet suicides, / and messianic ocean tides, / and racial roller-coaster rides / and other forms of boredom advertised as poetry."

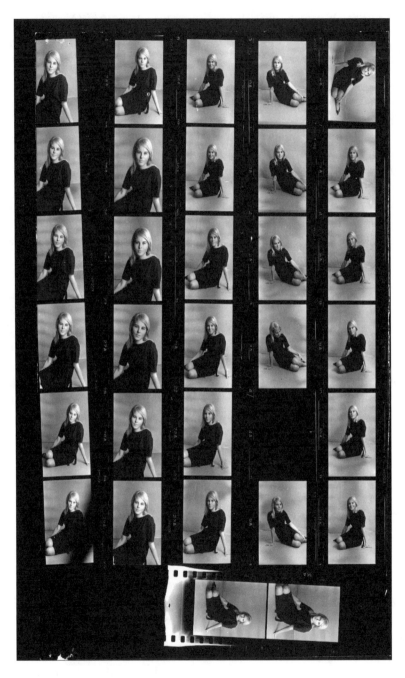

Filmstrip of Marianne Ihlen (held in the Cohen Papers, Thomas Fisher Rare Book Library, University of Toronto).

The theme of war continues in "First We Take Manhattan" (*I'm Your Man*). Cohen himself describes the song as a "demented, menacing geopolitical manifesto."[32] In it he is offering to take over the world with anyone who is willing to follow him. In "The Future," the threat is more sinister, colored with an excessive pessimism. Cohen calls for the resurrection of both good and evil, foreseeing the future as far worse than the past. He sings such lines as "Give me absolute control over every living soul":

> Give me back the Berlin Wall
> Give me Stalin and St. Paul
> Give me Christ
> Or give me Hiroshima
> Destroy another feotus now
> We don't like children anyhow
> I've seen the future, baby
> It is murder

This was the response Cohen had to the blind and uncritical optimism following the fall of the Berlin Wall in 1989. For him, it wasn't good news: "This is going to produce a good deal of suffering. You're going to settle for the Berlin Wall when you see what's coming next. You're going to settle for a hole in the ozone layer. You'll settle for crack. You'll settle for social unrest. You'll settle for the LA riots. This is kindergarten stuff compared with the homicidal impulse that is developing in every breast."[33] Cohen was very reluctant to inflict this gruesome song on the world, and thought at times that perhaps he had said enough about the decay and despair of a disintegrating social fabric in "Everybody Knows" (*I'm Your Man*).[34] Both songs convey an unrelenting, uneasy, uncomfortable vision of the reality behind the appearance. Cohen purports to be telling us what everybody already knows: all of the acclaimed progress in civil rights is an illusion ("Old Black Joe's still pickin' cotton"); the politicians' talk of economic and social progress is a facade ("Everybody knows that the boat is leaking, everybody knows that the captain lied"). The odds are stacked against the downtrodden; the poor get poorer, and the rich get richer. It is a society in which the certainties become unhinged; the good guys lose the war, and faithfulness is not compromised by a night or two of infidelity. The West has run its course, and its civilization is collapsing in on itself. The breaking of the ancient Western code is foreshadowed:

> And everybody knows that you're in trouble
> Everybody knows what you've been through
> From the bloody cross on top of Calgary

To the beach of Malibu
Everybody knows it's coming apart
Take one last look at this Sacred Heart
Before it blows
And everybody knows

Dictatorship

Cohen's attitude to politics was something like that associated with the Beat poets. The Beats were not political, in that they had no manifesto for change, but they were utopian in believing that the citizen-artists would become the leaders in a new society. The subject matter of Cohen's songs that express this theme of leadership and dictatorship was foreshadowed in an early 1970s' interview. In it, Cohen announced that "I want to take over the unconditional leadership of the world, I want to lead the world to a new sensibility and there has to be a leader, a figure to do it."[35]

We have already seen how Cohen was disillusioned by Castro's Cuba because it stood against everything that Cohen was—bourgeois, individualistic, and an aesthete. His visit to Cuba for political reasons and his involvement in the Yom Kipper War were aberrations of what was otherwise a life of political self-denial and an unwillingness to become involved in things overtly political. Cohen lived, for example, in Greece at the time of the coup of the generals there, and unlike many of his fellow Canadians, such as Lionel Rubinoff, he did not speak out against the Greek military regime, nor did he support George Papandreou, who later exiled himself in Canada. Greeks were subject to the right-wing dictatorship from 1967 to 1974. Cohen had moved out of his house in Greece after the coup. His public explanation was that there was something in the country and in himself that had changed, and he rarely went to Greece after that. As early as 1963 he was concerned about the political situation in Greece under Papandreou. He already sensed that it was moving to the right, becoming a less safe place to live, and that all opposition was being driven to desperate measures. Demonstrations, for example, were brutally suppressed, and Cohen feared that his kind would not be tolerated for long. One of his friends, Yorgo Lialios, was arrested for possession of two pieces of hashish and imprisoned in Pireus, which was notorious for harsh treatment of prisoners. Cohen said in a letter at that time: "We now hear that he won't be back for a while."[36] In the same letter Cohen quoted a poem on tyranny by the Hungarian poet Gyula Illyes, which he found indicative of the regime. He did not, however, advocate any political stance. His attitude was that he was currently living high until the ax fell. What else could be done?[37] Cohen was later criticized for having enjoyed the so-called fruits of democracy under Papandreou and for not taking a stand against the military regime.

We find, nevertheless, recognizably overt political themes in Cohen's work, such as the antitotalitarian "A Singer Must Die" (*New Skin for the Old Ceremony*). It is a song full of bitter irony, condemning artistic repression by the state. Cohen represents the persona of a wearied and worn down artist whose spirit is broken and who, like the suspect in a criminal interrogation after hours of mental torture, breaks down and confesses, not because of guilt, but to experience the relief of the process ending. It is in the context of fear that the singer is resigned to nonresistance—the manner of detention, one's own reflection in the tormentor's sunglasses, the knee in the balls, the fist in the face. The singer confesses in court that the totalitarian state's vision represents the truth, and his, a lie. He apologizes for contaminating the purity of the air with the words of his song and contemptuously, as if to wash his hands of politics all together, declares, "Yes and long live the state by whoever it's made."

Feminism

One feminist critic of Cohen has written, "Do you have an orifice and a pair of breasts? These are the essential if not sole requirements for a female character in a Leonard Cohen novel. Smooth skin helps, too. Intelligence and personality are of no consequence." She goes on to suggest that Cohen's writing is obscene and offensive to any female personality, and that for him, "sex is good only when it is dirty sex. . . . Fuck!"[38]

Michael Ondaatje argues that women in Cohen's early poetry and novels are always in various stages of undress; they lack individuality because they are all portrayed as the same: "Flesh, a favourite word of Cohen's, drowns out personality."[39] In Cohen's work, women are so often the medium through which some sort of fulfillment is attained, whether sexual gratification or religious salvation, or both simultaneously. In this sense, Cohen predominantly sees women in utilitarian terms. They are a means to an end, rather than an end in themselves. They provide direct lines to something else, and men connect by plugging in their penises.

Cohen has been compared with his mentor Irving Layton in this respect. For both, it is suggested, women are holes into which things are to be stuck; but whereas for Layton, the "hole" reads Kafka, for Cohen, it watches television, in particular *Star Trek*. The reduction of women to bodies for the gratification of men, however perverse these men may be, is to convey a dull one-dimensional image of women as excessively concerned with their appearance or with trivial preoccupations. This is what Mary Wollstonecraft, the author of *A Vindication of the Rights of Women*, complained of in the eighteenth century: that women, instead of being treated and respected as rational creatures with the same natural rights as men, are treated as if they are created for the gratification of men, with no preoccupation other than making themselves attractive for the opposite sex.

Tom Wayman complains that *The Energy of Slaves* is one whine after another about the troubles that "holes" get men into, such as getting filled by other people, "giving rise to all the whining anguish of poems of jealousy."[40] The point is, not that Cohen ought to be more feminist or politically correct, but that the obsession with the I, entangled in vague abstractions of threat, terror, and war, having no subject and no referent, exhibiting complete resignation, and implying that everything is boring except fucking, and that fucking is a useful distraction from politics, makes both Cohen (or his own self-portrait exhibited in the book) and his portrayal of women sad and uninteresting.

As Stephen Scobie points out, it is true that Cohen rarely portrays women as anything more than fulfillers of sexual demands that are more often than not bizarre. But it is also true that he rarely sees other men in any more flattering light. Cohen's vision is so self-centric that the other as individualized personality is eclipsed by his own. In fact, most of the characters he portrays are projections of his own self-reflected black romanticism.[41] In his first novel, *The Favourite Game*, the protagonist, Breavman, who is not Cohen's alter ego, but having experienced many of the same things as Cohen, sees women as reducible to thighs, genitalia, orgasms, and skin color. A reader's report on his first book remarks: "The astounding succession of girls becomes fascinating because Cohen pushes [Ernest] Hemingway right off stage when it comes to making his women not women but some kind of dream-object."[42] This vision of women was not substantially altered by the time he came to write *The Energy of Slaves*. Tom Wayman ridicules Cohen's view of women and politics as they are portrayed in this collection of poetry. The women are dehumanized and boring and are viewed in utilitarian terms, as a means to an end, without value in themselves. They have useful orifices for sticking things into. Politics comes across as some vague whimpering for or against the ill-articulated idea of revolution.[43] Scobie is, I think, right in insisting that although these things are true, the poems are about Cohen himself, not about women and politics, and they betray his own dehumanization and self-disgust at his stance toward both.[44] This self-loathing is almost simultaneously pronounced in his *Live Songs* (1973). In "Please Don't Pass Me By (A Disgrace)," recorded in London in 1970, Cohen exhorts the audience to return home transformed, to not be the person that they came as: "I'm not going to be. I can't stand him. I can't stand who I am."

The Holocaust

In his early work, images of the concentration camp obsess Cohen. When asked why, Cohen answered, "Cos I wish they'd let me out."[45] The most horrific aspect of war that Cohen confronts is the atrocities perpetrated by the Germans on the Jews. He offers us no injunctions—no prescriptions—but instead, once again, images that disturb and unsettle, such as the sinister, remarkable undertones of betrayal and survival disguised by the innocuous melodic accompaniment of "Dance Me to the End of Love," in which the implicit referent is the concentration camp orchestra comprised of Jewish musicians who perform as their fellow prisoners are marched to the gas chambers. "Lovers" (*Let Us Compare Mythologies*) confronts love and brutality in the concentration camp, where a stolen kiss is contrasted with the smashing of teeth to extract gold from the woman's mouth; as she is burned, the lover tries to kiss her flaming breast.

Cohen most famously confronts the theme in his 1964 collection of poems, the provocatively entitled *Flowers for Hitler*. One of the most disturbing poems in that collection is "All There Is to Know about Adolph Eichmann." Eichmann was the principal Nazi officer who delivered the policy of the "final solution of the Jewish question." During the Nuremberg trials, his name came up time and time again, and it became evident that his involvement in the brutality was considerable. Eichmann fled from Germany to Argentina before he could be tried. On the orders of David Ben-Gurion, the prime minister of Israel, Eichmann was kidnapped in Argentina on May 11, 1960, and brought to trial on April 11, 1961, in the district court in Jerusalem for his role in the "final solution."

The prime minister was determined that the trial showcase the extent of Jewish suffering. While there is no doubt of Eichmann's guilt, the fact of a nation, intent on revenge, resorting to illegal kidnapping, allowing no defense witnesses, and focusing on the suffering of the Jews rather than on bringing Eichmann to justice for what he did, tainted the whole proceedings.

Hannah Arendt covered the trial for *The New Yorker* magazine and published a book based on her observations. Its title, too, was deliberately provocative and shocking: *A Report on the Banality of Evil: Eichmann in Jerusalem.*[46] What did Arendt mean by the term "banality of evil"? It was Eichmann's ordinariness, his thoughtlessness and remoteness from reality, that wreaked havoc far more frightening than all the evil intentions put together. In Arendt's view, that was, in fact, the lesson one could learn in Jerusalem. But it was a lesson, not an explanation of the phenomenon or a theory about it.[47] Arendt maintained that the prosecution, despite its best efforts, failed to convince everyone that the man was a monster, but it was hard to escape the conclusion that he was a self-deluding, inconsistent fool. Arendt claimed that

> Eichmann could not be likened to Iago, Macbeth, or Richard II's villainy. He was ambitious for promotion, but would not have murdered his superiors to inherit their jobs. He had no evil motivation, and in fact he lacked imagination, he simply didn't realize what he was do-ing. . . . [O]ne cannot extract any diabolical or demonic profundity from Eichmann.[48]

Arendt's book generated controversy even before it was published. The mere suggestion that evil could be banal was for some a desecration of the memory of the victims of the Holocaust. Arendt was criticized for having taken any interest in what sort of person Eichmann was, and some maintained that he should not have been allowed to speak at all, the implication being that he should not have been able to defend himself at the trial.[49]

There were, of course, more considered discussions. Daniel Bell and Lionel Abel were two of many respondents to Arendt's controversial book.[50] Bell was more sympathetic but not uncritical. Abel was uncompromising, attacking what he saw to be Arendt's indictment of Jews for complicity in their own demise. He criticized her for applying an aesthetic rather than a moral standard to Eichmann and as a consequence grossly diluting the enormity of evil incarnate. Bell suggested that Abel had got it wrong and that Arendt's detachment came from applying a universal standard of justice applicable to Jew and German alike. Arendt explicitly maintained that "this trial had to take place in the interests of justice and nothing else."[51] Despite the fact that the crime was previously unknown and that the criminal was of the likes that no court, except Nuremberg, had seen before, Arendt contended that her report "deals with nothing but the extent to which the court in Jerusalem succeeded in fulfilling the demands of justice."⁵² And again, she said: "[O]n trial are his deeds, not the sufferings of the Jews, not the German people or mankind, not even anti-Semitism and racism."⁵³ However, the chief prosecutor, Gideon Hausner, had a wider agenda. His case was to play on what the Jews had suffered and not on what Eichmann had done. Nuremberg had not focused on the "final solution" but instead on the crimes committed by the defendants against various nations. The simple reason for this was that Eichmann was not there.

Abel criticized Arendt because he claims that in her analysis, Eichmann came off so much better than his victims. She portrayed Eichmann as a "clown," a vain man incapable of detecting contradictions in his speech and almost incapable of articulating his thoughts, because he had very few. He would make grand gestures, then immediately contradict them, as, for example, when he stated boldly that he would never take another oath because eventually, however sincere, there would be consequences. No one, he said, would ever make him take an oath again. Eichmann was then asked if he would like to give his evidence under oath, or if he preferred not to take an oath. He declared that he would give evidence under oath. There is no doubt that Arendt found him a pathetic man.⁵⁴

Abel contended that Arendt's judgment would have been sounder had she taken into consideration Simone de Beauvoir's point when writing of the war criminal Laval in 1946. In de Beauvoir's view, the man in the dock was weak and broken, worn down by the press attention and the incessant questioning, and perhaps had doubts about the rightness of what he did, whereas the real Laval, who needed to be on trial, was the one who wielded such power and who collaborated in the designs of Hitler. Arendt was accused of being insensitive to this distinction and of projecting the broken, sorrowful Eichmann back into his past role, without portraying his Nazism as a conspicuous ideological decision, but claiming that his sympathy to Zionism was reasoned. Bell pointed out that to have portrayed Eichmann as a "perverted sadist" and monster was too comfortable a judgment. It allows us to think that such behavior is an aberration and that the wickedness of Nazism and Stalinism, of torture and extermination camps, are the work of madmen who had hijacked the apparatus of the state and terrorized ordinary citizens into silence or acquiescence.

It was equally as contentious an issue as to whether the Holocaust should be represented in art at all. In the postwar years some writers thought the events so horrific that they defied representation in language. The social critic Theodor Adorno most famously argued that any attempt to represent Auschwitz was barbaric. The logical implication, Sandra Wynands has argued, is that any artistic re-creation of the Holocaust in the aesthetic realm may be seen as legitimizing it. It follows that, given that human beings derive pleasure from aesthetic representations, the Holocaust should not be represented in this way.[55]

In the same year as Arendt's book appeared, Irving Layton was calling upon poets to elucidate for us the horrors of the Bergen-Belsen concentration camp, and to speak out against the silence that threatened to banish such horrific episodes into forgetfulness. Layton maintained that poets should at least confront the challenge of making the unintelligible intelligible.[56] Cohen's treatment of Eichmann in "All There Is to Know about Adolph Eichmann" takes up Layton's challenge and at the same time aestheticizes Arendt's banality of evil and, as she claims to be doing, lays bear the facts:

ALL THERE IS TO KNOW ABOUT ADOLPH EICHMANN

EYES: .... *Medium*
HAIR: .... *Medium*
WEIGHT: .... *Medium*
HEIGHT: .... *Medium*
DISTINGUISHING FEATURES: .... *None*
NUMBER OF FINGERS: .... *Ten*
NUMBER OF TOES: .... *Ten*
INTELLIGENCE: .... *Average*

What did you expect?
Talons?
Oversize incisors?
Green saliva?

Madness?

What we get from both Cohen's and Arendt's studies is a grave warning about the extent to which human rights are illusory protections against states that deprive their citizens of those rights. The study of Eichmann shows that the gross violations of human rights that totalitarian regimes are capable of perpetrating do not depend on mad, psychotic lunatics, but on people like Eichmann, who many psychiatrists pronounced perfectly normal in his affections and attachments to people and who in his vanity, detached from reality, was swept along in the tide of the machinery of the "final solution," implementing his orders with dutiful enthusiasm. It is a warning that human rights are fragile and that states with far greater potential for centralization of power and communications constitute an ever-present threat.

Whereas this is an extreme case of ordinary people being capable of doing the extraordinary, it is something that permeates the whole of life.

The most "normal" of persons may desire, for example, the most "abnormal" sexual practices. As the narrator says in *Beautiful Losers*: "The reader will be shocked to see how abnormal are the tastes of the so-called normal person . . . how 'unusual' practices are passed along by seemingly innocent, normal sex partners."[57] There is a disturbing fragility to the thin veneer of civilization that veils, and barely keeps in check, the sordid and profane underworld partially submerged beneath the surface of everyday life.

The section in *Beautiful Losers* that describes a sordid encounter with Adolf Hitler is a continuation of the theme of how the Holocaust impinges upon the contemporary imagination. It is a brief but telling encounter in Argentina, a notorious haven for exiled Nazis, where Edith, at the age of twenty, whose husband, the narrator, remained to work in the House of Archives, and her mentor F, who devised the pretext of work in the archives to detain the narrator, have ventured for the sun and sexual experimentation. Hitler, disguised as a waiter, uses a passkey to open the door and enters the hotel bedroom, following a Danish Vibrator that had terrorized and ravished F and Edith, after which it had launched itself out of the hotel room window onto the beach to make its way to and enter the vast rolling waves of the sea.[58]

The cliché of comic-book Nazi imagery and sadomasochism and dominance enters the scene involving Hitler, F, and Edith.[59] In the scene, Hitler excites their sexual passion by issuing sordid commands, including an order to kiss his whip. He produces a bar of soap made from human flesh, and all three take a communal bath. Hitler then baptizes Edith and F with the soap. When they finish, Hitler charmingly dries their genitals, sighing with a hint of nostalgia that he had once had millions of them at his disposal.[60] When Hitler leaves, there is a sense that Edith and F have been complicit in their own degradation.

This portrayal by Cohen of victims complicit in their own humiliation, and even, to some extent, authors of it, was beginning to emerge in books about Nazi Germany detailing the extent to which the crowd psychology swept the vast majority away in a frenzy of enthusiasm for the Führer. Arendt's *Eichmann in Jerusalem* was savagely criticized for detailing the extent to which leaders of Jewish communities selected the victims, organized their evacuation, and were collaborators in the demise of their own people. Implicit in Cohen's account, which avoids the stigma of suggesting that Jews identified with their torturers, because neither Edith nor F is Jewish, is that anyone can become captive of the allure of the authoritarian personality and derive perverse pleasure from submitting to its will. In a similar vein, Cohen speculates on the ease with which external factors, such as the harsh terrain of Canada, the inhospitable landscape and the preachers of Nova Scotia, and staying too long in Winnipeg, can cause almost any ordinary person to become a murderer and mutilator of women.[61]

What we have been talking about, then, is the violation of human rights, the degradation of individuals by other persons. The point is that the most ordinary of people are capable of violating human rights on a massive scale, and that we are all a short step away from doing so on a much smaller scale. Why? It is in fact a matter of regarding the "other" as in some way equal, and not dehumanizing him or her. It is certainly the case that Jews, blacks, women, and more recently Bosnians have been dehumanized, which has been the justification for treating them as less than human. The issue, then, becomes not one of human rights, but who should have them. It is a matter of extending the moral community to incorporate those we have excluded. Richard Rorty has famously argued that the reason given for helping those persecuted, for example, the Jews in Nazi Germany, is rarely because the rescuers believed in a common humanity.[62] It is more likely that the individual was regarded as a member of a more localized community. Rorty contends that common humanity is rarely a strong motivation for heroic action. However, the evidence given by those who actually harbored Jews in Nazi Germany as well as by those who have studied the phenomenon is exactly because the rescuers believed that Jews were fellow human beings who were equal to all others.[63]

I have shown in this chapter that, although Leonard Cohen is generally viewed as expressing personal angst, the imagery of his poems projects political themes that are not as much injunctions to act, but expressions of emotion, or the delighting in images. His inspirational poetry does not aim to abate mystery, but instead marvels in it and celebrates its complexity and depth.

Endnotes

1. Leonard Cohen, *Musician Magazine*, 1988.
2. William Kloman, *New York Times*, January 28, 1968.
3. Cited in Stephen Scobie, *Leonard Cohen* (Vancouver: Douglas & McIver, 1978), ix.
4. Michael Gnarowski, introduction to *Leonard Cohen: The Artist and His Critics*, ed. Michael Gnarowski (Toronto: McGraw-Hill, 1976), 5.
5. Barbara Arniel, "Leonard Cohen Says That to All the Girls," *Maclean's*, September 18, 1978, 55.
6. Michael Harris, "Leonard Cohen: The Poet as Hero: 2," *Saturday Night* (June 1969). Reprinted in Gnarowski, *The Artist and His Critics*, 7.
7. Interview with Cindy Buissaillon on the show *Definitely Not Opera*, Canadian Broadcasting Corporation, August 26, 1995.
8. Quoted in Jim Devlin, ed., *Leonard Cohen in His Own Words* (London: Omnibus, 1998), 49.
9. Ibid., 57.

10. Maurice Ratcliff, *The Complete Guide to the Music of Leonard Cohen* (London: Omnibus, 1999), 43.
11. Cited in Harry Rasky, *The Song of Leonard Cohen: Portrait of a Poet, a Friend and a Film* (Oakville, Ontario: Mosaic Press, 2001), 58.
12. Ibid., 91.
13. Ibid., 102–103.
14. Devlin, *Leonard Cohen in His Own Words*, 59.
15. Karen Shoemer, "Leonard Cohen, the Lord Byron of Rock-and-Roll," *New York Times*, November 29, 1992.
16. Ian Pearson, "Growing Old Disgracefully," *Saturday Night* (March 1993).
17. Ibid.
18. Pico Iyer, "Portrait: Leonard Cohen," *Prospect* (October 1998): 44.
19. Cited in ibid., 45.
20. Cited in John Walsh, "Research. You Understand . . . Leonard Cohen," *Mojo* (September 1994): 56.
21. Tom Chaffin, "Conversations from a Room," *Canadian Forum* (August/September 1983): 10.
22. Devlin, *In His Own Words*, 23.
23. Richard Goldstein, "Beautiful Creep," *The Village Voice*, December 28, 1967, 20. Reprinted in Gnarowski, *The Artist and His Critics*, 43.
24. Ira B. Nadel, *Various Positions: A Life of Leonard Cohen* (London: Bloomsbury, 1996), 94.
25. Devlin, *In His Own Words*, 23.
26. Ibid., 60.
27. Buissaillon interview, August 26, 1995.
28. Robert Hilburn, "Telling It on the Mountain," *Los Angeles Times*, September 24, 1995.
29. Jim Devlin, *Leonard Cohen in Every Style of Passion* (London: Omnibus Press), 113.
30. Devlin, *Leonard Cohen, in His Own Words*, 17–18.
31. Ibid., 59.
32. Ibid., 60.
33. Shoemer, "Lord Byron of Rock-and-Roll."
34. Pearson, "Growing Old Disgracefully."
35. Susan Lumsden, "Leonard Cohen Wants the Unconditional Leadership of the World," available on http://www.itsystem.se/guitar/LC4.html.
36. Letter to Nancy, Hydra, Greece, August 22 (no year) (Leonard Cohen Papers, box 11, file 12, Thomas Fisher Library, University of Toronto).
37. Letter from Leonard Cohen to Esther Cohen, June 8, 1963 (Leonard Cohen Papers, box 11, file 12, Thomas Fisher Library, University of Toronto).
38. Dagmar de Venster, "Leonard Cohen's Women," in *Mother Was Not a Person*, ed. Margaret Andersen (Montreal: Content Publishing/Black Rose Books, 1972), 96–97.
39. Michael Ondaatje, *Leonard Cohen* (Toronto: McClelland & Stewart, 1970), 13.
40. Tom Wayman, "Cohen's Women," *Canadian Literature* 60 (Spring 1974): 90.
41. Scobie, *Leonard Cohen*, 11.
42. Leonard Cohen Papers, Thomas Fisher Library, box 10B, file 45.
43. Wayman, "Cohen's Women," 89–93.
44. Scobie, *Leonard Cohen*, 158.
45. Interview with Eli Mandel, cited in Ondaatje, *Leonard Cohen*, 35.
46. First published in the United States by Viking Press in 1963. A revised and enlarged edition appeared in 1965.
47. Hanna Arendt, *The Banality of Evil: Eichmann in Jerusalem* (Harmondsworth: Penguin, 1973), 288.
48. Ibid., 287.
49. Arendt answers some of the criticisms in the postscript of the 1965 edition of *Eichmann in Jerusalem*, 280–298. The danger of such show trials in countries bent on revenge rather than justice became manifest when Israel once again became the setting of the trial of an alleged Nazi war criminal in 1985. John Demjanjuk was extradited from the United States to Israel

and sentenced to death on the false finding that he was "Ivan the Terrible" of the Treblinka concentration camp. The proceedings were held in a theater as an avowed exercise in "Holocaust education"; the audience was allowed to express its emotions as survivors told their harrowing tales of how the accused over fifty years previously had tormented and tortured them. There was extremely prejudiced and hysterical media coverage, and forged documents were allowed to stand without scrutiny. The trial was a blatant attempt to use universal justice for political ends. It was some years before the elderly Demjanjuk was reluctantly acquitted on appeal. See Geoffrey Robertson, *Crimes against Humanity: The Struggle for Global Justice* (London: Penguin, 2000).

50. Daniel Bell, "The Alphabet of Justice: Reflections on *Eichmann in Jerusalem*," *Partisan Review* 30 (1963): 417–429; Lionel Abel, "The Aesthetics of Evil," *Partisan Review* 30 (1963): 211–230.
51. Arendt, *Eichmann in Jerusalem*, 286.
52. Ibid., 298.
53. Ibid., 5.
54. Ibid., 54.
55. Sandra Wynands, "The Representation of the Holocaust in *Flowers for Hitler*," in *Intricate Preparations: Writing Leonard Cohen*, ed. Stephen Scobie (Toronto: ECW Press, 2000), 199.
56. Irving Layton, *Balls for a One-Armed Juggler* (Toronto: McClelland & Stewart, 1963), xviii.
57. Cohen, *Beautiful Losers* (London: Jonathan Cape, 1970), 168–169.
58. Desmond Pacey makes much of Cohen's fascination with mechanisms. "A particular premonition of *Beautiful Losers* found in *The Spice-Box of Earth* is the mechanical mistress in "The Girl Toy," which points forward to the Danish Vibrator of the novel. This poem is also one of the first indications of Cohen's fascination with machinery, which becomes a thematic motif in both his novels. In the poem, as in the novels, Cohen's attitude towards the machine is ambivalent: It is at once frighteningly alluring." Desmond Pacey, "The Phenomenon of Leonard Cohen," *Canadian Literature* 34 (1967).

   In "Democracy," Cohen sings: "It is there they have the range and machinery for change," and in the *Billboard* interview, he says: "I was always trying to find, always trying to hook up something with a rhythm machine. It isn't like I just switched on, but I did. . . . I can envision a song a lot more completely when I've got some kind of dinky factory rhythm going on behind." Leonard Cohen, interview, *Billboard*, November 28, 1998.
59. Cohen, *Beautiful Losers*, 166.
60. Ibid., 182.
61. Leonard Cohen, "Ballad," in *Selected Poems 1956–1968* (Toronto: McClelland & Stewart, 1968).
62. Richard Rorty, *Contingency, Irony and Solidarity* (Cambridge: Cambridge University Press, 1989).
63. See Norman Geras, *Solidarity in the Conversation of Humankind: The Ungroundable Liberalism of Richard Rorty* (London: Verso, 1995), 7–46.

9

THE RELIGIOUS EXPERIENCE

Religion is another form of bondage which man invents to get himself to God. But that's why Christ came. Christ didn't preach religion. He preached the Truth, the Way and the Light.
—Bob Dylan, Santa Monica, 1979[1]

Religious fanatics, I find, are extremely good company. They seem to have very specific views and they seem to be in a state of attractive nervousness all the time.
—Leonard Cohen, 1974[2]

ob Dylan and Leonard Cohen both came from traditional Jewish backgrounds and were brought up to observe the customs of the faith, but neither felt completely comfortable with what he inherited and continued to search for a religious significance and meaning to life. They were both troubled souls, troubled not so much by self-doubt as with dissatisfaction, boredom, and the need constantly to be traveling both in body and mind. Neither was blessed with a calm soul, both sought solace in heavy self-indulgence, and both experienced periods of extreme remorse. Cohen, for example, once told a reporter from *USA Today* that it had taken him ten years to recover from his serious abuse of LSD. Dylan, too, confessed in an interview with Robert Shelton that he had been addicted to heroin at the time he was going out with Suze Rotolo but had managed to kick the habit. However, he was notorious up until the time of his motorcycle accident in 1966 for being in a permanent state of drug-induced confusion. During the recuperation period he turned to the Bible for solace, and its influence is evident in *John Wesley Harding*,

211

with its numerous biblical allusions. Both sought redemption in religion. Dylan had a brief flirtation with Buddhism, but Cohen's relation with it fluctuates and has dominated his spiritual awareness. As Jews, they both professed a belief in Jesus. Dylan's and Cohen's spiritual machinations, while obviously personal and related to their own personalities, are by no means unique. There is a long tradition in North America, the United States in particular, of Jewish writers, entertainers, and rock figures submerging their cultural identities by immersing themselves in alternative belief systems.[3]

Dylan and Cohen are serious students of the Bible, whose teachings have a special significance for both to varying degrees of intensity. When Dylan was a young man in Hibbing, Minnesota, the Bible stood on a stand in the middle of his bedroom, acting as a point of reference on his acquisitive journey. For both Dylan and Cohen, their religious intensity surfaces most forcefully in a particular album: for Dylan, it is *Slow Train Coming*; for Cohen, it is *Various Positions*, a title that itself imparts an ambivalence to the intense religious imagery it contains.

Religion has played an important role throughout Dylan's career, and his commitment is best viewed in terms of intensity on a continuum rather than as a series of conversions and discontinuities. His early albums abound with religious imagery and allusions, and the forms that many of his protest songs take are in the apocalyptic mode. "A Hard Rain's A-Gonna Fall," "When the Ship Comes In," and "The Times They Are A-Changin' " are all apocalyptic in their imagery. "When the Ship Comes In," for example, draws heavily on Exodus, with its references to the parting of the sea and the drowning of Pharaoh's men; "The Times They Are A-Changin' " draws directly on the Gospel of Matthew, where Jesus, referring to the Last Judgment, says "Many that are first will be last, and the last first."

Dylan's Spiritual Journey

Sara Lownds lived with her daughter in the Chelsea Hotel when Dylan first met her. He took an apartment there himself in order to be close to her. Lownds's whole demeanor was different from Dylan's in exuding a calm serenity and disarming equanimity. Although Jewish like Dylan, she was devoted to Zen and Eastern mysticism, which gave her an unassuming inner strength. Dylan had also become very friendly with Allen Ginsberg, who was a convert to Buddhism and who encouraged Dylan to explore its mysteries. Inspired by Lownds and Ginsberg, Dylan developed a passion for the *I Ching*, the ancient book of change. He told friends that it was the only book he had read that contained truths that you could believe in, adding that, of course, he believed in nothing.[4] His attraction to Eastern mysticism coincided with his self-absorption, almost to a pathological extent, in the drug culture.

Following his near-fatal motorcycle accident in 1966, Dylan released *John Wesley Harding*, which he later described as the first religious rock album. The religiosity in the album, however, was not inspired by the East, but instead set much of the message in a revived American folklore. Songs in this vein include "All Along the Watchtower," inspired by the Book of Isaiah, later famously recorded by Jimi Hendrix, and "I Dreamed I Saw St. Augustine," which laments the turning away from religion and Dylan's own complicity in it:

> I dreamed I saw St. Augustine
> Alive with fiery breath
> And I dreamed I was amongst the ones
> That put him out to death
> Oh, I awoke in anger
> So alone and terrified
> I put my fingers against the glass
> And bowed my head and cried.

The motorcycle accident forced Dylan to reassess his life, first by taking a detour through Christianity, then by turning toward Judaism for direction. He embraced his Jewish heritage with the fanaticism with which he had absorbed the American folk heritage. This reaffirmation may have been occasioned by the death of his father in June 1968. Dylan had returned to Hibbing for the funeral and took his brother by surprise in reciting the Kaddish prayer.[5] He reaffirmed the heritage he had rejected, learned Hebrew, and visited Israel a few times. He was at the Western Wall on his thirtieth birthday, wearing a yarmulke, and had made tentative plans to buy an apartment in Israel or even join a kibbutz. He became associated with Rabbi Meir Kahane's Jewish Defense League in 1970, which once again was testimony for Dylan's critics that he had sold out and was now becoming right wing. The Left that gradually came to support Yasir Arafat's Fatah movement after the 1967 Arab-Israeli War and had criticized Dylan for abandoning politics was appalled by his Zionism.

At the end of 1972, having not played an advertised concert since 1969, with the exception of the 1971 Concert for Bangladesh, at which he was a surprise guest, he and a Canadian girlfriend stayed with Leonard Cohen for a few weeks. Cohen had just returned from Israel and his brief service with the Israeli Air Force. Cohen remembers that he and Dylan discussed both Christianity and Hasidism during this visit at a time when Dylan described his quest in music as mathematical and his attitude as oddly pro-Arab and Zionist. Dylan's enthusiasm for Judaism was short lived, and he resented the fact that once again he was being claimed by a group of people who wanted him to lend his voice to their cause. He declined many invitations to speak on Judaism on the grounds that he had nothing to say about it and that he felt no affinity with the people who invited him. Just as he felt uncomfortable with the organized protest movement, he was uneasy about organized religion, preferring instead a personalized Judaism.

It was shortly after this that he began moving more seriously toward Christianity. His most popular success following this was "Knocking on Heaven's Door" from the soundtrack of Pat Garrett and Billy the Kid (1973). The Rolling Thunder Revue, although an unlikely road to Damascus, seems to have had a profoundly spiritual effect on a number of its participants, including Dylan. Almost immediately after the tour four of the musicians—T-Bone Burnett, David Mansfield, Roger McGuinn, and Steve Soles—became born-again Christians, and almost a dozen eventually became Christians or renewed their commitment to Jesus.[6] In a rare interview Dylan gave in 1975, it is clear that he saw his life directed by divine intervention. Speaking of his earlier career, he talked fatalistically. He claimed that the Bob Dylan myth and his receptivity to it were the creation of God. He declared himself to be unconcerned with what people thought about him because he believed himself to be following God's will.[7] By 1977 he was denying his Jewish heritage completely. He told Ron Rosenbaum that "I've never felt Jewish . . . I don't have much of a Jewish background."[8] He made an even stronger disavowal in Sydney, Australia, in 1978 when he said that his blue eyes showed that genetically he was not Jewish. He claimed that he had Cossack blood in him.

It was in 1979, however, that his newfound religious fundamentalism found full expression in Slow Train Coming, for which he won his first Grammy in 1980 for Best Male Rock Vocal Performance for the single "Gotta Serve Somebody." The reasons for his conversion to born-again Christianity are, of course, complex and the subject of considerable speculation. Most fundamental, however, seems to have been a resurfacing of the fear of death that he had experienced after his motorcycle accident. Although there were numerous rumors of its seriousness, ranging from paralysis to his demise, it does not seem to have been as life threatening as legend has it. Nevertheless, it frightened him and forced him to reassess his life. Following the accident, he gave up touring in order to spend more time with his young family.

After the motorcycle accident, he not only became a family man, he also became intensely interested in astrology. In an interview in *Newsweek* and shortly after in *Rolling Stone*, Dylan said that he was unable to read anyone else's astrological chart, but that a good friend of his had told him about the influence of Saturn: "It's a big heavy obstacle that comes into your chain of events, that fucks you up in a big way. Came into my chart a few years ago and just flew off again a couple of months ago."[9] It was the lifting of this burden that inspired him to tour again.

Dylan had become terribly affected by Elvis Presley's untimely death at a young age in August 1977 and by the extent to which Elvis had become a parody of himself—reclusive, obese, even grotesque. Dylan described his reaction to Elvis's death as a breakdown. He reexamined his whole life and was unable to talk to anyone for a week. Elvis and Hank Williams, he believed, had paved the way for what he was doing, and Williams himself had died at the age of twenty-nine from a heart attack induced by hard living, whiskey, and drugs. When Dylan was struck down with pericarditis, a potentially lethal infection of the heart muscle, in 1997, he later joked that "I really thought I'd be seeing Elvis soon."[10] Dylan was thirty-six when Elvis died; he was very conscious that forty was on the horizon and that he was becoming an aging rock star. His life was empty and lonely without his wife and children (he and Sara had separated; they divorced in 1977), and it seemed to have no direction.

Helena Springs, a cowriter of songs with Dylan and a backup singer with his band from 1978 to 1980, seems to have been one of the catalysts of his change. He had phoned her to discuss the problems he was having, and she suggested to him that he pray. Dylan became intensely interested in the concept of prayer and explored its every facet, absorbing everything he could, just as he had with folk, country, and blues music in his early days. When he had exhausted that line of exploration, he once again moved on.[11]

Mary Alice Artes, who was Dylan's girlfriend at the time of his conversion, was certainly instrumental in precipitating the process of immersion. She belonged to a religious group called the Vineyard Fellowship in Tarzana, California, and Dylan became baptized into its community. A number of musicians, some from the Rolling Thunder Revue, also worshiped there. C. S. Lewis's *Mere Christianity* seems to have been doing the rounds among musicians at the time, and Lewis's rhetorical argument that either Jesus was who he said he was or he was a raving lunatic clinched the argument.

Dylan enrolled in the Vineyard's school of discipleship in Reseda, California, and studied the Bible intensely for three and a half months, five days a week. The pattern of total immersion is a familiar feature of Dylan's psyche; he had gone through a similar process about five years earlier in the personal exploration classes of Norman Raeburn. Just as that period of reflection, deriving from an obsessive search for knowledge, culminated in a new phase of songwriting, his newfound fundamentalism manifested itself in his art, two songs of which expressed gratitude to Artes for bringing Jesus into his life, "Precious Angel" and "Covenant Woman." He recorded the songs for *Slow Train Coming* in May 1979.

Dylan felt that he had been called to follow, and that he had found the meaning to his life that had so long eluded him. Determined to share that meaning, he transformed his concerts into evangelical celebrations. He believed in the Second Coming and was influenced by the particular version espoused by Hal Lindsay in *The Late Great Planet Earth*. Lindsay's diagnosis and prognosis were pessimistic: Armageddon, the war to end all wars, was on the horizon and would be generated in the Middle East by Iran and its new ally, Russia. Before the total destruction of the human race, Christ would return to save humanity. Dylan preached this with such fervent conviction that even his mentors in the Vineyard Fellowship were taken by surprise. At concerts he told audiences that "[w]alking with Jesus is no easy trip, but it's the only trip. . . . Nobody ever told me Jesus could save me. I never thought I needed to be saved."[12] Dylan had come to believe, after a close study of the Book of Revelation, that ever since the time that Adam and Eve were expelled from the Garden of Eden, things had progressed down a slippery slope destined for Armageddon. He did not see his belief in Christ as incompatible with his Jewish background, however, and in this respect he concurred with sects within Judaism who thought of themselves as Messianic Jews.

That *Slow Train Coming* was so intensely religious should not have come as a surprise. Dylan's early albums, beginning with the first, *Bob Dylan*, were obsessed with death and God. This obsession could be explained by the fact that the material he sang simply reflected the religious element in the country-blues music he sang. This wouldn't explain why Dylan chose the particular songs, however. *Slow Train Coming* is indicative of the personality that we see throughout his career. When he moves on, he leaves something behind, and usually in a way that is demonstrative and not always free of ambiguity. Here he is moving on from his Jewish background, without rejecting religion, adopting Christianity, and eventually leading to a phase where he becomes a born-again Christian. It was in an interview in 1980 that Dylan publicly affirmed his conversion in declaring that "I truly had a born-again experience. If you want to call it that. It's an over-used term, but it's something that people can relate to."[13] The concerts immediately after his conversion included only his new religious songs, but gradually he reintroduced some of the earlier material into his repertoire, which itself became imbued with a religious aura. Take, for example, "Like a Rolling Stone," probably Dylan's most famous single, in which, at times, there is a venomous, accusatory tone. In the new version, all anger is dissipated and replaced by compassion and forgiveness, delivered in a more somber and melodic voice, transforming "Miss Lonely" from the author of her own self-destruction and degradation to a lost soul having taken a wrong turn en route to God.

In his fundamentalist phase, Dylan preached the idea of divine immanence. Take, for example, the song that was recorded by Dylan in October 1963 but not released until 1985 on *Biograph*. It was "Lay Down Your Weary Tune," recorded earlier by the Byrds in the United States and by McGuinness Flint in Britain. In the song, the wonderment of nature is applauded, as God is seen to animate and inhabit it:

> I gazed down in the river's mirror
> And watched its winding strum.
> The water smooth ran like a hymn
> And like a harp did hum.
> Lay down your weary tune, lay down,
> Lay down the song you strum,
> And rest yourself 'neath the strength of strings
> No voice can hope to hum.

This degree of religious intensity also turned out to be a phase Dylan was going through. It was, he claimed, "part of my experience. It had to happen. When I get involved in something I get really involved."[14] In 1982 he was rumored to have returned once again to Judaism. He was believed to have been studying with the Lubavitch Hasidim in Brooklyn, and he took a trip to Israel for the bar mitzvah of his son. His former wife, Sara Lownds, was still very much of the faith, and all his children had been brought up within it, so it should have been no surprise that their father attended one of the most important religious events in his son's personal spiritual growth. Throughout the next two decades Dylan was reported to be supporting this or that Jewish cause by, for example, appearing at Jewish telethon charity events, visiting a synagogue, and playing various concerts in Israel. Throughout this time he never explicitly renounced his belief in the Messiah. In his view, Jesus was a Jew who most Jews refused to recognize.

The 1983 *Infidels* marks his return from born-again Christianity, which had so thoroughly permeated the previous three albums, *Slow Train Coming*, *Saved*, and *Shot of Love*. The religious themes, though still evident to a certain degree, are not so blatant. For example, the references in "I and I" are to God's answer to Abraham, "I am that I am," and that no man can remain alive if he looks upon His Face. In "Man of Peace," Dylan is repeating the traditional Christian exhortation to be vigilant in resisting the works and temptations of Satan, who is to be found in the most unlikely guises, even that of a man of peace. In his live performances Dylan still made his religious affiliations explicit, and even though the imagery and tone of much of his religious writings is that of the wrath of God, it is to Jesus he looks for redemption. In his 1986 Australian tour, backed by Tom Petty and the Heartbreakers, Dylan gave an introduction to a song off the album *Saved*. He told the audience that everyone has heroes, and, to applause, he said that maybe theirs were Mel Gibson, Michael Jackson, or Bruce Springsteen. Having built up the emotions of the audience by placing before them their secular idols, he deflated them by saying, "Anyway, I don't care nothing about any of those people." The song that he sang was about his own hero, Jesus Christ, and it was "In the Garden."[15]

Despite the success of *Slow Train Coming*, seasoned admirers of Dylan complained that he was finished and had nothing more to say. Greil Marcus characterized the albums of this period as "increasingly lifeless works that had all but destroyed the subjective, critical voice with the imposition of a received ideology."[16] For Marcus, it also heralded a serious decline in Dylan's writing powers. The songs were, for him, "insultingly shoddy" and one dimensional: Jesus is the answer, and if you don't believe, there's no hope for you. Dylan was not taking a genre, as he had with the folk tradition, and making it his own; instead, he was preaching a received doctrine in a humorless and uninspiring, hectoring tone.[17] This was not just a jibe against finding religion, because Marcus could admire the inspiration, for example, in Van Morrison's album *Into the Music*, in which he sings of being elevated by the power of the Lord. Noel Paul Stookey, on the other hand, who had also found God, thought *Slow Train Coming* was particularly inspiring because it "beseeches a decision from the hardest-hearted. . . . It is an inspiration to all brothers and sisters."[18] Leonard Cohen, in addition, thought that the songs of Dylan's religious fundamental-ism phase were some of the most beautiful to enter the gospel music landscape.

The songs emanating from Dylan's religious fundamentalism constitute a reversion to what I have called art as magic. They are certainly more prescriptive than his earlier finger-pointing songs in that they offer not only a diagnosis of the problem but also an answer.

The religious theme still surfaces in Dylan's recent work, for example, the despondent 1997 "Trying to Get to Heaven" on the Grammy Award–winning *Time Out of Mind*, which includes the line "Tryin' to get to heaven before they close the door." It is an album that expresses resignation, world weariness, and coming to terms with mortality. In the same year Dylan contracted the potentially fatal infection histoplasmosis. On recovering, he toured again and accepted an invitation to perform before Pope John Paul II in Bologna, Italy. Dylan sang "A Hard Rain's A-Gonna Fall," "Forever Young," and "Knocking on Heaven's Door." More recently there is again speculation about his reversion to Judaism.[19]

There is, then, an essential dialectical tension in Dylan's spiritual journey, a fundamental exploration of Christianity followed by periods of reflection from the standpoint of Judaism. It is this constant pull toward Judaism after passionate flirtations with Christianity that characterizes much of Cohen's spiritual quest, with the added complication of Zen Buddhism.

On Top of Mount Baldy

As a successful poet and novelist, Leonard Cohen was claimed most vociferously by the Canadian Jewish community. He was a voice that spoke to the new generation of Jews. The publication of *The Favourite Game* had been celebrated by the planting of a tree in Israel, sponsored by the Jewish National Fund of Canada. Cohen's presence at public discussions sponsored by Jewish organizations was seen as a sure way of gaining publicity, but it was always a high-risk strategy. Cohen delighted in being publicly outrageous, and just as Bob Dylan was pleading to his elders to get out of the path of social change, Cohen preached that the Jewish establishment subverted and inhibited their inherited religious principles. In a public debate at the Jewish Public Library in Montreal in January 1964, Cohen accused his elders of talking merely of group survival and of the social institutions of the community, such as special education. In forgetting about their cosmic purpose to bear witness to monotheism, Cohen argued, Jews were becoming just another ethnic group. The individualism of the prophet was being vanquished by the priest. Rabbis and businessmen had surreptitiously imposed conformity and smothered the prophetic element in Judaism. Cohen further outraged his elders by claiming that the Jewish community had become like a British square of old—

highly armed and well equipped with artillery, but nothing in the center of the square to defend. Instead of addressing his assertions, Cohen's critics resorted to character assassination, by identifying him with the actions and characters in *The Favourite Game*.[20]

Throughout Cohen's work, from the early poems to his latest offerings, two themes dominate with alacrity and in intricate entanglement: the quest for an elusive God and the search for respite or comfort in sexual fulfillment. The Beat Generation, in Kerouac's view, was essentially a religious generation in which Beat meant "beatitude" and not "beat up." Many of the Beats were desperate to believe, but were loath to do so through conventional religions. The mystical side of the Beat Generation was at its strongest on the West Coast in the works of Kenneth Anger, Jordan Belson, Wallace Berman, Bruce Connor, Jay Defeo, and Harry Smith.[21] The Beats explored the extremes of lofty spiritualism and realistic squalor, the ecstatic and the horrific in experience, but did not translate them directly into politics.

One commentator suggested in 1969 that Cohen's songs are about "piety and genital pleasure."[22] There was a tension between reverence for the regulative life and complete obedience required in Judaism, something Cohen sought later in increasingly prolonged periods in a Buddhist monastery, and irreverence toward the certainty of absolute truth that the Torah espoused. In March 1978, in an interview broadcast by the Australian Broadcasting Corporation, Cohen asserted that only two things interested him: women and God. In his view, the song has to be all-embracing; it must not be onesided, or it becomes distorted. If God is left out of sex, it becomes pornographic, and if sex is left out of God, it becomes self-righteous and pious. This is a quality he saw not only in his own songs, but in other songs whose simplicity captures the sublime. Fats Domino's "Blueberry Hill," for example, has the same quality: "I found my thrill on Blueberry Hill / The moon stood still on Blueberry Hill." The song is exquisite because you comprehend everything about the moment, a tipping of the balance, back and forth, between the secular and the spiritual.[23]

It was the combination of God and sex that drew singer Jennifer Warnes to Cohen's music. Having joined a convent immediately after high school, she saw in Cohen someone trying to unite an intense love of God with sexual desire, something that she repressed in her youth. Warnes, having sung as backup singer on several of Cohen's tours and done vocals on *Recent Songs* and *Various Positions*, was responsible for reviving Cohen's waning career in 1986, when she released a collection of his songs entitled *Famous Blue Raincoat*.

Among the criticisms of Cohen's first book of poetry, *Let Us Compare Mythologies*, was the observation that there was a too liberal and graphic use of sex and violence juxtaposed with religious themes.[24] Religious and sexual epiphanies have almost always been closely entwined in his work. The two themes together are characteristic of how the sacred and the profane merge and dissolve. In *The Favourite Game*, for example, Bertha, in return for playing her flute, demands that Breavman, the main character, say something "terribly, horribly dirty." Breavman complies with, "Fuck God, fuck GOD, FUCK GOD."[25] In *The Spice-Box of Earth*, the theme is continued in "The Priest Says Goodbye," in which the priest is the lover experiencing uncontrollable desires of lust. He is on fire, like a burning holy tree. In "Celebration," fellatio is portrayed as a ceremony in which the semen becomes a blessing, and the act is compared with the ancient Roman worship of the phallus.

Cohen's second novel, *Beautiful Losers*, exemplifies these themes. Linda Hutcheon goes so far as to say that "*Beautiful Losers* parodies not only [the] Bible but also sex manuals and pornographic fiction."[26] In the opening pages, F, the mentor of I, is reported to have said that he had not heard of a female saint that he did not want to screw: "[F]ind a little saint and fuck her over and over in some pleasant part of heaven. . . . [F]ind one of these impossible cunts and fuck her for your life."[27] The underlying thread that holds together *Beautiful Losers* is the choice that each character makes to lose himself or herself for the sake of a higher cause,[28] with the exception of I, whose cause is simply the loss of self.[29]

The title of the book refers to those who, despite appearances, attain the beauty of "sainthood." To the ordinary person, viewing them through the eyes of conventional standards, they are losers or victims. Their beauty is achieved by somehow entering into communion with God. The loser, however, in Cohen's special sense, is not a victim of circumstance, but has chosen to surrender himself or herself and ordinary life for a noble cause. Catherine Tekakwitha, the seventeenth-century Iroquois virgin saint and the subject of I's obsessive sexual longing, suffers an excruciatingly painful death by torture and starvation. Edith, I's wife and another of F's conquests, commits suicide by gaining access to the bottom of the elevator shaft of their small apartment building. F goes mad, is committed to an asylum for the criminally insane, and there meets his end. Mary Voolnd, a nurse at the asylum to which F is committed, is savaged by ferocious police dogs. From the point of view of eternity and in the eyes of God, the characters are not losers in the ordinary sense of the term at all. Catherine Tekakwitha gives herself up in holy matrimony to Christ, attains sainthood, and miraculously heals the sick. Edith's suicide is belatedly acknowledged by I for the lesson it is and directs him to his own sublime example. Mary Voolnd voluntarily becomes the sexual object of F, when he is at his most undesirable, and reveals to him that he has been recognized as the first president of the republic. F deliberately subordinates himself to I as his teacher and mentor, and in return is rewarded by I with a vision of salvation. I is reduced to a destitute state, filthy and wretched in the woods.

Beautiful Losers is a profoundly political statement; at the same time, it is disorienting and disturbing because it constitutes a complete denial of the principle presuppositions of human agency in the West. As Stephen Scobie has indicated, we start in the West with the individual's acceptance of personal responsibility for his or her own individuality.[30] What I does in the novel is to abjure that responsibility, and in doing so the reader is invited to entertain a complete reversal of Western values. What is more, the work itself, as Douglas Barbour suggests, represents, an attack on reason, time, and history.[31] Its narrative certainly transcends time in elapsing three centuries into an eternal present, denies history in rejecting chronology, and suspends reason or belief in portraying events outside of time.

Cohen's family kept kosher, observing the traditional Jewish practices, attending the synagogue on the Sabbath, and performing the traditional rituals on Friday evening. His maternal grandfather was Rabbi Solomon Kintsky Klein, who had famously compiled the 750-page *Thesaurus of Talmudical Interpretations*. Rabbi Klein was influential in Leonard Cohen's education, regularly accompanying the boy to the library in order to ensure that he had a thorough grasp of the Old Testament. It was the Book of Isaiah that most impressed Cohen, perhaps because of the powerful imagery of the wrath of God it contains, as opposed to the New Testament's emphasis on the love of Jesus. Cohen grew up during a time when Jews were being deprived first of their citizenship and then of their rights, including the right to live in large areas of continental Europe. Cohen's parents shielded him from much of the news coming out of Germany at the time, but he could not help but be touched by the horrors that had occurred as he grew into a young man.

The name Cohen is venerated in Jewish culture, and Leonard Cohen's parents taught him that he was descended from Aaron, the high priest, and was expected to flourish into a leader of men. His poetry and lyrics betray the ambivalence of the burden and privilege that this carried. The references to leadership and controlling the world, as well as to submission, ricochet off interviews and lines of poetry and song. By the age of six,

Cohen knew the rudimentary conventions of Judaism. He attended after-school classes at the synagogue, where he learned the history of the Jews and their ancient scriptures, and received his bar mitzvah in 1946.[32] Cohen described his upbringing as religious, but not fanatic or oppressive.[33] He himself developed a sense of destiny from the impression created of being chosen. He generated for himself a mythology fueled by the strength of his superego.[34] The title of his first book of poems, *Let Us Compare Mythologies*, implied that we all create mythologies for ourselves. The dominant theme throughout is a comparison of the Hebraic mythology of his family background with the Christian mythology, both French and Anglo Catholicism, of his surroundings in Montreal. In this book we encounter a theme that was to be enduring, namely, the quest for an elusive and mysterious God always just beyond comprehension.

Cohen's second book was *The Spice-Box of Earth*. The spice box has particular significance in Jewish religion, particularly in the ceremony of havdalah which, in conjunction with a candle, brings the Sabbath to a close. As L. S. Dorman and C. L. Rawlins suggest, "whatever we may make of Leonard's Judaism, he is a man seized by its traditions."[35] His writings are replete with references to Judaism and biblical allusions because, as he explained in 1972: "For me it is more important to explore old experiences before you develop a whole overwhelming backlog of new experience."[36] "Who by Fire," for example, is based on an old Hebrew prayer that is sung on the Day of Atonement and includes the lines "Who by fire?," "Who by sword?," and "Who by water?" The melody is based on one that Cohen had heard in the synagogue as a boy.

By January 1964 Cohen was already enough of a celebrity at home to cause controversy in what he said in an address on the future of Judaism in Canada. As we saw earlier, in a public debate he berated the Jewish community for its excessive attachment to commerce at the expense of the arts and culture of traditional Jewish heritage. He also accused the community of neglecting young Jewish artists.

At the time, Cohen was heavily experimenting with drugs, including opium, peyote, and hashish. He had also become curious about the book *Dianetics*, the basis of Scientology. His flirtation with *Dianetics* was short lived, although it had a lasting effect on him.[37] Indicative of his unending quest for spiritual enlightenment, Cohen had joined the California cult of Scientology. It did not take him long, however, to become disillusioned with the pronounced faith of its leader, L. Ron Hubbard, but it took Cohen longer to extricate himself than it took him to be lured. (It was in fact at a Scientology convention in New York City that Cohen had met Suzanne Elrod, the mother of his son, Adam.)

Cohen's self-absorption in the mid-1960s generated a religious imagery of his personal quest that was almost self-delusory. He wrote of a generational loss of faith that had undermined everything that had been passed down. Each individual was encapsulated, and the capsule that Cohen inhabited was that of a cantor, a priest of a nascent catacomb religion. As one of the many singers or priests in that religion, he was also one of the creators of the liturgy at the foundation of the church.[38]

In a 1969 interview Cohen explained that he saw religion as a means for achieving strength and for making the universe less inhospitable.[39] He genuinely believed that there is a power to get in touch with, and he felt no discomfort, unlike many of his contemporaries, in calling it God. He also felt comfortable about using the masculine pronouns *He* and *Him*. Cohen sincerely believed that he had felt the grace of God.[40]

It is not an overstatement to suggest that Cohen is saturated in religion and mysticism, absorbing the spiritual lessons of both the East and the West. His early public concerts, for example, took on the air of a religious experience. In his first Toronto appearance at York University in 1967, Cohen lit candles at the front of the stage and led the audience in chanting to achieve a reverent state of mind. He remarked in 1974 that he found himself completely at home in the company of religious fanatics because of the specificity of their views and their permanent state of nervousness. Later he stressed the importance of accepting religious diversity. He maintained that all places of worship give solace and comfort to worshipers: "I don't think it serves anything or anybody to become an enemy of organised religion."[41] Even his concerts took on the air of religious experiences. The *New York Times,* for example, in commenting on the 1993 tour, suggested that in the live performances "romance and religiosity [are] entwined. . . . For Mr. Cohen, the concert is a somber ritual." The *Los Angeles Times,* in remarking on the infrequency of Cohen's live performances, suggested that they "take on the air of a pilgrimage, with the faithful approaching him more as a spiritual leader than a mere musician. . . . "[42]

Cohen's religious journey seems to have been characterized by inner conflict, which constitutes a dialectic between Judaism, Christianity, and Zen Buddhism. His interest in Zen Buddhism was fueled while he was at Columbia University for a short period in the mid-1950s, when he became familiar with the burgeoning counterculture of the Beat poets, who were questioning all of the prevailing images of the age, including religion. This interest was renewed when he attended the wedding of an old friend from Hydra, Steve Sanfield, who appeared to have found inner peace after becoming attracted to the Rinzai version of Zen Buddhism through a Japanese mission in a Southern California suburb.[43] It was at the Buddhist wedding ceremony that Cohen first met the man who was to become his spiritual teacher intermittently over the next thirty years, Joshu Sasaki Roshi. The ceremony incorporated meditation, ritual, and the copious consumption of Japanese sake. As David Sheppard remarks: "Spiritual ceremony, hedonism and the ritual of love taken together constituted an irresistible cocktail of attractions."[44] Cohen's description of why he first went to Roshi's Zen Center is typically mysterious and vague. He said that he had got himself into the sort of trouble that no one can talk about. He stayed there for a month, but the rigor and discipline were too much for him to bear. Walking around in the snow at night in open sandals and in meditation seemed like deliberate torture, revenge for World War II by the Japanese master on the idealistic youth of America.

It was after his son was born, and after the release of the much derided *Songs of Love and Hate*, that Cohen first went to the monastery, which had now moved to Mount Baldy in the San Gabriel Mountains north of Los Angeles. He meditated there for three weeks in 1972, observing the strict regime imposed by Roshi, which started at 3:00 A.M. Two years later, Cohen went on a tour of Japanese monasteries with Roshi. After touring in 1976, he returned to Montreal for prolonged periods and reimmersed himself in the Jewish faith. Just as he had never wholly embraced Buddhism, he had never wholly rejected Judaism. He then helped to establish a Zen Buddhist meditation center in Los Angeles and would often go there to meditate for a few hours.

Cohen came close to renouncing Buddhism altogether, however, in 1988, after his recovery from a severe mental breakdown. He attributed the breakdown to his involvement in Zen and warned his listeners during a radio interview to steer clear of Buddhism because it was "dangerous."[45] He nevertheless continued to practice Zen and later explained his cautionary note: the danger was in thinking that it can provide salvation.

Periodically, Cohen would subject himself to the Zen Buddhist regime as practiced by Roshi and his followers at Mount Baldy. This need to be controlled after losing control—the need for complete submission—is a theme that surfaces in his work, just as it does in his life. "If It Be Your Will" (*Various Positions*) is the poetic apotheosis of this disposition: "If it be your will / that I speak no more / and my voice be still / as it was before."

The regime that he disciplined himself to follow, rising at 3:30 every morning and driving to South-Central Los Angeles, one of the poorest and most dangerous parts of town, in order to meditate, was not motivated by optimism. To subject oneself to such a disciplined regime, Cohen has argued, one has to be driven there by misery: "It is confusion and suffering that lead you to these stern measures."[46] A deep sense of self-doubt drives the individual to disciplined meditation. In the process, Cohen has said, you may discover a self that you cannot abide, and that is why you drop it.

A prolonged retreat to Mount Baldy in 1993 was the culmination of over twenty years of friendship with Roshi. The idea of total abstinence as the redeemer of the soul was a belief firmly ingrained in Cohen. He had often fasted and had frequently abstained from those things in which he had overindulged. A life of debauchery had led to remorse and a longing for absolution from sin. During such times Cohen would try to conduct himself on the models of saints that he had read about and abstain almost completely from the pleasures of the flesh. As early as 1969 Cohen contended that "I've always had an attraction to that ascetic kind of life. Not because it's ascetic, but because it's *aesthetic.* I like bare rooms."[47]

Cohen left the Mount Baldy monastery as an ordained monk shortly before his sixty-fifth birthday and returned to recording, releasing *Ten New Songs* two years later. He tried to underplay his commitment to Zen, saying that he was always happy with the religion with which he was born and that it was his personal attachment to Roshi that had drawn him to the monastic life. It was not a spiritual thing, he claimed, but instead one of the many attempts that he had made over the years to come to terms with clinical depression.

Despite flirtations with other religions, Cohen has always maintained his Jewishness, or at least a diluted version of it. He is able to pray in Hebrew, but he has also seen something significant in the image of Christ on the cross. His most famous song, "Suzanne," is replete with religious imagery, reflecting the varied affiliations of the different Montreal communities, the Catholicism of the French-speaking majority, the Protestantism of the English-speaking minority, and a significant Jewish presence. The image of Jesus and the Virgin Mary appear in this song:

> And Jesus was a sailor
> when he walked upon the water
> and he spent a long time watching
> from his lonely wooden tower
> ....
> And the Sun pours down like honey
> on Our Lady of the Harbour

The religious imagery in his songs is almost always accompanied by tortured or harrowing images of love and metaphors or allegories of war: "I've seen your flag on the marble arch, / but love is not a victory march, /

it's a cold and it's a broken hallelujah!" ("Hallelujah," *Leonard Cohen Live*, shorter version on *Various Positions*). Of this song, Cohen says that he is trying to convey that we live in an imperfect, tainted world with shattered lives and broken hearts; despite all that, we have to stand up and cry out "Hallelujah."[48] But religion is not necessarily the source of salvation. In *Beautiful Losers*, for example, the character I accuses the Roman Catholic Church of Quebec of being responsible for precipitating all sorts of depravity, including ruining his sex life, placing his penis in a religious relic box, building green masturbation toilets, and causing him to refuse to let Edith go down on him properly.[49]

Love is depicted as irresistible but regrettable, a beautiful and sordid temptation. Irving Layton took Cohen's attitude to love to be one of his weaknesses. He described Cohen as a narcissist who hates himself. Cohen is something like the Jean Jacques Rousseau in *Confessions* who is absorbed by the pleasures of the flesh yet ridden with guilt, and desperate for absolution and redemption. The difference is that Rousseau wanted to transform society and its institutions in order to make better and more moral citizens, whereas Cohen is in search of personal salvation.

Sex in Cohen's songs is a motivational drive, which is reminiscent of the solitary individual in Thomas Hobbes' state of nature whose life is an unending quest of one pleasure after another. The lover is both the perpetrator of the crime and the victim, sometimes repentant, sometimes defiant: "When they said repent, I wonder what they meant" ("The Future"). The religious imagery is often irreverent and disturbing, giving rise to expectations of holiness and purity, but instead conveying something more tainted. In "Sisters of Mercy" the tone and solemnity of the lyrics evoke the order of nuns and their charitable and holy deeds:

> All the Sisters of Mercy
> They are not departed or gone
> They were waiting for me
> when I thought that I just can't go on
>
> ("Sisters of Mercy," *Songs of Leonard Cohen*)

The song is in fact about two women, Barbara and Lorraine, whom Cohen had met during a snowstorm in Edmonton, Canada, and whom he had taken back to his hotel room. The seriousness and solemnity of the song have, to some extent, been destroyed for many people because it was used on the soundtrack for Robert Altman's *McCabe and Mrs. Miller* (1971), where the referent of the song became prostitutes in a whorehouse.

There is much of a redemptive character in Cohen's lyrics in juxtaposing sex and religion, especially when the union is understood as an expression of something higher or divine. Referring to the pleasures of sex in religious terms may, from an ordinary view, seem blasphemous and irreverent, but I think we can be more generous of spirit than that. Cohen's view of religion is not what is called divine transcendence—a benevolent God outside of our experience, the dispenser of mercy. Cohen instead subscribes to divine immanence; that is, God manifests Himself in all human relationships—we are all divine in our own different ways. This was aptly expressed by the philosopher Henry Jones when he was questioned about his alleged denial of the divinity of Christ. His reply was that he denied the divinity of no man.[50] In other words, God is immanent in everyone. There is some evidence for this view in an interview Cohen did with Harry Rasky. Like F. H. Bradley, the idealist philosopher who argued that we have a right to employ whatever ideas work for us, Cohen contends that for most of the time our everyday conception of a transcendent, or objective, God to which we stand as subject/object, is a "satisfactory device, to satisfy many human experiences." He qualified this by saying: "But there are other conditions in which we don't have that subject/object relationship. It dissolves and we experience ourselves as the content of everything that arises. And some people call that God. It is just another kind of experience in which there is no subject and object."[51] From this viewpoint, "Sisters of Mercy" can be appreciated as a religious experience rather than a sordid episode. Similarly, "Hallelujah" may be interpreted in the same way: "I remember when I moved in you, / and the holy dove was moving too, / and every single breath we drew was Hallelujah!"

Various Positions was Cohen's most intensely religious album. It became clear from later interviews that at the time of its release, in 1985, he had come to see himself as some sort of religious leader or prophet, but had come to realize that in fact he was not prepared to be the martyr, the Joan of Arc, that jealous religions crave. He told *LA Style* in 1988 that

> I had a lot of versions of myself that I had used religion to support. If you deal with this material, you can't put God on. I thought I could spread light and I could enlighten my world and those around me and I could take the Bodhisattva path, which is the path of service, of help to others. I thought I could, but I was unable to. This is a landscape in which men far stronger than you, far braver, nobler, kinder, more generous men of extremely high achievements have burnt to a crisp on this road. Once you start dealing with sacred material you're gonna get creamed.[52]

In the song "The Future," Cohen sings, "I'm the little Jew who wrote the Bible," by which he means that humanity has produced this holy book and that the landscape we inhabit is a biblical one and of our own making. Organized religions, he suggests, serve a useful purpose in providing real solace for millions of people. From within these religions they provide comfort, but in relation to each other they are antagonistic. They act like territorial states, and Cohen thinks this sinful.[53]

Cohen has always been ambivalent about his relation to Zen, and despite his meticulous subscription to a strict regime, he has been reluctant to admit he is a wholehearted convert, even though he is an ordained Buddhist monk. He says, for example, that he is not really sure what the ideas of Zen are or whether as he has received them they are authentic to the tradition.[54] Although the influence of Zen Buddhism is not as overt as Judaism and Christianity in the lyrics of his songs, the contemplative mood and demeanor of meditation is. Roshi sat in on one of the recording sessions of *New Skin for the Old Ceremony* in 1974, and after sleeping through most of it, he advised Cohen to sing more sadly. Cohen has recently commented that when he played *Ten New Songs* for two Zen monks, one said that it was equivalent to a two-week session of intensive meditation, and the other simply kept his eyes closed, opening them only when his glass was filled.

If one were to attribute a philosophy to Cohen, recognizable within the Western tradition, it is philosophical idealism. In this philosophy the absolute, the undifferentiated whole of experience, of which we ourselves are fragments, is the only thing that is real. Everything else is somehow an expression of this whole. The implication is that finite individualities— things and persons—are abstractions, fictions that are presupposed in certain forms of discourse. Thus, in history, for example, we presuppose the category of the past, and that events are somehow related to each other; in Newtonian mechanics, we presuppose that everything has a cause. In practical life, we presuppose an individual who is free, capable of making choices, and therefore of being responsible for actions. The alternative would be that we are parts of a greater whole, somehow caught in a much grander and larger plan, orchestrated by a God who lives in and through us. Idealism is an intensely spiritual philosophy and has been identified with mysticism. The ideas of its exponents have often found a hospitable climate in Asia and the Far East. The typical criticism of absolute idealism was that the individual somehow becomes absorbed into the whole. This is in fact the position that Cohen has moved toward, not through a familiarity with idealism, but through Zen Buddhism. The severe regime on Mount Baldy was designed to overthrow individualism and to divert the monks from thinking about themselves and matters that are irrelevant and produce anxiety. It provided the kind of space in which to get lost, a retreat from the world and its distractions.

Take, for example, Cohen's "A Thousand Kisses Deep," in which the life of our conscious thoughts and strivings is portrayed as a delusion, and that in losing our grip on this false "reality," we "slip into the Masterpiece" or grand design that is found "a thousand kisses deep." This is not what Cohen means by inner feelings that cannot be trusted because they come and go. It is something more fundamental. In an Internet discussion of October 16, 2001, he affirmed that at this level the individual dissolves. He maintained that

> a thousand kisses deep is that fundamental intuitive understanding, usually wordless, which is beyond opinion and belief. It is the unspoken conviction that things are unfolding according to a pattern that the intellect or the emotions cannot discern. This conviction is accompanied by a loosening of the unconditional affirmation that an individual entity exists and that it determines its own fate.

This is not the aberration of a life disappearing into the mist, but was immanent in the thought processes of the young Cohen. From very early on his flirtations with different disciplines, including yoga, the Hebraic tradition, Christianity, and Zen Buddhism, were attempts to control his mind, attempts that were in fact to no avail: "It's not that a man chooses the gods that he worships—it's the gods who choose him."[55] In describing *Beautiful Losers*, Cohen explains how the most beautiful parts of the book are those that achieve this self-loss or absorption into a greater whole: "There [are] certain moments when the lyricism and the spontaneity and the boldness allow the expression to be without self-regard, without self-consciousness, and once that happens, once that moment happens, then the embrace is absolute."[56] This sense of becoming absorbed into a higher order is paralleled with a sense of becoming absorbed in the sensual. In "You Have the Lovers" (*The Spice-Box of Earth*), the dance of love is portrayed as a ritual in which self-consciousness is lost in a mystical union. In an interview with Angelica Houston in 1995, Cohen suggested that dissolution is something we all want. We long for the experience of self-loss, of forgetting who we are. It is both fulfilling and frightening, because it is what we want but cannot sustain.[57] As Desmond Pacey suggests, in Cohen "the state of sexual fulfilment is virtually synonymous with the state of grace: the fulfilled lover feels himself to be a part of a universal harmony."[58]

Dylan and Cohen have exhibited very different attitudes toward religion, although both think that the spiritual quest ultimately leads to revelation and answers their very different questions. For Dylan, religion ultimately reveals the answers to all those questions he first posed in "Blowin' in the Wind." But even though Jesus played such a prominent role in his life, it was the vengeful God of the Old Testament, the God of fire and damnation, that he predominantly preached. Souls could only be saved by completely following the path of righteousness. Whereas Dylan maintains that God's work is all around us, He is nevertheless transcendent and standing over us all in judgment of our sins. Dylan's religious fundamentalism constituted an even more austere finger-pointing phase than his early protest songs, in which the problems were clearly identified but the answers rarely unequivocal. In God Dylan found the answers, and like Moses returned from the mountain with the Decalogue in hand, he was determined that everyone should be subject to them. Christian fundamentalism constituted Dylan's most injunctive phase, and one that most severely conformed to R. G. Collingwood's idea of art as magic.

Cohen's attitude to religion has been experimental, and whatever temporary truth he found was personal and self-exploratory. Because his God is immanent, the Spirit permeates everything, making even the sordid sacred. God inhabits all flesh, and this is why Cohen has drawn such a close relationship between sex and religion, between the sacred and the profane. Ultimately, however, Cohen has needed the discipline of religion to suppress the profane, to subdue and tame the demands of the flesh.

Endnotes

1. Quoted in *Bob Dylan, in His Own Words*, ed. Christian Williams (London: Omnibus, 1993), 88.
2. Quoted in *Leonard Cohen, in His Own Words*, ed. Jim Devlin (London: Omnibus, 1998), 11.
3. See E. Anthony Rotundo, "Jews and Rock and Roll: A Study in Cultural Contrast," *American Jewish History* (September 1982); and Michael Alexander, *Jazz Age Jews* (Princeton, NJ: Princeton University Press, 2002).
4. Andy Gill, *My Back Pages: Classic Bob Dylan 1962–69* (London: Carlton, 1998), 72.
5. Larry Yudelson, "Dylan: Tangled Up in Jews," *Washington Jewish Week*, 1991. Reprinted in *The Bob Dylan Companion*, ed. Carl Benson (New York: Schirmer Books, 1998), 172.
6. Scott M. Marshall (with Marcia Ford), *Restless Pilgrim: The Spiritual Journey of Bob Dylan* (Lake Mary, FL: Relevant Books, 2002), 21.
7. Jim Jerome, "Bob Dylan: A Myth Materializes with a New Protest Record and a New Tour," *People*, November 10, 1975. Reprinted in Benson, *The Bob Dylan Companion*, 131.
8. Ron Rosenbaum, "Born Again Bob," *New York* September 24, 1979. Reprinted in *The Dylan Companion*, ed. Elizabeth Thompson and David Gutman (New York: Da Capo Press, 2001), 235.

9. Interview with Ben Fong-Torres, January 12, 1974, in *Knocking on Dylan's Door,* by the editors of *Rolling Stone* magazine (London: Michael Dempsey, in association with Cassell and Co., 1974), 106.

10. David Frank, "Sometimes Down, Never Out," *The Globe and Mail*, August 15, 2002.

11. Helena Springs, interviewed by Chris Cooper, 1978. Reprinted in *Wanted Man*, ed. John Bauldie (New York: Citadel Underground, 1991), 126.

12. Bob Dylan interview, May 7, 1980. Reprinted in Clinton Heylin, "Saved! Bob Dylan's Conversion to Christianity," in Bauldie, *Wanted Man,* 132.

13. Robert Hilburn, "I Learned That Jesus Is Real and I Wanted That," in Benson, *The Bob Dylan Companion*, 164.

14. Yudelson, "Tangled Up in Jews," 174.

15. Bob Dylan, *Live Down Under* (Down Under Records, 1986). The first three hundred copies of this album included a seven-inch interview disk. All the albums included a poster headed "Bob Dylan Sydney 1986."

16. Greil Marcus, "Dylan as Historian," in *The Dustbin of History* (Cambridge, MA: Harvard University Press, 1995), 81.

17. Greil Marcus, "Amazing Chutzpah," *New West*, September 24, 1979. Reprinted in Thompson and Gutman, *The Dylan Companion*, 237–240.

18. Noel Paul Stookey, "Bob Dylan Finds His Source," *Christianity Today*, January 4, 1980. Reprinted in Thompson and Gutman, *The Dylan Companion*, 240–242.

19. Zoe Brennan, "Bob Dylan's 'Secret Wives' Are Revealed," *London Sunday Times*, March 15, 1998, News, 10.

20. "Poet-Novelist Says Judaism Betrayed," *Canadian Jewish Chronicle*, January 10, 1964.

21. Lisa Philips, "Beat Culture: America Revisioned," in *The Beat Culture and the New America* (New York: Whitney Museum, in Association with Flammarion, 1996), 30.

22. Ira Mothner, *Look*, June 10, 1969.

23. Brian Cullman, "Sincerely, L. Cohen," *Details for Men* (January 1993).

24. Allan Donaldson, "Review of *Let Us Compare Mythologies*," *The Fiddlehead* 30 (November 1956): 30–31.

25. Leonard Cohen, *The Favourite Game* (Toronto: McClelland & Stewart, 1994: first published 1963), 15.

26. Linda Hutcheon, *Leonard Cohen and His Works* (Toronto: ECW Press, 1992), 19.

27. Leonard Cohen, *Beautiful Losers* (London: Jonathan Cape, 1970; first published 1966), 12.

28. This theme is pursued in Desmond Pacey, "The Phenomenon of Leonard Cohen," *Canadian Literature* 34 (1967): 5–23.

29. The qualification is pursued in Stephen Scobie, "Magic Not Magicians: *Beautiful Losers* and *The Story of O*," *Canadian Literature* 45 (1970). Reprinted in *Leonard Cohen: The Artist and His Critics*, ed. Michael Gnarowski (Toronto: McGraw-Hill, 1976).

30. Ibid., 110.

31. Douglas Barbour, "Down with History: Some Notes Towards an Understanding of *Beautiful Losers*," in Gnarowski, *The Artist and His Critics*, 141.

32. L. S. Dorman and C. L. Rawlins, *Leonard Cohen: Prophet of the Heart* (London: Omnibus Press, 1990), 25–27.

33. Devlin, *Leonard Cohen in His Own Words,* 7.

34. Dorman and Rawlins, *Prophet of the Heart*, 32.

35. Ibid., 91.

36. *Leonard Cohen in His Own Words*, 51.

37. Paul Barrera, *Leonard Cohen: Came So Far for Love* (Andover, NH: Agenda, 1997), 22.

38. Sandra Diwa, "After the Wipe-Out, a Renewal," *The Ubyssey*, February 3, 1967.

39. Michael Harris, "Leonard Cohen: The Poet as Hero: 'I Wanted Very Much to Have This Conversation,' " June 1969, available at http://www.itsystem.se/guitar/LC.interview.html.

40. Michael Harris, "An Interview with Leonard Cohen," *Duel* (Winter 1969).

41. Cited in David Sheppard, *Leonard Cohen* (London: Unanimous, 2000), 115.

42. Quoted in Columbia Records press release, November 15, 2000: "Columbia Records to Release *Field Commander Cohen: Tour of 1979*."
43. Sheppard, *Leonard Cohen*, 31.
44. Ibid., 32.
45. Cited in Ian Pearson, "Growing Old Disgracefully: Page Two," *Saturday Night* (March 1993).
46. Richard Guilliat, "An Interview with Leonard Cohen," *Sunday Times Magazine*, December 12, 1993.
47. Michael Harris, "An Interview with Leonard Cohen," *Duel* (Winter 1969).
48. "A Master's Reflections on His Music," *Los Angeles Times*, September 24, 1995.
49. Cohen, *Beautiful Losers*, 47.
50. H. J. W. Hetherington, *The Life and Letters of Sir Henry Jones* (London: Hodder & Stoughton, 1924), 43.
51. Quoted in Rasky, *Song of Leonard Cohen*, 29.
52. Quoted in Columbia Media Department undated press release accompanying the release of *Ten New Songs*.
53. Devlin, *In His Own Words,* 12.
54. Arthur Kurzweil and Pamela Roth, "Leonard Cohen, *Stranger Music: Selected Poems and Songs*," *The Jewish Book News* interview, available at http://www.serve.com/cpage/LCohen/interview.html.
55. Sandra Diwa, "After the Wipe-Out, a Renewal," *The Ubyssey*, February 3, 1967.
56. Brain Cullman, "Sincerely, L. Cohen," *Details for Men* (January 1993).
57. Angelica Huston, "Leonard Cohen," *Interview* (November 1995).
58. Desmond Pacey, "The Phenomenon of Leonard Cohen," *Canadian Literature* 34 (1967): 7.

CONCLUSION

There can be no detracting from Bob Dylan's portentous effect on popular music. The fusion of poetry and melody, first acoustically, then through rock, prepared the way for a whole range of serious music within the popular idiom. As David Sheppard suggests: "Dylan legitimised intimate, elaborate, and sometimes pretentious lyrical flights in the context of popular music."[1] Without him, it is inconceivable that the Beatles could have developed beyond the trite, bouncy songs of the early '60s or that David Bowie could have taken song narrative to new heights. Leonard Cohen was the beneficiary of this liberation, taking seriousness to new limits and entangling it with melancholy and depression. The angst of Federico García Lorca and of the Beat Generation found musical expression in Cohen's eclectic combination of melodic forms, anchored to the French *chanson* tradition. That angst subsided into a deep melancholic sadness, on the way to attaining serenity in the contemplative mood of *Ten New Songs*.

Dylan and Cohen were not willing spokesmen for their generation, but their voices have resonated in the mute souls of the disenfranchised, disconcerted, and disillusioned youth of the world, dismayed that the defeat of fascism in World War II had given rise to a paranoiac fear of communism in the cold war. Securing freedom in the face of tyranny in the international sphere served to accentuate the degree to which freedom was denied significant minorities domestically. The civil rights movement that both Dylan and Cohen supported cried out, not for special privileges, but for recognition of the humanity of blacks. The two singer-poets were both integrationist, and neither went down the road of radical separatism demanded by the black power movement. They feared the insidious influence of the military-industrial complex, but they were not pacifists. They feared the insanity of war, the implications of which in the 1960s appeared to be complete destruction of the planet. They opposed such insanity overtly and subtly, in imagery that the popular song had never previously aspired to attain. That very same facility with words, the use of language like the brushstrokes on a painter's canvas, enabled them to produce some of the most beautiful love songs of the twentieth century. They were, in other words, masters of emotional expression. The durability of their artistry is evident in the obvious and acknowledged impact that they both have had on succeeding generations of songwriters and in the enduring character of their own success. Throughout, religion played a significant part in their lives, and continues to do so, informing the substance of their songs to different degrees of subtlety and intensity. While in Dylan's case the religious intensity alienated many of his loyal followers, it did not do irredeemable harm to his long-term career. One might say that both Dylan and Cohen are both resurrection men. Having achieved considerable success, they also experienced a significant period in the wilderness, only to return, in Cohen's case in 1988, and in Dylan's case in 1997, triumphant.

The general political lessons to be drawn from this study are fairly simple. Popular music can be political at a number of different levels: (1) The message of the song can be overtly political and include recommendations about how to improve the world. (2) The political message of a song may describe or lament a situation of injustice that intends to evoke a particular mood, with the effect that the audience feels the same sense of revulsion or anger. This may reflect the mood of a counterculture against bigotry, hatred, and racial prejudice or merely be a comment on the system that generates such injustices. (3) A song may be inspired by a political situation and through a series of images evoke a mood that is indicative of a more universal struggle, such as the search for freedom, the sense of despondency in a chaotic world, a feeling of triumph over adversity, or optimism in human progress. Such songs may be subversive in questioning prevailing structures of authority, such as the relations between men and women, blacks and whites, heterosexuals and gays.

Aesthetically, this book has indicated the importance of the questioning activity in the interpretation of texts, and in particular the sensitivity needed to the appropriateness of the questions. The distinction made between art as magic or art with a practical purpose, art as the expression of emotion, and art as the delighting in and contemplation of images that are not propositional, and the further distinction between imaginative art and inspirational art enabled me notionally to distinguish different types of poetic utterance in the works of Bob Dylan and Leonard Cohen in terms of a vocabulary that allowed comparison in terms of identities and differences. I tried to show that the distinctions with which I worked were not artificial abstractions when applied to the works of Dylan and Cohen, but surfaced, sometimes only barely above the horizon, when they were asked to explain or justify the meaning of particular works.

In addition, throughout, I have tried to characterize the context in which these icons of popular song emerged and became almost deified. The context of folk and blues influences; the folk music and avant-garde culture around Greenwich Village and the division between traditional and contemporary song, and between jazz and folk; the hootenanny craze, the Eichmann trial in Jerusalem, nuclear disarmament, civil rights, and the reactions against them in the form of the John Birch Society and McCarthyism, all served either as referents for songs, that is, enhancing the meaning by identifying the event or persons to which the words refer, or as the inspiration that generated or precipitated images about which questions of meaning may have been inappropriate.

What I also tried to do, was not only to introduce aesthetic theories, but also to provide a firmer theoretical basis for the discussion of some of the issues that the book raised. Among the theories invoked were the varieties of hermeneutics, the distinction between origins and originality, the meaning of philosophical idealism, and the distinction between a transcendent and immanent God. All, I hope, served to illuminate the particular aspect of the work of Dylan and Cohen under discussion.

Endnote

1.   David Sheppard, *Leonard Cohen* (London: Unanimous, 2000), 109.

Index

"As Tears Go By," 81
Attar, 140
Auden, W. H., 151
Aufray, Hughes, 2
Austin, John, 180
Australian Broadcasting Corporation, 220
Auteur theory, 75–78
Authenticity, 120–24
Avalon, Frankie, 128
Aznavour, Charles, 2

B
"Baby, Let Me Follow You Down," 80
"Baby, Let Me Take You Home," 80
Baez, Joan, 8, 85, 94, 105, 170, 182
  commercialism, 55
  Dylan, tours and concerts with, 57, 74–75, 86–87
  Farina, Richard, and, 52
  protest, ABC, 32
  protest songs, 177
  Rolling Thunder Revue, 54
  success of, 89
  Town Hall concert, 60
Baez, Mimi, 52, 87–88
Baldwin, James, 51
"Ballad in Plain D," 160, 183
"Ballad of a Thin Man," 179
"Ballad of Donald White," 171, 177
"The Ballad of Frankie Lee and Judas Priest," 185
"The Ballad of Medgar Evers," 177
"Ballad of the Absent Mare," 140
A Ballet of Lepers (Cohen), 19
"Banality of evil," 204, 206

The Band, 81, 91, 94, 138, 151
  farewell concert, 54
"Banks of Marble," 105
Ban the Bomb movement (Great Britain), 39
Barbour, Douglas, 161–62, 222
Bard, David, 138
Bard, Stanley, 138
Bargeld, Blixa, 2
Barrera, Paul, 161
Barthes, Roland, 76
Barth, John, 14
Barwick, Bill, 101
The Basement Tapes (Dylan), 65, 151, 154
Baudelaire, Charles-Pierre, 16
Bay of Pigs, 19
BBC, 63, 81
BBC World Service, 178
Beardsley, Doug, 161
Beat Generation, 50–51, 185, 220, 235
Beat movement, 29–33
  drugs, glamorization of, 53, 54
  film poster, beatniks, *31*
  magazine cover, *56*
The Beat Generation (Haas), 56
Beat Girl (film), 56
Beatles, 51, 79, 81, 83, 84. See *also* Lennon, John; McCartney, Paul
  metamorphoses, 93
Beatniks. See Beat Generation
Beat poets, 15, 17–18. See *also* Beat Generation
Beautiful Losers (Cohen), 13, 14, 19, 20, 103–4, 113, 118, 139, 152, 207, 210n. 58, 221–22, 230
Beauty at Close Quarters (Cohen), 103

Beck, Jeff, 89
Beecher, Bonnie, 86, 143
Behan, Brendan, 137
Behan, Dominic, 86
Belafonte, Harry, 55, 85
Bell, Daniel, 204
Belson, Jordan, 220
Ben-Gurion, David, 203
Bennett, Tony, 76, 99
Berlin Wall, 195, 199
Berman, Wallace, 52, 220
Bernhardt, Sarah, 137
Berrigan, Ted, 51
Berry, Chuck, 28, 73, 76, 128
Berry, Dave, 89
Big Bopper. *See* Richardson, J. P.
Bikel, Theodore, 134, 170
Billboard, 45
Biograph (Dylan), 62, 171, 217
"Bird on the Wire," 105
Birney, Earle, 17
Bitter End (New York City), 61
The Black Freighter (Brecht), 8
"Black Girl," 84
Blacklisting, 32, 62, 84–85. *See also* McCarthyism; McCarthy, Joseph
Black Muslims, 122
Black Panther Party for Self-Defense, 36, 37, 122
Black Power, 36
Black romanticism, 17
Blacks. *See also* Civil rights movement; Racial inequality
  identity, 120–21
  as invisible men, 128–29
  music of, 28–29, 123, 129–30
  place as minority, 120
  prisoners, 125
  voter registration campaign, 121, 134, 178

Blake, William, 143
  Poetical Sketches, 2–3
  Songs of Experience, 3
  Songs of Innocence, 3
Bleecker Street (New York City), 61
Block, Allan, 50
Blonde on Blonde (Dylan), 65, 67, 93, 140, 154, 160
Blood on the Tracks (Dylan), 71, 93, 148
Blood Wedding (Lorca), 151
Bloomfield, Mike, 83, 88
"Blowin' in the Wind," 59, 61, 79, 119, 131, 134, 170, 176, 178
"Blueberry Hill," 220
Blue, David, 94
Blues as poetry, 1
Blues Breakers, 82, 161
Boas, Franz, 35
Bob Dylan, 126, 216
"Bob Dylan's Dream," 79, 126
Boggs, Dock, 119
Bolan, Marc, 3
"The Bomb." *See* Nuclear war, fears of
Bono, Sonny, 27
Book of Mercy (Cohen), 161
"Boom Boom Mancini," 96
Boone, Pat, 76, 128
Bootleg Series (Dylan), 126, 150, 169, 175
"Boots of Spanish Leather," 8, 179
Boston Globe, 14
Bound for Glory (Guthrie), 7
Bowering, George, 14
Bowie, David, 235
Boyd, Joe, 97n. 46
Bradley, F. H., 153, 228
Bragg, Billy, 7, 123

Cézanne, Paul, 156
Chabrol, Claude, 76
Chad Mitchell Trio, 55
Chansonier, 137
Chapter Hall (New York City),
　60
Charles, Ray, 99
Checkmates, 89
The Chelsea Girls (film), 138
Chelsea Hotel (New York City),
　3, 75, 96n. 5, 113, 136–39,
　191–92, 212
"Chelsea Hotel No. 2," 146, 191
Chester McNaughton Prize, 10
Chiasmus, 71
Child, Francis, 125
"Chimes of Freedom," 10, 160,
　180, 183
City Lights (San Francisco), 51,
　52
Civil defense, 172
Civil rights movement, 35–37,
　42, 121–22
　Brown decision and, 129
　radicals, 122
　segregation, protests against,
　119, 121, 131, 170, 177
Clancy Brothers, 51, 55
Clarkson, Adrienne, 144
Cleaver, Eldridge, 37
Cochran, Eddie, 128
Coffee House Benevolent Associa-
　tion, 58
Coffeehouses, 51, 58
COFO. *See* Council of Federated
　Organizations (COFO)
Cohen, Esther, 124
Cohen, Leonard, 99–116, *100,*
　189–210. *See also specific works*
　Beat poets, view of, 17–18
　breakdown, 114

Canada Council and, 13
"Captain Mandrax" name, 79
Chester McNaughton Prize, 10
Cuba, 194–95, 197, 200
dictatorship, attitude toward,
　200–201
Dylan, Bob, comments on, 6
education, 15
French tradition, 2
Ginsberg, meeting in Athens,
　54
Greece, 200
Holocaust, fascination with, 19,
　203–8
influences on work, 16
Isle of Wight Festival (1970),
　107, 111
jazz, 101–11
Judaism, 19, 219–31
manic depression, 113
Playboy, on, 4
poetry as verdict, 2
poetry reading, flyer, *106*
poster for poetry and jazz, *102*
psychiatric institutions, concerts
　at, 113–14
reading tour, 1963, 17
religious convictions, 193–94,
　219–31
Scientology, 223
voice, 117
war images, 192–200
website, 115
women, view of, 201–3
Zen Buddhism, 193–94, 224–
　25, 229, 230
Cohen, Marsha, 104
Cohen's Greatest Hits, 44
Cold war, 50
Cole, Nat King, 130
Collected Poems (Cohen), 151

Collingwood, R. G., 21, 144,
    182, 183, 231
  art as magic, 185–86, 190
  The Principles of Art, 155–59
  Speculum Mentis, 157
Collins, Judy, 32, 105, 108, 170
Colombo, John Robert, 20
Columbia Records, 45, 61, 87,
    132
Columbia University, 17, 19, 101
Communism, fears of, 37, 39–40.
    See also Blacklisting; McCar-
    thyism; McCarthy, Joseph
Concert for Bangladesh, 213
Confessions, 227
Conformity, 30
Congress of Racial Equality
    (CORE), 36, 121, 131
Connor, Bruce, 220
"The Coo Coo Bird," 26, 126
Cook, Bruce, 91
"Copper Kettle," 40
Corcoran, Neil, 4
Cordwell, John, 91
CORE. *See* Congress of Racial
    Equality (CORE)
Corman, Roger, 56
"Corrina, Corrina," 87
Corso, Gregory, 136
  Chelsea Hotel, 138
  Paris trip, 52
  poetry of, 17
Coughlin, Father Charles E., 41
Council of Federated Organiza-
    tions (COFO), 121
"Covenant Woman," 216
Cranston, Maurice, 2
Croce, Benedetto, 183
Crotty, Patrick, 151
Cuban missile crisis, 184, 195
Cultural cringe, 124

D
Dali, Salvator, 19
"Dance Me to the End of Love"
    (Cohen), 19, 196, 203
Darin, Bobby, 76
"Darwin Cory," 40
Davey, Frank, 2
Davis, Bette, 138
Davis, Reverend Gary, 59
Day, Aidan, 145, 149
"A Day in the Life," 145
Dean, James, 69, 73
Death of a Ladies' Man (Cohen),
    99–100, 139, 140–41
Death of a Lady's Man (Cohen),
    10, 20
"The Death of Emmett Till," 168–
    69, 171, 177
de Beauvoir, Simone, 205
Defeo, Jay, 220
Demjanjuk, John, 209n. 49
"Democracy," 27, 109, 195
Denisoff, Serge, 167–68
"The Deportees," 129
De Quincey, Thomas, 53
Desire (Dylan), 93
"Desolation Row," 66, 160,
    184–85
Dianetics, 223
Diller, Phyllis, 50
Dilthey, Wilhelm, 149, 152
Diwa, Sandra, 16
The Dom, 107, 139
Domino, Fats, 220
Donne, John, 150, 152
Donovan, 80, 89
Don't Look Back (Dylan), 43, 55,
    80, 178
"Don't Think Twice, It's All
    Right," 126, 179, 180
Doors, 97n. 46

Kaye, Maury, 101
Kazee, Buell, 119
Keating, Senator, 40
Keats, John, 3, 5
Kennedy, John F.
 assassination of, 135–36
 desegregation and, 177
 inaugural speech, 39
 Vietnam War, on, 38
Kennedy, Robert, 136, 177
 assassination of, 184
Kermode, Frank, 6
Kerouac, Jack, 136, 173
 Beat Generation, term, 50, 220
 Beat movement and, 30
 Chelsea Hotel, 138
 imitation of, 6
 jazz poetry readings, 101
 poetry of, 17
 On the Road, 18
 The Subterraneans, 55–56
Kesey, Ken, 5
Kettle of Fish (New York City),
 94
"Kevin Barry," 105
King, Martin Luther Jr.
 assassination of, 136, 184
 "I Have a Dream" speech, 134
 opponents, 122
 Southern Christian Leadership
 Conference (SCLC), 36, 121
Kingston Trio, 32, 55, 85
Kinnard, J. K., 128
Klein, A. M., 15, 101, 151
Klein, Rabbi Solomon Kintsky,
 222
Kloman, William, 189
Knocked Out Loaded (Dylan), 72
"Knocking on Heaven's Door,"
 214, 219
Koch, Kenneth, 51

Konikoff, Sandy, 90
Konrads, 89
Kooper, Al, 83, 90, 136
Korea, 42
Korean War, 36, 50, 193
Kosovo, NATO intervention, 35
KQED-TV, 182
Kramer, Daniel, 80
Kristofferson, Kris, 111, 138, 191
Ku Klux Klan, 169
Kymlicka, Will, 120

L
*Ladies and Gentlemen, Mr. Leonard
 Cohen* (film), 17, 43, 103
Laine, Frankie, 99, 100
Landau, Jon, 184
"Land of Plenty," 26, 109–10
Langhorne, Bruce, 87, 88
"Last Thoughts on Woody
 Guthrie," 8, 10
The Last Waltz, 54
LA Style, 228
The Late Great Planet Earth (Lind-
 say), 216
Laval, Pierre, 205
"Lay Down Your Weary Tune,"
 217
Layton, Irving, 101, 103, 206,
 227
 collaboration with Cohen, 19
 influence of, 16
 philosophy of, 162
 poetry reading, flyer, *106*
 reading tour, 17
 women, view of, 201
Leadbelly. *See* Ledbetter, Huddie
 (Leadbelly)
Leavis, F. R., 153
Le Cercle de Minuit (television
 show), 20

The Performing Self (Poirier),
77–78
Perkins, Carl, 128
Peter, Paul, and Mary, 8, 58, 85,
170
"Blowin' in the Wind," 61, 79,
134
commercialism, 55
Gerdes Folk City, 59
Lees, Gene, on, 119
Pet Shop Boys, 154
Pettus, Terry and Berta, 31–32
Petty, Tom, 218
Phone Booth (New York City),
84
Picasso, Pablo, 152
Pinter, Harold, 27
"Pirate Jenny," 8
Pitney, Gene, 81
Planet Waves (Dylan), 72
Playboy, 4, 161
"Please Don't Pass Me By (A Dis-
grace)," 203
Poe, Edgar Allan, 49
Poetical Sketches (Blake), 2–3
Poetry Society of Great Britain, 3,
6
Poirier, Richard, 77–78, 145
Political correctness, 61
"Political World," 173
Politics and popular culture, 26–
46. *See also specific topics*
Popular culture
and auteur theory, 75–78
and politics, 26–46. *See also spe-
cific topics*
Porco, Mike, 50, 57–59, 94
"Positively 4th Street," 145
Pound, Ezra, 5, 10, 136, 184
Powell, Tony, 44
"Precious Angel," 216

Prendergast, Tom, 57
Presley, Elvis, 28, 73, 76, 129
death of, 215
drafting of, 128
radicalism, 34, 39
Pretty Things, 79
Price, Alan, 80
"Priests," 105
"The Priest Says Goodbye," 221
The Principles of Art (Collingwood),
155–59
Prisoners, 125
Protest movement, Vietnam War.
See Vietnam War
Provincetown Playhouse, 49
Pynchon, Thomas, 14

Q
Q Dylan, 43

R
Race riots
Birmingham, Alabama, 41
Los Angeles, 36
Racial inequality, 169, 171. *See
also* Civil rights movement;
Segregation, protests against
Raeburn, Norman, 71, 216
Rasky, Harold, 4, 228
Ratcliff, Maurice, 146–47, 192
Rauschenberg, Robert, 51
Rawlings, Adrian, 7
Rawlins, C. L., 223
Rawls, John, 135
Ray, Johnny, 99
Ray, Nicholas, 76
Rebel Without a Cause (film), 73
Recent Songs (Cohen), 107, 140,
151, 220
"Rededication," 152
Red Scare. *See* Communism, fears
of

"Sugar Baby," 26
Sullivan, Ed, 40, 80, 131
"Summer Days," 26
Summer Holiday (film), 34
Surrealism, 1
"Suzanne," 27, 105, 149, 191, 226

T
"Take These Chains from My Heart," 99
Take Thirty (television show), 105, 144
"Take This Longing," 139
"Take This Waltz" (Cohen), 10, 19
"Talking World War II Blues," 133, 172
"Talkin' John Birch Paranoid Blues," 40–42, 131–32, 169
Taplin, Jonathan, 139, 146
Tappettes, 103
Tarantula (Dylan), 8, 9, 83
Taylor, James, 93
Tenant, Neil, 154
Ten New Songs (Cohen), 25, 26, 44, 109, 112, 115, 229, 235
Ten O'Clock Scholar (Minneapolis), 54, 86
Ten Ox-herding Pictures, 140
Terry, Sonny, 30, 123, 128, 130
"That Girl Belongs to Yesterday," 81
"There But for Fortune," 180
"There is a War," 193, 197
Thesaurus of Talmudical Interpretations, 222
"Things Have Changed," 46
"This Land Is Your Land" (Guthrie), 27
Thomas, Caitlin, 7, 137

Thomas, Dylan, 51, 70, 137–38, 151
"Vision and Prayer," 2
Thomas, Henry, 134
Thompson, Virgil, 138
Thoughts of a Landsman (Cohen), 10
"A Thousand Kisses Deep," 230
Till, Emmett, 168–69, 171, 177
Time Out of Mind (Dylan), 26, 46, 73, 219
"The Times They Are A-Changin'," 170–71, 176, 179, 212
The Times They Are A-Changin', (Dylan), 8, 81, 151, 170
"Tintern Abbey" (Wordsworth), 152
"Tombstone Blues," 160, 184
"Tom Dooley," 85
Tom Paine Award, 135, 179
Tom Petty and the Heartbreakers, 218
"Topical Song Workshop," 87
Tork, Peter, 58
Toronto Daily, 104
Toronto University, 103
"To Sing for You," 80
"Totem Pole," 89
"Tower of Song," 111
Town Hall (New York City), 31, 32, 60, 74
Train, John. *See* Ochs, Phil
Trainspotting (Trocchi), 18
"The Traitor," 107
Traum, Happy, 3
"Travel," 152
Travers, Mary Ellen, 85. *See also* Peter, Paul, and Mary
Treblinka, 210n. 49
The Trial (Kafka), 73
Trocchi, Alexander, 18–19, 53

York University, 224
"You Have the Lovers," 230
Young Adam (Trocchi), 18
Young, Israel (Izzy), 31, 57, 58, 60
Young, Neil, 96
"You're Gonna Make Me Lonesome When You Go," 148
Yurchenco, Henrietta, 6

Z
Zen Buddhism, 193–94, 212–13, 219, 224–25, 229, 230
Zevon, Warren, 96
Zimmerman, Robert Allen. *See* Dylan, Bob
Zionism, 205, 213